LEADERSHIP THROUGH SUPERVISION

1946 YEARBOOK, ASSOCIATION FOR SUPERVISION AND CURRICULUM DEVELOPMENT OF THE NATIONAL EDUCATION ASSOCIATION

1201 Sixteenth Street, N. W.
Washington 6, D. C.

Copyright, 1946, by the
ASSOCIATION FOR SUPERVISION AND CURRICULUM DEVELOPMENT
NATIONAL EDUCATION ASSOCIATION
1201 Sixteenth Street, Northwest
Washington 6, D. C.

Price $2

CONTENTS

CHAPTER

1 Exploring Educational Frontiers, *William Van Til* . . . 1

2 Supervision in the American Scene, *Marguerite Ransberger* . 17

3 Analyzing Our Problems, *Lelia Ann Taggart* and
   Mary C. Evans 27

4 A Look at Our Best, *Lelia Ann Taggart* and *Mary C. Evans* 77

5 Tomorrow's Assignment, *Fred T. Wilhelms* 115

1946 YEARBOOK COMMITTEE

Contributors:

    Lelia A. Taggart, *co-chairman*, Director of Education, Santa Barbara County, California

    Fred T. Wilhelms, *co-chairman*, Associate Director, Consumer Education Study of the National Association of Secondary-School Principals, Washington, D. C.

    Mary C. Evans, General Supervisor, Santa Barbara County, California

    Marguerite Ransberger, Supervisor, Elementary School of Lompoc Union, California

    William Van Til, Director of Publications, Bureau for Intercultural Education, New York, New York

Advisory Committee:

    Hollis L. Caswell, Director, Division of Instruction, Teachers College, Columbia University, New York, New York

    Ruth Cunningham, Assistant Professor of Education, Teachers College, Columbia University, New York, New York

    Paul R. Hanna, Professor of Education, Stanford University, California

    Gordon N. MacKenzie, Director, Institute for School Experimentation, Teachers College, Columbia University, New York, New York

    Gladys L. Potter, Supervisor of Elementary Education, Long Beach, California

1

Exploring Educational Frontiers

WITH earth-shattering impact, an atomic bomb dropped on Hiroshima. The blast reverberated thru chancellories and state departments in Moscow, Chungking, Tokyo, London, Washington, and thru homes of little people thruout the world. A war was ended and an age begun.

In the historians' chronicles 1945 will go down as the year of the destruction of Nazism, of agreements reached by a Big Three in the heart of Prussia, of Japan's surrender before an allied soldier had set foot in her homeland, of emerging agreements in Europe and in the Orient. In the scholars' books, 1945 will be an unforgettable year. Yet, even with these great historic events to its credit, 1945 may be immemorially recalled as the year in which man first harnessed the incalculable power of solar energy and entered upon the atomic age.

No age is completely new, and the atomic age is no exception. Into an era of giant power, man brings sad, familiar baggage—his social problems. Into the new world he brings his controversies, his power politics, his conflicting national and imperial drives, his unemployment, his poverty in plenty, his failing economic systems, his bigotries and group hatreds, and his frightening moral irresponsibility. His major weapons are the democratic way of life, the religious tradition of western culture, and his increasing knowledge of the emerging social sciences. They may yet prevail—if his faiths are strong enough, his new understandings deep enough, and his will to put both to the task unremitting.

Again, we in American schools, granted honorable discharges from wartime curriculums, turn back to the task of education for democratic living in a society where the power of billions of wild horses has been

---

By WILLIAM VAN TIL, *Director of Publications, Bureau for Intercultural Education, New York, New York*

turned loose. Unbelievable energy is in the hands of people who have not yet learned to live together even in the simple environment of home or office. If we really believe, as we affirm, that the world's chance for lasting peace rests upon making true democracy operative for all people everywhere and upon developing social intelligence to match man's achievements in science and technology, our task in American schools is clear. We must equip young people to respect the worth of the individual, to work together for common purposes, and to apply the method of intelligence to the difficulties we face in living together, to the controlling of our material environment, and to the use of our mounting scientific and mechanical inventions and discoveries for the welfare of mankind. In short, our major function should be to help young people understand and practice the democratic way of life in a technological age.

Again the race between education and catastrophe is on—a recurring contest which has been run before in this twentieth century. We of the schools must enter the struggle in full realization that education has in past contests been a consistent loser, defeated in the teens of the twentieth century by a catastrophic war which mobilized sixty million men, more than half of whom were killed, missing, wounded, or taken prisoner; defeated in the twenties and thirties by an organization of the peace which did not work; defeated in the thirties by a worldwide depression in which the gaunt spectre of poverty stalked thru many lands; defeated in the forties by total war fought with frightful weapons and barbarity at a staggering cost yet unmeasured. The late forties and the fifties loom ahead with their challenge to establish a workable peace rather than an uneasy interval between wars, their challenge to establish full employment and economic security rather than the mockery of destitution and enforced idleness in a land which possesses the technological means for producing abundance and prosperity.

As we enter the postwar world, one fear dogs those of us charged with the schooling of the young: we know our educational efforts to be one of the major factors operating in a society which strives desperately to achieve human control over its technology. Will our efforts be too little and come too late?

We cannot afford schools which placidly instruct the young for cultured living in a horse-and-buggy society. As the Educational Policies Commission has pointed out, too many children in our schools, in this age beset by its urgent and real human problems, are learning that "the square of the sum of two numbers equals the sum of the squares plus twice their product; that Millard Fillmore was the thirteenth president of the United States and held office from January 10, 1850, to March 4, 1853; that the capital of Honduras is Tegucigalpa; that there were two Peloponnesian Wars and three Punic Wars; that Latin verbs meaning command, obey, please, displease, serve, resist, and the like take the dative; and that a gerund is a neuter verbal noun used in the oblique cases of the singular and governing the same case as its verb."[1]

Even in those modern schools which come closer to grips with reality than the school thus satirically portrayed, the question must still be raised whether some fatal lag is yet evident. Many are the supposedly forward-looking schools which first taught conservation of natural resources after the problem had reached the advanced stage of legislation to fight the destruction of land and water resources that had made dustbowls of once fertile countryside. Many are the modern schools where an economics deviating from the severe classical canons of *laissez faire* was first taught, well after the economic crash of the twenties demonstrated classical economics to be a realm of ghostly shadows. Many are the schools which began to concern themselves with intercultural education after rioters had swept down the broad boulevards of the community, looting and beating as they went. Can we deal with today's problems in the school? Can we even, as wise men, foresee and offset tomorrow's possible problems? Or must we forever, in laggard fashion, deal only with ex post facto analyses of yesterday's debacle?

Cultural lag has carried over into our relationships with students. Many a perplexed teacher of the 1930's taught as tho before him in class were the youth of the 1920's, fairly sure of a job, frequently accepting the doctrine that this is the best of all possible worlds, fascinated by the gay living of the period Charles A. Beard characterized as the golden glow of American civilization. Such teachers were baffled by the youth who actually sat before them, youngsters who knew too well that jobs had mysteriously vanished from their ken, that education was no longer a sure key to economic success, that they inhabited an imperfect world which regretted to see them mature and join the long lines of job hunters in a glutted labor market. To many teachers, the unwanted generation of the 30's was sullen, radical, defeatist, and baffling. To the bewildered depression children, much of what they were taught made little sense beyond the walls of the classroom sanctuary.

In the struggle to bring school instruction to bear upon the significant social and individual problems of today, the supervisor and curriculum worker occupy key positions. Perhaps more than any other group serving the schools, they are the people to whom teachers look for foresight. Since they know intimately the day-by-day workings of classroom life, they are not so inclined toward breathtaking flights into impossible classroom Utopias as mere educational theorists are likely to be. Yet they are at the

---

[1] Educational Policies Commission. *The Purposes of Education in American Democracy.* Washington, D. C.: National Education Association, 1938. p. 147.

same time in a position to take a broad view of education based upon their thinking about society, the youngsters in the schools, and the direction in which they believe education should move. For they are not so harassed as are administrators by the immediate need for raising funds and reconciling diverse community pressures. And they are not, like many teachers, so closely bound to a particular group of students that the broad problems of education for a democratic society become obscured.

Each supervisor and each curriculum worker must make his judgment as to learning experiences best suited to the social education of students. In determining such learning experiences for a postwar world, the educator must reexamine three sources of curriculum content which interact and play upon each other:

1. Our culture, with particular reference to conflicts, trends, and predictable problems.
2. The needs, problems, and tensions of the young people within whom learning is to take place.
3. A philosophy of guiding values which determines purposes of learning experiences.

The substance of this chapter is an examination of each of these sources in curriculum building. It deals, also, with the appropriate centers of learning experience for postwar young people which must be included in the social education program if it is to serve the new age.

The Culture of Our Times

Learning experiences in postwar America certainly must be based in part on the kind of culture which characterizes the times. Postwar grows out of war and prewar; hence it is important to recognize the major conflicts which have marked our time and promise to mark the future. Trends are worth examining, for these remorselessly march onward. We need, too, to attempt to recognize major social problems, even tho this necessarily involves the hazardous business of prediction.

Conflicts Cloud the Way

The overshadowing conflict of our days has been war. It remained for the twentieth century to raise war to its preeminent place among mankind's occupations. New weapons have erased the distinction between combatants and noncombatants, soldiers and civilians. Whole cities have been Coventryized, given the Hamburg treatment, vaporized. Populations have been captured and enslaved. War belongs to everyone. Today, the energy of Mars has been expended, temporarily at least, permanently if man proves intelligent enough to exorcise this unwanted god. But in the very effort to organize a lasting peace, conflict continues.

The campaign for lasting peace has been heralded by a wealth of preliminary plans, skirmishes in theory which preceded the Big Three conferences, and the San Francisco Charter meeting. Scholars and diplomats have debated Continentalism, the Balance of Power, the Atlantic System, the Good Neighbor Policy, Union Now, a resurrected League of Nations, a new United Nations Organization, and World Federation. In practice, the die has been cast for a United Nations approach. Within that broad term, the struggle for a lasting peace goes on, with the issue in doubt. The United Nations approach may become a new Holy Alliance, may dissolve with shifts in balance of power, may become the seed of an international fraternity of nations, may develop into organic union. Whether the Soviet Union or the United States moves toward isolation or toward world collaboration; whether Germany is de-industrialized, partitioned, policed, or resurrected as a power; whether the Balkans become communist, capitalist, or retain feudal vestiges; whether America sets up outposts in the Orient; whether India becomes independent or stays in the British orbit; the fact remains that an inescapable area of conflict in the postwar world is that of the organization of the peace. We in the schools must deal with it again and again and again thru historical and contemporary study. Education's failure to do this has in the past resulted in the endless repetition of the tragedy of war. Its failure to do so this time may plunge the world even beyond the misery and chaos of war into total destruction of civilization.

Another inescapable conflict of the years immediately ahead is the struggle among groups for power and income. Conflicts between social classes are worldwide. They lie behind revolutions, behind both democratic and authoritarian movements. They lie behind elections such as the one which swept the British Labor party into power in England. In America three significant groups struggle for relative advantage in the social structure—business, labor, and agriculture. Groups which are smaller numerically and less significant in terms of organizational strength, such as teachers and doctors, play their roles in the struggle, occasionally independently of the big three social groups, but more frequently as satellites. The stakes at issue are frequently economic; the struggle is one for income or power. Each group attempts to increase its share of worldly goods, thru tactics as varied as labor's use of collective bargaining and the strike and industry's use of price-fixing and restriction of output.

Paradoxically, the struggle in our nation goes on in an environment of potential plenty. A great technology has been erected upon a powerful resource base. Total war has resulted in a production miracle in America which is scarcely appreciated as yet. Faced with the choice of making guns or butter, American productive capacity matter-of-factly turned out both in amazing quantities for practically the duration of the war. What we need now is an accompanying distribution and consumption miracle so that the goods and services we have learned to produce in abundance may serve not only those in above average income brackets, but all of our citizenry, rich and poor, powerful and humble.

This land of plenty has known mill towns which have become ghosts during depression. It has known farms abandoned and lying idle for lack of purchasing power. It has known ports where boats have ridden idle at anchor. It has known schoolteachers without salaries, cities without recreation facilities, men pounding the streets seeking work. It has known the lowering shadows of insecurity as factories have rusted away.

Struggle Begets Solutions

The struggle for power and income is reflected in social, political, and economic controversy. In the postwar world, five conceivable courses for the organization of American domestic life are shaping up. One calls for *laissez faire,* an unhampered, unrestricted capitalism following what are termed natural economic laws. A second course calls for governmental intervention to free the capitalist economy from the fetters of monopoly and restrictive practices and to restore the free market of *laissez faire* theory. A third course reflects the hopes of some modern businessmen who see a need for reconciliation of labor, industry, and government in an economy marked by low prices and highly expanded output. A fourth course is that of mixed economy in which private enterprise produces to its maximum and is supplemented where necessary and in periods of crisis by the compensating public enterprise sector of the economy. A fifth course is that of planned economy thru central government with price determination, production quotas, and coordinated all-out production and distribution in an economy which steadily becomes more socialized in character.

As the wheels begin to turn in reconversion, the rumblings of the struggle for power and income again make themselves heard. Related conflicts to come are already making many black headlines in today's newspapers. In varied classrooms domestic, economic, and social problems must be discussed and studied. Whether the young people now in the schools live out their life spans depends upon the resolution of problems of the peace. Upon resolution of domestic economic conflicts depends the quality of living, the very quality of food, health, and shelter for those young people.

Trends Are Discernible

There are some recognizable trends along the road we are traveling. They are, in general, agreed upon by a large consensus of social scientists. Some trends we may like; others we may think a menace. In any case, we shall do well to be aware of them and direct them as we can.

Certainly one persisting trend is technological advance, a still accelerating trend. One need only to turn to studies by Lewis Mumford, Roger Burlingame, or Stuart Chase, or see the news and advertising columns of any major newspaper, for documentation. A companion trend to technological advance is increasing interdependence. Time and space have shrunk thru the airplane and radio. We have learned that there are no people resembling Chamberlain's classic description of the Czechs, "a foreign people about whom we have no concern." The web of relationships has become fragile; a Japanese foray into the East Indies meant that Americans wore out their shoe leather as they had not since the inception of the wizardry of Detroit. Conversely, a race riot in Detroit made East Indians more willing to accept the Japanese heel.

Twin trends, long established and recently encouraged by war, are nationalism and imperialism. As the technologically advanced civilizations grow more discouraged with the fruits of nationalism, other nations such as China, India, and Egypt, seem still more determined to try it out. As the fruits of imperialism drop from venerable mother trees such as England, other nations seem ready to bear a crop. Imperialism and the dynamic new nationalisms are trends which cross each other and promise trouble.

Companion trends within our own United States are the increasing concentration of economic power in the hands of the relatively few and a trend to centralization in government. Again these seem to be trends at cross purposes, for a strong government determined to move swiftly toward economic security may conflict with the power of the two hundred corporations which controlled almost half of the corporation wealth of the United States when Berle and Means made their classic study, *The Modern Corporation and Private Property*, in the 1930's. War has supplied renewed strength to both trends. Already-powerful business organizations have been entrusted with the bulk of war contracts and have been acquiring government-built plants. Far-reaching economic controls and planned government coordination have been essential to the United States, as to every belligerent.

Still another trend which should be mentioned is the steady movement toward collective action in our society. Today is the era of competing propagandas; a wit has remarked that an optimist is a man who belongs to no pressure group. In an impersonal urban civilization where apartment dwellers do not know the residents across the hall, the old neighborhood groupings break down. The job becomes increasingly important as the center of one's self-organization, dominating one's day, determining in large part friends, patterns of entertainment, even interests. Economic urges and constant rubbing of shoulders with folks who are truly akin usually condition thinking into patterns which national organizations then represent with all of the pressure power at their command. This has been true of business interests; it has become increasingly true of agricultural and laboring interests and of the myriad of subgroups which make up the pictures of American social organization.

The World's Uneasiness Enters the Classroom

The supervisor and curriculum worker must take into account such conflicts and trends if the social foundations of the educational program he proposes are to be firmly based. He must attempt to visualize resultant problems, such as the divergent roads proposed for the American economy; the problem of conflicting interests of workers, management, and government; the fight for full employment and economic security; the competing economic theories of the Soviet Union, Great Britain, and the United States; the emergence of areas formerly backward technologically such as Latin America and China; the clashes in interest of great powers; the problems of enduring peace organization; the attempts to harness powerful resource bases for construction and destruction; the bewilderment of men as to what to believe; the struggles among ideologies and world views. He must be eager that young people consider predictable and emerging problems, by definition controversial, within the classroom. Studying conflicts, trends, and problems; discussing, applying values, and learning to act on them whenever possible, is essential to a program of postwar social education. Propagandized and emotionalized mass thinking resulting from pressure group tactics should not be tolerated in American society. Our young people must learn to examine controversial issues with intelligence and foresight, to reserve judgments until evidence has been carefully weighed. In other words, they must learn to think for themselves so that they will never, like the lost generation of German youth, be emotionalized into accepting as valid, false doctrines and anti-democratic ideologies.

The Youth In Our Land

Centers of learning cannot be based simply upon an analysis of the culture, however searching such an analysis might be. Fundamentally, we are dealing with human beings; more specifically, we are dealing with young people who have their own problems, needs, and tensions which must be respected. Abstract ideas can enter into the learning experiences of students only as they are comprehended by the young people themselves and related to their own drives and purposes. A primary task for the postwar supervisor and curriculum worker, then, is to understand these children and adolescents for whom our educational machinery exists.

We shall not at this point enter into a discussion of the relatively stable needs of children and adolescents, for many studies already exist to help the educational worker who wishes to understand child development. We shall, however, comment upon some of the problems and tensions of young people which manifest themselves at various stages of societal development.

Concerns Are Outgrowths of the Culture

It is important to recognize that the concerns of young people, like the concerns of adults, are in large part culturally conditioned. They are conditioned by the ways of living which the people of the culture hold to be important, the conflicts and trends of the culture, and the folkways and mores which the people accept. A culture which holds to social ownership of the means of production, frowns on wealth accumulation, and defends its way of life against invaders deep into home territory, produces a youth different from the young person in the culture which lauds individual accumulation and is divorced from invasion by ocean barriers. Even biological drives are in large part socially conditioned. American youth in the first half of the 1940's did not express biological needs in the patterns so familiar to the 1930's: the necking in the back seats of cars, the stop at the hamburger drive-ins. The reasons were social: the male partner was no longer in the community because of the social phenomenon called war; the car could not be used because of the social phenomenon called gas rationing; the hamburger drive-in had long been closed because of a dual social lack, cars and meat.

The concerns of young people change in large part with cultural changes. Their problems shift as the culture moves into depression, prosperity, war, or reconstruction. Today's relevancy becomes tomorrow's anachronism. We can reasonably expect that the young people who are the students of the postwar American school will have problems, concerns, and tensions somewhat different from their predecessors among school generations.

The point may be illustrated by a contrast between the characteristics and concerns of adolescents in the 1930's and adolescents in the first half of the 1940's. There exists a valuable body of materials concerning the needs and problems of youth of the 1930's. Studies conducted by the American Youth Commission and two recent commissions of the Progressive Education Association, for instance, have been invaluable. Few studies of youth were made during America's frantic war years; the student of needs must depend largely upon observation and reporting.

The commissions have documented the fact that economic depression was the major characteristic of the social situation in which adolescent youth found itself in the 1930's. The major characteristic of the first half of the 1940's was war. Each was a pervasive influence upon the particular generation. Let us note how the distinct universe inhabited by American adolescent youth was affected by these two traumatic social events.

War Glorifies Youth

Consider family relationships and employment status. In his family, the war youth is cherished and prized, because patriotism and the tragic sense of time combine to make him a focus of family concern. He is the potential fighting man in a war where casualty lists are expected to be high. Or he is a part- or full-time wage earner holding a job because of his youth, strength, and adaptability. The adolescent girl, too, is prized. She too may be a wage earner. Or, if not, there are jobs to be done at home while her mother is busy with salaried or civilian defense work. There may be less time for the family group to be together at home than ever before; yet when it is together, there is a deep feeling of belonging and of mutual interdependence.

In employment, war youngsters are essential. They not only belong—they are the focus of production. They are the users of the weapons of death. Whether fliers, Waves, welders, or laborers, they are consciously glamorized by a society fighting its own extermination. The armed services and civilian occupations compete for them. They are the big show. Peter Arno points up the situation in the irrepressible *New Yorker* magazine with a cartoon which shows the board of directors presenting the office boy with a watch in recognition of his long-time service to the firm, six weeks of faithful attendance.

In a war period, younger children suffer more than older, since home life may diminish. Lower-income families see for the first time an opportunity to accumulate while the "getting is good," tho normal home living goes by the board. So the ten-year-old girl may take care of the baby of the family while mother and dad work the swing shift.

In Depression Adolescents Get in the Way

The family status of the depression youth affords an interesting contrast. In his home, as in society at large, he is a burden. He remains in school until well after he is old enough to get a job. He works infrequently and he contributes little or nothing to the family income, already markedly reduced. Yet he eats with regularity. He is about the house more than is good for family morale. The family radio is tuned in continuously; newspapers are read and reread to the point of boredom. When he goes out with little change in his pockets, he finds that recreation costs money. Like James T. Farrell's *Studs Lonigan*, he wants to "do something" but finds nothing to do. The adolescent girl, too, is constantly about the house. She is constantly allured by the smart world of fashion, spurred by advertising to unattainable wants, diligently fostered by a business civilization gone dry. She remains unmarried for a longer time than parents regard as usual. In his home, the depression adolescent lacks the sense of belonging which the wartime adolescent has found, however briefly.

The lack of status in employment of depression youth is well summarized by *Reorganizing Secondary Education*, a study of the 1930's. "Under current economic conditions, young hands are a drug on the market. There aren't enough jobs to go around. Therefore the adolescent is told there is no place for him as an adult in an adult world ... Without an economic function and the early prospect of marriage he is robbed of a sense of significance in his life. He is really no longer a child; yet he is excluded from the status of adulthood."[2]

Uncertainty Faces Youth Today

If we admit, then, that the needs of young people are in large part culturally conditioned, we must recognize that the needs of postwar adolescents are different from the needs of the wartime adolescents with whom we have worked during the 1940's. For suddenly, almost overnight, the wartime status of youth is withdrawn. On the days when America awaited official confirmation of the Japanese surrender, it was symptomatic that the radio, spurred no doubt by OWI, injected a significant note into a repeated filler inserted between programs. The announcement simply urged youth to return to school in the fall.

Gone is youth's priority in the labor market. Gone is competition for his services. Gone is glamor. Advice to youth now? Stay in school. Youth accustomed to high regard as fighters and war workers, actual or potential, must find places of lesser status. We may meet in America's high schools a generation of adolescents who feel that they have been cheated of heroic roles. School may seem less glamorous than more manly tasks. Youth will move from being the highly prized essential person in the economy to an ordinary young person. This shift, at least, seems inescapable.

While no one can foretell for sure, there exists also a strong possibility that the psychological transition which youth must make will be even more severe than the shift from a privileged status to an ordinary role. If American society cannot provide full employment, if indeed it is overwhelmed by the modern plague of joblessness, in a short span of time the youth who was essential will become a nuisance. Again he will compete for jobs with heads of families. Again his own family will find him too much with them. In such a society he will be able to take little solace from the men in their twenties returned from the war, for they too will chafe restlessly, at least at first, in office or factory jobs, or grow bitter if they find their civilian reward to be unemployment. It is realistic rather than alarmist to point out that fascism was born among German youth under somewhat similar circumstances in the 1920's.

---

[2] Thayer, V. T.; Zachry, Caroline; and Kotinsky, Ruth. *Reorganizing Secondary Education.* New York: D. Appleton-Century Co., 1939. p. 104-105.

It would seem, then, that supervisors and curriculum workers in a postwar world will have to take careful stock of the needs and problems and tensions of this generation of young people and to develop programs based on both felt and predicated needs, on both personal and social needs. Whatever the major needs and tensions of postwar young people have to be, the task of supervision is to recognize problems of the young and help provide social education which makes sense to a new generation of students, culturally conditioned to be different from their predecessors who sat at the same desks and tables.

The Search for Direction

Whether the culture be one marked by the violence of war or by the readjustments of a shattered world in peacetime, learning experiences must be closely related to understandable purposes of education. The supervisor who has reexamined the nature of the culture and the needs of this generation of young people must also define his philosophy of education. Curriculums must be chosen and learning experiences developed with reference to a sense of direction. Schools can neither take all knowledge, without selection for their province, nor pretend that moral issues and value judgments are not the business of education.

Viewpoints Spring from Many Sources

Thru the years educators have debated the sources from which a direction for education may be derived. Some claimed to find the source of direction from within the individual's organism. Rousseau and primitive progressive educators, for instance, believed that guidance as to the good life emerged inscrutably from the inner workings of the child. However no bodily organ has yet been discovered which generates and hatches values which are by their very nature good, regardless of the social philosophy of the surrounding culture.

Some religionists and humanists take their clue to a philosophy of education from the supernatural, deemed to lie beyond human sensory perception. Philosophers of Plato's persuasion teach that "ideas" exist beyond time and space and that our human concepts are but dim reflections of eternal essences. The seeker for educational direction must consider the absolutistic assumptions of such interpretations.

Still other educators find their direction from long vanished golden ages. Classicists frequently prize the self-mastery, balance, and urbanity of Periclean Greece and the Renaissance. Questers for truth are referred to listings of great books. But critics comment on the kinship of the classical ideal to the ideals of a leisured aristocracy at the pinnacle of a pyramid broadly based on slave workers. Too, the writers of the great books, in which elusive truth is assumed to be contained, contradict each other.

EXPLORING EDUCATIONAL FRONTIERS

Still other educators find direction in the State, assumed to reflect popular ideals. The State, they say, is the great investor in education, supporting schools to perpetuate itself. Consequently, the State should determine the direction which permeates the school program. But the power politics State of actuality is frequently based on privileged-group ideals and Machiavellian purposes which cry to the high heavens for examination, not inculcation. Perpetuation of State purposes may be simply perpetuation of the *status quo*.

The educational historian will report that such conflicts over direction in education have continued in our times. But the historian must also be struck by a growing consensus among twentieth century educators in America upon another philosophy of education than those described above. For many have found a source of direction for education within a philosophy of experimentalism which has at its core faith in democracy as a distinctive way of life.

Our Commitment Is to a Living Democracy

Historian after historian recognizes democracy as the basic commitment of the American social experiment. Report after report, educator after educator, conceives our major educational purpose to be the understanding and practicing of a continuously scrutinized democratic way of life. One might repetitiously quote from reports of the Educational Policies Commission, from reports of the commissions of the Progressive Education Association, and from previous yearbooks of the Association for Supervision and Curriculum Development.

Perhaps the educational historian will record that it was the convergence of three traumatic developments of our time which forced Americans to reexamine their values and to reaffirm the importance of democracy as a social philosophy. These developments were, of course, the depression, the rise of the fascist way of life, and the total war. The Dewey school of thought had tended the democratic plant; social developments brought the philosophy to bloom. As it grew clearer that the social question of the day was, as Mussolini put it, "we or they," a torrent of literature on democracy poured from the presses.

The experimental philosophy of democratic living demands an appropriate education—one which stresses the dignity and worth of the individual, calls for working together for shared purposes to extend associated living, continuously promotes the general welfare, and proceeds thru the method of intelligence. Consequently, supervisors who accept democratic living as their ultimate and pervasive assumption are accustomed to determining and reconsidering their values. They will assume that in the immediate postwar era contemporary social thought may help them to reexamine further the democratic values which afford them their directions in education. The desirability of frequent reexamination is shown by a notable twentieth century shift in democratic concepts. In redefining the promise of democracy, a group of social scientists in Ohio State University wrote: "Two conclusions appear to be clear. First, that while the philosophy of individualism which emphasizes the worth of the individual and his right to an opportunity for the full development and free expression of his personality is as true as ever, and is still the goal of American life, individualism as a method of achieving the good life is no longer practical. Second, that if we are to realize the goal of securing for the individual those conditions of life to which Americans have always aspired, we must abandon the philosophy and the practice of trying to achieve that goal only by individualistic means. Social responsibility and collective action for decent incomes, for security, for health, for recreation, for education, constitute, under the conditions which our modern complex and interdependent mode of living and working impose, the only practical road to the goal of individualism."[3]

There Is New Ground To Be Broken

Democratic-minded supervisors, who have thought thru their values, may feel that there is little new ground for them to break in the area of philosophy of education. Actually, there is a postwar educational frontier going begging for their best efforts. Who is better equipped to help teachers in the intelligible and intelligent application of values to the educational experiences of students? The democratic philosophy has been inadequately translated into educational action.

Many educators can now glibly recite the value pattern to which they subscribe, indicating their acceptance of a relativistic rather than an authoritarian viewpoint, their readiness to contrast conflicting world views such as the anarchical attitude which confuses freedom with doing as one pleases, the authoritarianism of the various totalitarian outlooks, and the true democratic way. But many teachers and supervisors have not yet learned to make such understandings operate in actual curriculum content. After lip service to philosophy, they make a flying mental leap to a curriculum utterly irrelevant to professed purposes.

There is seldom malice aforethought in this arbitrary leap. It is sheer lack of know-how. When teachers see possibilities for developing democratic practices in a classroom environment, they eagerly avail themselves of opportunities. Many American schools are commendably developing microcosms marked by wholesome human relations. But few schools have helped students to understand and appreciate the values which underlie

---

[3] Ohio State University. *Democracy in Transition*. New York: D. Appleton-Century Co., 1937. p. 29.

desirable social practices in the schoolroom. Few have helped young people to apply democratic standards readily and consistently to personal everyday actions and to social problems. Educators are slowly discovering how to help young people to live together. But the intellectualization of this process, the comprehension and application of a consistent set of values, is scarcely explored territory in education.

Experience Centers Afford Sound Learning

Only a seventh son of a seventh son could foresee the most appropriate experience centers for every social education curriculum. Experimental-minded educators, seventh sons or not, deny that any pattern can be prescribed which is universally useful. Communities differ in this continental America; neighborhoods differ within communities; schools differ within neighborhoods; classes differ within schools; individuals differ within classes. The ways in which schools handle social education programs differ widely: some channel it thru history and social studies subjects; others thru an integrated social studies sequence; others thru core curriculums; while still others emphasize a social education program which permeates all phases of the curriculum. Therefore, educators must individually analyze the culture which provides the social foundation of education; learn the needs, problems, and tensions of the young people with whom they work; determine and apply a philosophy of education which will guide their endeavors. These insights, with a conception of content for implementation, the educator brings with him to a teaching situation where, after the give and take of teacher-pupil planning, actual (not paper) curriculum experiences materialize.

Among the centers of learning experience, the following are suggested as of probable postwar educational concern:

1. Personal development and self-understanding
    (life and growth, sex and marriage, personality, psychology, mental hygiene)
2. Home, school, and friends
    (the family, housing, immediate educational problems, school government, age-mate relationships)
3. Health
    (diet, exercise, posture, rest, heredity, medical care, disease)
4. Time on our hands
    (recreation, use of leisure time, expanding interests)
5. Goods and services
    (consumer education concerning food, clothing, shelter, economic organization, advertising, standards)
6. Racial, religious, ethnic, social-economic relationships
    (intercultural education concerning minority groups, prejudice, human relations)

7. Our vocations
    (varieties of work, work experience, vocational choice, job preparation)
8. Education
    (further education, varieties of schools, self-education, role of education, educational support)
9. Proposed roads for the American economy
    (*laissez faire*, restoration of free market, business leadership, mixed economy, governmental planning)
10. Workers, management, and government
    (historical development, consolidation, conflicts)
11. Propaganda and public opinion
    (sources of our ideas, agencies of communication, propaganda technics)
12. Ways of living in other nations
    (China, Russia, Latin America, British Empire, Germany)
13. War in the modern world
    (backgrounds, causation, alignments, conscription, weapons, results)
14. Efforts toward enduring peace
    (attempts to organize peace, disruptive factors, nationalism, imperialism)
15. Human and natural resources in modern civilization
    (resource bases, technology, science, cultural lag, human behavior)
16. World views and ideologies
    (religion, democracy, fascism, communism)

Such a list is intended only to stimulate thought and attendant disagreement on needed emphases in the years immediately ahead. It is not a final, comprehensive list. Fundamentally, educational experiences must be adapted to the problems of American City and to John Smith's needs as well as to the culture of America in the atomic age and to generalized child and adolescent needs. No list, however, can substitute for the fundamental task of the supervisor as he works side by side with teachers—to examine the culture, the needs of young people, the unfinished business of philosophy, and to develop centers of learning experience which are valid for a specific community-neighborhood-school-class situation in which teachers as well as children and youth are continuously learning.

2

Supervision in the American Scene

To whom shall American education turn for leadership during this transition period when new concepts must be gained and new insights developed? Certainly a position of leadership belongs to classroom teachers. These are people who devote their lives to the training of the young, who work tirelessly to strengthen democratic principles, whose precepts help to shape the destiny of the politicians, generals, scientists, writers, artists, laborers, and theologians of today. Their days and nights are filled with the urgent necessity of preparing young people to meet the present and the future.

Administrators, too, rightfully play a role of leadership in the schools of our land. These are men and women who have training in financial affairs and are adept at meeting the public. They are anxious to have their schools meet the needs of modern society and of the individual who lives in the new world. And they make progress rapidly as they see the road ahead which education should follow. But their burdens are heavier than before. They are inextricably entangled in pressing financial problems and the minute details of organization that accompany any period of accelerated progress.

Both classroom teachers and administrators are ready to move into a new era of living. They are ready and able to assume responsibilities and to share them. Both groups, however, are weighted down with the intricacies of their daily work. Who is to share with them the responsibility of reading, exploring, of thinking in frontier areas, and of pointing the educational direction? There is an educational leader who works shoulder to shoulder with both the administrator and the classroom teacher. He is the supervisor.

By Marguerite Ransberger, *Supervisor, Elementary School of Lompoc Union, California*

The Ideal Supervisor Is a Versatile Person

What kind of person is this *ideal* supervisor for American schools? He is a composite of all the finest qualities of supervisors who have ever served the schools. Above all he has a sincere belief in the importance of his unique educational functions. His work, his training, and his personality are geared, not only to the local and immediate problems of pupils, teachers, and administrators, but to the many social problems of the era in which we live. He is a frontier thinker, a philosopher, whose enthusiastic faith in democracy as a way of life is contagious. He is a dreamer, daring to dream of a world free of prejudice, hatred, and poverty. He is a man of action, working consistently in the classrooms of America to make his dreams come true. He is a friend, discovering in each individual with whom he works a personality worthy of recognition and understanding. He is a student of the social sciences, noting and seeking to understand the trends of civilization. He faces the future courageously. The advent of the atomic age challenges but does not completely daunt him.

The ideal supervisor-leader is a dynamic person, with sufficient force to influence other people. He has enough vitality and energy to work thru the hours and over the wide areas thru which he may travel. He may be discouraged at times, but the face he turns to the world is strong. He inspires those with whom he works with a like faith in the destiny of education for democratic living.

The ideal supervisor-leader recognizes creative ability in others because he is, himself, creative. He senses human needs and seeks to fulfil them. Knowing the importance of education in the United States and the importance of thinking in advance areas, he has deliberately cultivated within himself a sensitivity to new ideas. He is creative enough to constantly reorganize his experiences and to develop plans, procedures, and new meanings to share with his colleagues. The creative supervisor is a pioneer on the greatest frontier of all, the unexplored and unknown continent of thought, and he has the inspiring opportunity of helping pupils and teachers to develop the capacity, each in his unique way, to express impressions gained thru seeing, hearing, feeling, and imagining.

The supervisor knows what responsibility means. If he makes a promise he fulfils it to the best of his ability at the specified time and place. He knows that an essential of responsibility is sharing it with someone else; therefore he shares his with others, being careful to do his own part effectively. He uses his own time wisely and is conscious of the value of the time of others.

No set of formulas will work in every situation. For this reason, the supervisor is both flexible and adaptable. He meets a change of plans with equanimity, understanding that out of new procedures may grow better situations. He realizes that change is inevitable and is aware that as he meets change so will the advance of education find those with whom he works ready to adapt themselves to new plans and procedures.

The supervisor has a keen sense of humor. Without it, his attempts to cultivate the other desirable traits of ideal supervision would be in vain. A smile may set the day right for a weary, discouraged teacher. A genuine chuckle at the right moment may be the turning point in some doubting urchin's life. The saving grace of being able to laugh at himself will save the supervisor from becoming a weighty bore endowed with wonderful purposes but so dull that people flee from his path. His sense of humor is kindly and based upon subtle shadings. He laughs with, not at, people. Laughter is one of the most potent aids of the good supervisor, for laughter shared makes the whole world one.

The supervisor is no hermit soul living on an intellectual Olympus. He is a social being who participates actively in the affairs of men. His interest in people makes him an acceptable member of any group of which he may be a part, whether it be a professional group with interests similar to his own or a lay group with many and varied interests which he can share or can learn to share.

The supervisor-leader is sincere in his dealings with his fellowmen. His sincerity of purpose guides him thru the morass of doubt and of self-appraisal. It helps him to inspire others with his own idealism. He realizes that education faces its most difficult years, and he has faith in its worthiness to meet the challenge.

His Jobs Are Manifold under Many Titles

How can the supervisor possibly comprehend the problems of the harassed superintendent whose desk is piled with report forms and whose patrons are howling for reduction of taxes? What does he know about the crowding of classrooms and the impossibility of making social adjustments between the Van Ristocrats and the Alley Dwellers? Philosophers may philosophize and dreamers may dream to their hearts' content, but do they ever deal in realities?

The supervisor-leader has faced these problems. He knows the joys and sorrows, the loves and hatreds of the teachers and children, for their problems are his concern. He knows the trials of the administrator, for he has worked cooperatively with the superintendent and has carried administrative responsibilities. He knows the social and intellectual problems of the classroom because he has been a classroom teacher.

For the man who has been called *the supervisor* in these pages is not one man, but many men, of many kinds of backgrounds, in positions under many titles. He is the supervising principal. In large systems he is the director of curriculum or of education. He is the general classroom supervisor or the specialist in specific subject areas. He is the head of a department. He is visiting counselor in rural areas and consultant to the staff of city schools. He is the instructor who is responsible for training of teachers in a college or university. He is the state supervisor who participates in professional discussions or leans against the rail fence to talk to a rural board member who has halted his plow to deliberate upon the affairs of some isolated school. His titles are as many and varied as the sections of this nation in which he works or as the individuals whom he meets in his daily travels.

But, whatever his title, this leader has chosen to be a supervisor because he loves children and believes in people, and above all else because he has an abiding faith in the destiny of the democratic way of life. He is a man of vision because he is a citizen of a land of inveterate dreamers, and he sees before him a world in which the American Dream may be realized for all people and for all times. But, he is also a realist, and he knows that the American Dream of a united people enjoying peace and plenty may not be realized without hard work and unrelenting faith. He works with teachers to develop the basic understanding that schools are established to meet the needs of the culture of which they are a part and that they must meet these needs or lose their significance. The supervisor advances beyond the methods of yesterday to help schools function in the world of today.

He Searches for Values

The supervisor continually examines his philosophy of education so that he knows under which principles he operates. With the coming of the atomic age he sat down and reconsidered his philosophy in light of the new powers, potentialities, and resultant responsibilities thrust upon mankind. He critically examined each of his goals and discarded those that were no longer essential. He retained those that were basic to an understanding of the principles that have guided men thru periods of stress and strain and are as rich as when they were first conceived. He redefined his philosophy until he felt that it would guide him in helping people to face the new era and join the march into the future. The supervisor knows that he may not foist his recently defined philosophy ready-made upon anyone else. He knows, too, that it is not complete—that it can be enriched and modified by the thinking of others. The supervisor-philosopher and the teacher work together as individuals, or as members of a larger group, comparing values deemed essential. Her close contact with children enables the classroom teacher to bring stimulation which clarifies the supervisor's thinking and broadens his vision. He, in turn, offers to the teacher new concepts for guaranteeing to children the inalienable rights of childhood and youth. As a result of group thinking, teachers and the supervisor together see these as:

The right to face the problems of today realistically in order that problems of ten, twenty, or even thirty years hence may be faced with the same realism.
The right to develop self-respecting personalities that will make valuable cultural contributions.
The right to master the skills and tools basic to the leading of an effective life in a democracy.
The right to be helped to realize that the democratic way of life is not a birthright which may be taken for granted but an ideal ever-changing in its implications, that must be worked toward.
The right to understand, utilize, adapt, or change the natural world so that life may be greatly enriched for everyone.
The right to develop an appreciation of the unique worth of the personalities met in daily living, so that all people who are part of the world culture may live together effectively.
The right to know and to acknowledge the contributions of the past to the heritage of the present thru a presentation of phases of social life and growth.
The right to definite knowledge upon which to base the choice of a career among the multitudinous choices that may be offered in the new stage of human development.
The right to creative self-expression.
The right to a common fund of cultural appreciations and shared understandings thru exploration of the treasures of literature, art, music, and science.

Of these rights the supervisor and teachers are ever conscious as they work with parents, other teachers, administrators, children, and youth in developing the citizen capable of living effectively as a member in a world democracy.

The supervisor sees his work objectively in relation to a certain group of teachers and children and makes provisions for individual differences among the persons with whom he works. He has faith in the freedom of all men and respects and values their opinions as he expects his in turn to be respected and valued. He believes that respect for personality is the cornerstone of freedom and the assurance of freedom for everyone. The supervisor-philosopher realizes that collective action for the development of mutual respect and freedom among peoples can come only from individuals who work together harmoniously.

Many People Cross His Path

The supervisor is a student of human relationships and has consciously worked and studied to develop within himself insights and understandings concerning the forces that motivate human beings. He is a teacher of teachers as well as indirectly a teacher of children and youth. He is genuinely sympathetic but never maudlin in his sympathy. He knows that personality is the direct result of the impact of individual experiences. When he meets a defiant child or a troubled teacher, he looks beneath the surface and seeks to learn something of the individual's background that will give him a basis for understanding obvious symptoms. Family responsibilities, financial worries, social pressures, peer relationships, whether it be teacher or child, these are crucial parts in the total life picture.

He realizes that the youth of a literate and enlightened people must develop a command of basic skills sufficient to render them effective in their chosen ways of life. He knows that the nature of a child makes it impossible to teach effectively many new concepts at once; that if a child is introduced abruptly to a number of special studies, an emotional block may be formed that will make his future one of educational frustration. He knows that the true center of the correlation of school subjects may not be science, literature, history, or geography but the child's own social setting. He knows that integration takes place within the individual. He knows that the world community begins and ends with the child's own environment; but that as the child grows in understanding of relationships close to him, his horizon may expand to include those just beyond, until finally it reaches those far away. The supervisor brings to the teacher a variety of materials which he has found basically sound that will help the teacher to see the necessity for developing within the child a readiness for each new experience thruout his school career. He knows that readiness is not a principle that belongs to the beginning days of school alone but is a prerequisite to each experience with which the child or the youth is confronted thruout the period of his education.

Because the supervisor has a basic understanding of the laws of learning, he knows that the learning process is much the same at any stage of human development. As the teacher is working with the child she is increasing her store of knowledge in much the same way that the child is increasing his. As the supervisor-leader works with the teacher his own horizons are also broadening. The learning process is continuous. As the teacher works with the child to develop a readiness for reading or for mathematical experiences, so the supervisor works with the teacher to develop a readiness for supervision.

The supervisor-leader in developing teacher readiness for supervision works to make the teacher feel that he is a friend and a sincere one. He is interested in her ideas and attainments. The curriculum is not his and he has not developed it working alone in a secluded office. The teacher works with him exploring the latest materials developed in other school systems. They study, read, and think together. They discuss the evolving material with experts who are called in to give assistance. Often the teacher is the expert and she guides group thinking, for there are areas in which her experiences make for understandings not fully grasped by supervisor or consultant. Together they evaluate supplemental materials from which they may make selections, in order that decisions may be more valid and work ever more effective. Having been closely identified with curriculum development, the teacher feels that she shares responsibility for the success or failure of new ventures. As they work with the developed curriculum the teacher and supervisor evaluate it and explore strengths and weaknesses. Then when the inevitable change that is the accompaniment of human progress occurs, they are ready to go ahead with understanding of life in an expanding society.

That leadership is relative to the situation in which it operates or to the job that needs to be done is the conviction of the supervisor. But it is not enough that he alone be convinced of this. It must permeate teacher groups working and thinking together. Within the group itself there needs to be recognition of all of the varieties of potential leadership which different teachers possess. In one group there is Alice Brown's leadership in thinking thru a problem; Jane Thomas' fine understanding of children; Fern Master's broad outlook on life growing out of living among peoples of many cultures; Jim White's keen awareness of community thinking; Eloise Stone's genuine friendliness and concern for others; Dick Johnson's ability to pour oil on troubled waters. Each of these is a leadership peculiar to the individual.

The supervisor recognizes various types of group leadership as well. As older and younger teachers pool their ideas and experiences, each of them gains. The younger teacher, accepting help from the experienced teacher in the next room or in the next school, in turn assumes leadership as she offers some of the materials that have been brought to her attention in recent college experiences. Both teachers are the stronger for the exchange. The older teacher has unconsciously imbibed some of the idealism and enthusiasm of youth, while the younger teacher has gained new respect for the understanding of the individual child possessed by the older teacher.

The supervisor-counselor believes in the improvability of human beings. It matters not to him whether a child or teacher be large or small, black or white, Catholic, Protestant, or Jew. He sees only an individual who is the center of an ever-expanding social pattern. He realizes that a change in voice inflection or a lift of an eyebrow may change a child's attitudes toward his peers, but that a child has no natural racial or class prejudices and antipathies. These are the doubtful gifts of age to youth. The supervisor's belief in the democratic way of life makes him deeply aware of the danger of the instillation of ready-made prejudices, and he works with his fellow teachers toward the development of desirable attitudes and discouragement of undesirable tendencies.

He Is a Link between School and Community

The supervisor is a key liaison officer between the schools and the community. He realizes that the community in which a school is situated is the center of the world for the youth who attend that school. This single community is a picture of other communities that differ in only a few characteristics. As such, the community should be a laboratory for the child or young person who in actuality is a citizen of the world. The youth should know the businesses in his community and be familiar with the processes by which they are conducted. He should have a basic understanding of the industries upon which the community life is based. The supervisor not only participates in community affairs as does the administrator but encourages the teachers to be active community participants.

The supervisor knows what helps individuals need in choosing their way of earning a livelihood. He knows of the occupations that are open to youth in the immediate environment. He has knowledge of vocational choices open to young people today or knows where such information may be secured. If the system in which the supervisor works has a functioning guidance program, he turns his information concerning the youth in a definite school over to the guidance director and renders such assistance as the counselor requests. If there is no special guidance director, the supervisor must make available to the teacher and the youth the material that will help each individual make a wise choice in relation to his potentialities and the community in which he expects to live.

The supervisor is keenly aware of the problems of local government, industry, agriculture, labor, business, and management. He can speak the language of lay people. He is deeply interested in the problems of the individuals who support the school because their problems are his and because they influence the effectiveness of the education offered in the schools. Since he is interested in the problems of the school patrons, he interprets the school to community members and together they work on the problems of the community's school. He and the people who work with him are recognized as experts in the field of education and, as such, they accept responsibility for guidance in educational thinking. They help doctors, farmers, storekeepers, housewives, and politicians understand and evaluate what the school is trying to do. But they, in turn, recognize that only as all community members think together and share insights into community life will education truly be a part of the culture in which it exists.

He Rises to Demands of Society

The supervisor bears the responsibility for guiding educational efforts. He must be ready to explore new areas. He must keep abreast of the developments of science, politics, business, and labor. He is a positive force in the development of desirable social change. He wishes to implement the development of a literate and thinking citizenry of the world state. In order to do this he must be acquainted with a wide range of literature. He finds time to read, to explore, and to think. He reads critically and weighs material for its value to the people with whom he works.

He reviews the literature in a variety of fields, discarding that which is trivial and filing for later consideration that which may be valid. He knows the sources of materials and knows how to select those which are scientifically accurate and which will meet the needs of a specific situation. He has a knowledge not only of materials which will help a teacher to broaden her horizons but he knows pupil materials, as well. When he steps into a classroom where boys and girls are struggling with a problem for which they cannot find adequate material to guide them to a solution, he can tell them where to turn.

The leader knows that educators have been accused, perhaps justly at times, of having their heads in the clouds and of being unaware of a world outside the cloistered walls of the school. He knows that education is the center of the culture by which it has been established and can last only so long as it serves the culture effectively. Today, no man can live alone. The same forces affect the lives of all. The teacher of today must know something about the political scene because what happens there influences her classroom practices. She must know something about the ideas most prominent in current magazines, books, and motion pictures because they directly influence the thinking of the child or the youth with whom she works. She must know of the latest scientific developments because these influence the ways of life in any community. But the teacher is so busy that she has little time to explore the countless materials concerning such impacts upon the personality of her students. The supervisor reads in these fields and studies the most pertinent materials, that he may intelligently recommend the best to his co-workers.

He knows that audio-visual aids are important equipment for every school system. They may be as important as books. The supervisor carefully studies these new materials, knows which are currently available, and likely to be the most valuable in a specific situation. Some of these aids are so new that they are misused as often as they are used effectively. If they are to take their rightful place in the classroom and become as much a part of the equipment as tables, chairs, desks, and books they must be used in such a manner never in danger of being interpreted as frills. The supervisor surveys this field critically, so that the experiential backgrounds of children may be richer than they have ever been before and school may become the joyful place that Johnny so eagerly anticipates before he starts.

The supervisor realizes that today the average adult cannot conceive of the potentialities of atomic energy. There are no words with which to describe such possibilities. The proper symbols have not yet come into being because mankind has had no experiences upon which to base such understanding or to develop the essential descriptive phrases. This inability to comprehend lends to the supervisor a forceful means of explaining to teachers, administrators, and school patrons the need of experiences upon which a child may base his understanding of the symbols that he is expected to read and interpret to a gratified circle of teachers, friends, and relatives.

The conception of supervision considered in this chapter is that of educational leadership. It should be appreciative, recognizing and encouraging strengths; it should be cooperative, utilizing the leadership ability of all; it should be creative, inspiring creativeness in others; it should be objective but always human. Above all, ideal supervision exists only as it recognizes the importance of all people as individuals with a rightful place in today's culture.

3

Analyzing Our Problems

It is the purpose of this chapter to define the major goals of presentday American education, to present the handicaps supervision faces, to examine types of organizational provision for supervision together with supervisory services rendered, and to outline the areas in which advance and development are needed. Evidence presented in the following pages was gathered by means of questionnaires sent during 1945 to individuals in more than two hundred and sixty communities, representing every state in the Union, from a study of recent professional literature, and from an analysis of curriculum materials produced by outstanding school systems. Data included in this chapter unless otherwise stated are taken from responses to the above-mentioned questionnaires.

Altho almost half of the questionnaires were sent to supervisors, directors of curriculum, and instructors in teacher-training institutions, included in the mailing list were supervising principals of both secondary and elementary schools, city and county superintendents, staffs of state departments of education, and a selected group of teachers. Recipients of the questionnaires were chosen from the membership list of the Association for Supervision and Curriculum Development, a department of the National Education Association, and from school systems reported in recent professional literature as doing outstanding educational work. The committee responsible for the questionnaire deliberately made its list of recipients selective, since its purpose was to discover the thinking and practice of the most competent leaders thruout the country.

Few critics of our public schools have charged educational leaders with a lack of zeal or good intent, but the criticism frequently is heard that educators are confused and in disagreement as to just what their role in American culture should be. Even among school people, many conflicting opinions are heard. Some point to recent military successes as evidence

---

By Lelia Ann Taggart, *Director of Education, Santa Barbara County, California,* and Mary C. Evans, *General Supervisor, Santa Barbara County, California*

of the efficiency of American public education, while others give army records on illiteracy as evidence of inefficiency and waste. Some say that our schools are so experimental and progressive in their methods that they overlook the necessary and obvious task of teaching skills and abilities, while spending their energies on visionary attempts to fulfil other social functions. Others charge that our schools are too bound by tradition to face modern social problems realistically.

It is not easy for education to steer a clear course thru all this jumble of praise and blame, but it is necessary for educators to come to some commonly accepted standards if the American system of education is to continue to serve the nation effectively. The accelerating mobility of our people requires increased coordination of educational services. This means that educational leaders, until now intent on improving the individual schools or systems in which they work, must feel an increasing responsibility for sharing with other schools and other systems their best thinking and their most promising ways of working. American education does not need uniformity of methods, but educators thruout the country do need to become increasingly aware of common problems to be faced and common goals to be attained.

What Are the Goals of Supervision Today?

The first item on the questionnaire was concerned with the goals upon which present programs of supervision are based. Eleven broad statements of goals were given and recipients were asked to check these in the order of importance as far as their specific school systems were concerned, adding other goals considered especially significant.

It is fully recognized that the goals listed are closely interrelated and that no one of them can stand alone. However, a consciousness of the steps, or goals, which are possible and desirable to attain, and a sense of their relative importance are prerequisite to the realization of any philosophy of education. To say that all aims are equally worthwhile and, therefore, should be equally emphasized at all times and under all circumstances is like saying, "We want to be good," without any fundamental understanding of the ideas and actions that "being good" necessarily involves.

Goals of Present Programs of Supervision

  A. To make American public schools an effective means for maintaining and extending American democratic ideals.
  B. To implement a system of guidance designed to produce pupils who are physically and mentally well adjusted and who have social competence.
  C. To help boys and girls understand and deal with personal and social problems which have meaning for them now, so that they may, as adults, be prepared to face issues which will necessarily arise.

ANALYZING OUR PROBLEMS 29

Fig. 1
RELATIVE IMPORTANCE OF GOALS OF PRESENT PROGRAMS OF SUPERVISION AS RATED BY SELECTED GROUPS OF SUPERVISORS, STATE SUPERINTENDENTS, CITY AND COUNTY SUPERINTENDENTS AND TEACHERS.

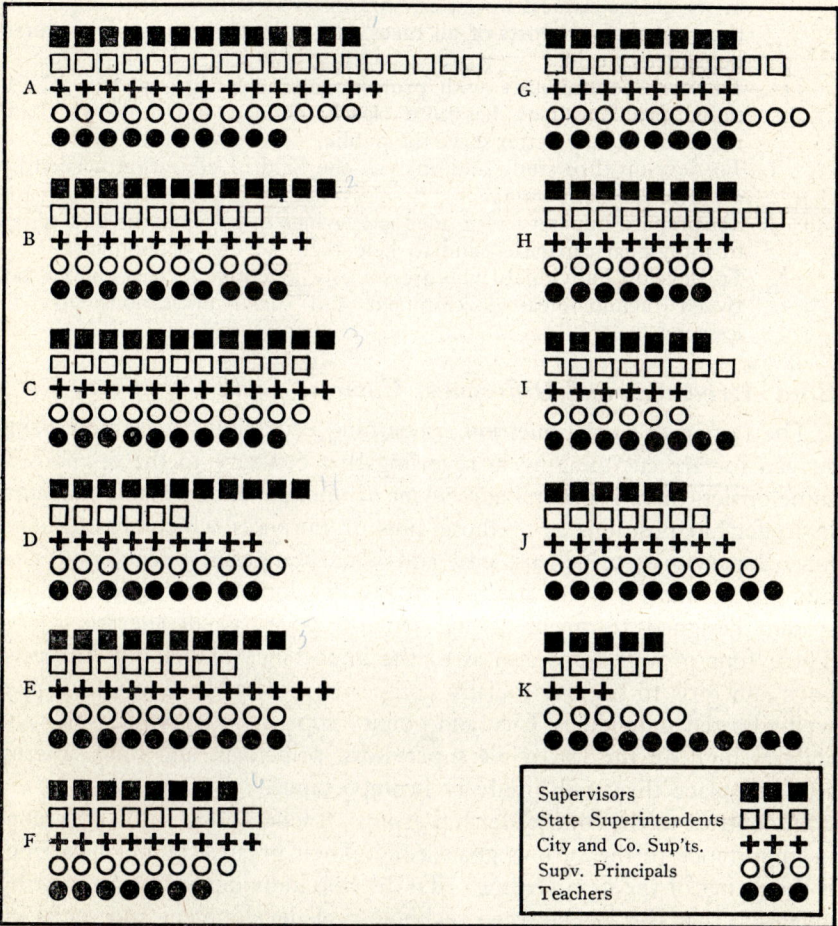

(Each unit in the above graph represents one percent of the total weighted score of goals as rated by the five groups of individuals responding to the Yearbook questionnaires. The eleven goals as listed in the questionnaires were numbered in order of importance as judged by each respondent. Those goals rated first in importance were valued at eleven points, those second at ten points, those third at nine points, and on down to the eleventh place receiving one point)

D. To develop in pupils those attitudes necessary to effective human relationships, overcoming bigotry, race prejudice, and class hatred.
E. To develop increasing efficiency in the teaching of skills and knowledges.
F. To work toward equalization of educational opportunities for all children.
G. To develop individuals who will be able to live effectively in a world in which mechanical inventions and discoveries have made imperative the cooperative efforts of all races and nationalities in a highly interdependent world.
H. To work continuously with professional and lay groups that educational problems may be more clearly defined and dealt with, and that schools may better serve the public.
I. To develop thru study and analysis the kind of education needed by a particular community.
J. To prepare pupils to earn adequate livings in occupations best suited to individual capacities, and to help them achieve economic literacy.
K. To develop individuals who are socially inventive so that the lag between technological development and social institutions may be lessened.

Both Agreement and Differences Come to Light

The responses to the question concerning educational goals now being striven for are encouraging in revealing that contrary to the opinions of some critics, there is general agreement of opinion among many educators in leadership positions as to those aims or purposes which should come first. Supervisors, principals, city and county superintendents, and state superintendents lay great stress upon the development of an educational system designed to maintain and extend American democratic ideals. These four groups agree also as to the importance of helping American boys and girls to become socially competent and to develop into happy, well-adjusted individuals. City and county superintendents rate skills and abilities high on the list, while supervisors, principals, and state superintendents place them only midway in importance.

In contrast to the four leadership groups, teachers assign little difference in importance to the various goals listed. Their greatest point of variance is the rating of the item reading: "To develop individuals who are socially inventive that the lag between technological development and social institutions may be lessened." Teachers placed this goal first on the list in order of importance. They are in agreement with city and county superintendents that the skills are of great significance. In their rating of other goals, teachers are more concerned with the personal and social adjustments of pupils than are the other groups.

It is not the purpose of this chapter to speculate as to the reasons for divergencies of opinions, but it is significant that the groups working most directly with youth and children are particularly aware of the need for helping them to achieve satisfactory personal and social adjustments. It might be well, on the other hand, to ask why the teacher group failed to assign significant differences to the values of the various educational aims. Is it because leadership has failed to inspire teachers to think thru and express a philosophy of education? Is it because teachers are so subject to pressure to work toward goals set by administrators or supervisors that they have not been able to clarify their own thinking? Is it possible that the duties and functions required of teachers keep them so occupied with the minutiae of their work that it is difficult for them to get a broad vision of educational problems?

State superintendents, as might be expected, see as of great importance many of the broader educational problems such as equalization of educational opportunities, the development of public understanding and support of education, and the adaptation of educational theory and practices to the problems of the postwar world.

School people may well scrutinize more closely the item given last place on the list of goals by all but the teacher group: "To develop individuals who are socially inventive that the lag between technological development and social institutions may be lessened." The war has greatly accelerated the already astounding pace of technological invention, and has brought about an unprecedented social upheaval, affecting the lives of the majority of individuals thruout the world. Undoubtedly, if our way of life is to endure, it is imperative for mankind to solve a host of grave social problems long present in our social order, but which the war and its aftermath have brought to a head. It should certainly be asked whether modern public education should not dedicate itself to much more energetic attempts than heretofore to develop individuals equipped to solve such problems and eager to do so.

Any rating of a list of educational goals can only be tentative, with current and localized problems and perplexities a potent factor in the placing of a goal either first or last on the list. Nevertheless, the responses show clearly that many educational leaders recognize that schools have responsibilities that go far beyond the teaching of skills and knowledges, important as these are. Teaching of skills and knowledges will still absorb a large portion of the school's time and attention, but they will need to be taught in a functional setting and learned much more thoroly than they have ever been before. Otherwise broader and more socially significant educational aims cannot be achieved.

List Is Broadened To Include Other Goals

A survey made of recent educational literature in order to determine educational goals as reflected in the writings of the nation's leading educators showed that they placed vocational training and the development of

Fig. 2
MAJOR GOALS OF EDUCATION AS RATED BY A SELECTED GROUP OF NATIONALLY KNOWN EDUCATORS

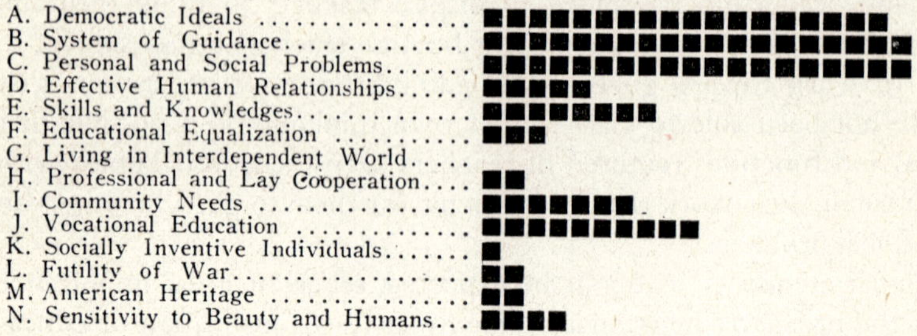

A. Democratic Ideals
B. System of Guidance
C. Personal and Social Problems
D. Effective Human Relationships
E. Skills and Knowledges
F. Educational Equalization
G. Living in Interdependent World
H. Professional and Lay Cooperation
I. Community Needs
J. Vocational Education
K. Socially Inventive Individuals
L. Futility of War
M. American Heritage
N. Sensitivity to Beauty and Humans

(Each unit represents one percent of the total number of opinions collected)

economic literacy much higher on the list than any of the groups included in the questionnaire. This raises the question of the degree to which modern social and educational problems have as their roots economic causes. If economic factors play as significant a role as a number of our best-known educational thinkers believe, it may be that educators on all levels will need to give much more attention to socio-economic issues.

A number of these individuals also listed as of major importance goals not included in the questionnaires. Among those most frequently named were the development of:

> A recognition of the futility of war as a means of settling disputes.
> An appreciation of America's cultural and racial heritage.
> An appreciation of beauty and a sensitivity to human suffering.

There can be little argument in this atomic era but that war as a means of settling disputes is futile. The only alternative left is international co-operation. Yet newspaper headlines daily make it appallingly evident that the peoples of the world are ill-prepared for effective cooperation. Beulah Amidon makes the problem vivid in the following questions:

> By what failure in the educational process are young people turned out, so insecure and so undiscriminating that they flock to rabble-rousers? What educational gaps let in hate and prejudice? What quickens curiosity? Strengthens integrity? Distinguishes truth from propaganda? Encourages neighborliness and good will? Turns knowledge and training into the stuff of action?

> The dictators have their answers. They have devised an education to warp young and old alike to their goals. In the long view—but the times obscure the long view.

> What are the American answers? What are we trying to do through

the schools we keep? What is our goal for the hugest system of public education in the world? What is the purpose of its enormous expenditures of time, effort, and money? Are the schools equal to their task—not to condition docile followers, but to educate free men?[1]

Our national idols have long been the scientists and the industrialists—the go-getters and the men who get things done. Certainly no one would belittle their contributions. But we cannot escape the fact that, unless social scientists and specialists in human relationships receive corresponding recognition, the leadership necessary for the very survival of our civilization cannot be achieved. The schools should not only examine their responsibility for developing such leaders, but should also seek to develop in all pupils, followers as well as leaders, those basic traits, attitudes, and appreciations that will make such leadership possible.

A great deal has been said in recent years about the importance of educating American children to know and appreciate the social order in which they live. Some act on the belief that an increased number of American history courses will accomplish this. Others stress final examinations in civics and government as a sort of intellectual passport to American citizenship. What we should want American children to learn from such courses and examinations is not a series of historical events, a set of important dates, or a collection of governmental and historical data, however useful and interesting these may be. What we do want them to learn and take pride in is the meaning of the democratic heritage, the efforts thru the past years to fulfil it, and the struggle ahead in which these children may take their part in bringing the American Dream closer and closer to realization, not only for our own people, but for all people everywhere.

Many of today's children have been nourished on hatred, fear, and ugliness. And this is true not only in the war-torn countries of the old world. Every day countless American children sit thru motion pictures in which violence and destruction are made as vivid as the art of the screen can make them. Educators, witnessing the reactions of children to such pictures, may well question whether they will ever love beauty and become really sensitive to human suffering. It seems obvious that we cannot expect to create in children a love of the good and the beautiful or sensitize them to human suffering by means of classroom teaching alone. Education must make itself felt in all forces which influence child behavior, from the home and the church to movies and the comics.

---

[1] Amidon, Beulah, editor. *Democracy's Challenge to Education*. New York: Farrar and Rinehart, 1940, p. 4.

What Handicaps Effective Supervision?

Qualified People Are Hard To Find

City and county superintendents, principals, and supervisors who responded to questionnaires showed a belief that the major handicap supervision faces is that of securing adequately trained personnel. Obviously, before making a real analysis of the problem, it is necessary to determine the characteristics of adequate training for supervision. Requirements for certification in the field of supervision vary widely from state to state. They range from a record of successful teaching experience to a minimum of a master's degree plus a record of successful teaching experiences and the completion of a specified number of units of graduate study related to the problem of supervision. Responses to the questionnaires show that of the total number of individuals questioned, one hundred and twenty four have earned degrees beyond the A.B.; seventeen have the Ph.D. or Ed. D. degree, and a considerable number more have covered at least some of the work toward their doctorates. Twenty-four of the group have earned A. B. degrees, leaving only a very inconsiderable number without some form of educational degree.

Altho the questionnaire respondents were a selected group, it seems safe to conclude that the time supervisors have spent in training for their work has, on the whole, been adequate. The question arises, then, whether or not the training many supervisors have undergone has been the best type to equip them for educational leadership. If adequately prepared personnel is not available, where does the fault lie? Is it possible to set up preservice experiences in colleges and universities that will develop the philosophy and technics essential to effective educational leadership? Is there also need for improved methods of discovering individuals who show evidence of potential leadership abilities and of guiding them into public-school supervision?

A remark frequently heard is that only those who have been outstandingly successful as classroom teachers should be employed as supervisors and that, even then, supervisors should be required at regular intervals to return for a year of classroom teaching in order to keep close to the problems of teachers. The questionnaires show that in actual practice 50 percent of the supervisors questioned did enter supervision directly from the classroom. An additional 30 percent entered thru administrative positions of various kinds. Seventeen percent were instructors in teachers colleges before they became public-school supervisors. The remaining 3 percent were research specialists and school librarians. Only one lone individual had entered supervision directly from training. It would seem, then, that any inadequacy of personnel can hardly be due to a lack of practical

Fig. 3

DEGREES EARNED BY SUPERVISORS REPRESENTED IN
THE 1946 YEARBOOK STUDY

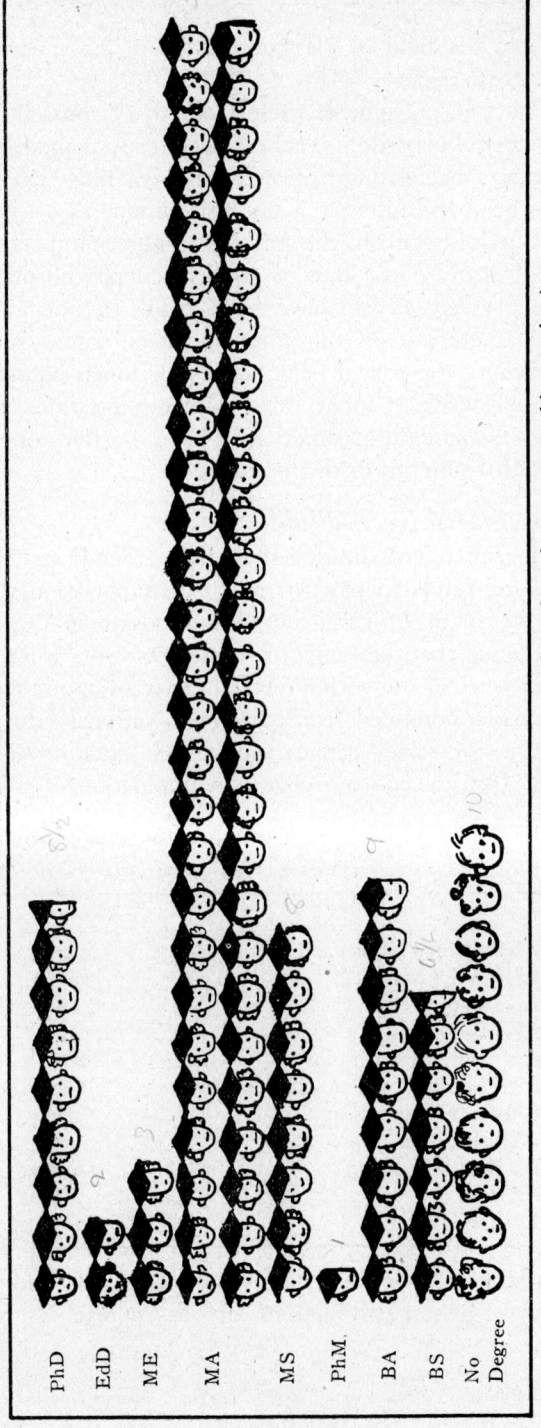

(Each symbol represents one percent of the total number of responses to this question.)

experience in the field of classroom teaching or a background of other educational experience.

It may be well, in light of these facts, to ask ourselves whether or not highly successful classroom teachers necessarily make the best supervisors. Granted that a background of successful teaching may be a decided advantage to a supervisor, may it not also be true that a general practice of selecting supervisors from the ranks of highly competent teachers results in depriving many classrooms of good teachers who make only mediocre supervisors? What efforts have been made to isolate and define those qualities characteristic of our most successful supervisors? What phases of their training have such successful individuals found most helpful to them in their work as supervisors? What suggestions, if any, might our best leaders in the field of supervision have to offer concerning preservice experiences for supervisors of the future?

Funds Aren't Always Available

State superintendents headed their list of handicaps facing supervision with "lack of funds to pay for adequate supervision services." A study made of the status of rural-school supervision in the United States in 1944[2] points out that the range of rural supervisors' salaries in this country is from $1300 to $6000, with a median salary of approximately $2400. The following table, compiled from data in a National Education Association bulletin gives the salary ranges for various kinds of supervisory services in cities of from 30,000 to 100,000 in population.

TABLE I—SALARIES PAID VARIOUS SCHOOL SUPERVISORY OFFICERS, 1942-1943, TWO HUNDRED AND FOURTEEN CITIES 30,000 TO 100,000 IN POPULATION[3]

	Median	Maximum	Minimum
Director of Vocational Education	$3365	$5500	$2181
Director of High Schools	3302	4300	2300
Director of Kindergartens	3000	3800	1955
Director of Primary Grades	2970	5500	1620
Director of Intermediate Grades	2950	4500	1500
Director of Research, Tests, and Measurements	2870	5155	642
Director of Physical Education	2808	5500	1215
Director of Music	2544	5500	1005
Director of Visual Education	2510	3600	1200
Director of Art	2365	4360	1260
Chief Attendance Officer	2150	4388	425

The question of salaries for supervision services cannot be dealt with apart from the general problem of salaries for teachers. Supervision, how-

[2] University of Georgia. *Status of General Rural School Supervision, United States.* Athens: the University, 1944. (Mimeo.)

[3] National Education Association, Research Division. *Special Salary Tabulations 11-B.* Washington, D. C.: the Association, July 1943. p. 18.

ANALYZING OUR PROBLEMS

ever expert, cannot be expected to affect the school systems markedly when teachers are overworked and underpaid. The problem of providing funds for all types of educational service can be solved only by arousing the interest and concern of the public, and thus obtaining more adequate public funds for education in general. Such articles as that appearing in *Reader's Digest* for October 1945, "Teachers' Pay—A National Disgrace," may do more to help the situation than carefully prepared articles in educational journals.

Many salaries offered supervisors are inadequate to attract the kinds of individuals needed for school leadership. While they are higher in general than teachers' salaries, supervisors' expenses are so great that in many instances their net incomes are less than those of the teachers they supervise. Supervision needs to ask to what extent the problem of the financing of supervision services has its roots in the failure of administrators to assign proper status to supervision. Administration, on the other hand, should examine staff salaries to see whether or not the services they expect from supervisors coincide with their own evaluation of those services in dollar and cents terms.

Careful evaluation of the various types of supervisory services, analyses to determine which types of supervision seem most likely to assure lasting benefit to the children in the schools, and compensation at least in some measure commensurate with the preparation of supervisors and the duties expected of them are the obligation of administrators in providing desirable supervision services for any school system.

Theory and Practice May Be At Odds

A considerable proportion of the supervisors and supervising principals responding to the questionnaires felt that the second most serious problem in supervision is the failure of leaders to translate the educational philosophy to which they subscribe into meaningful school practice. However, an examination of the functions frequently or regularly performed by supervisors seems to show little inconsistency between worthwhile supervisory aims and actual practice.

TABLE 2—FUNCTIONS FREQUENTLY OR REGULARLY PERFORMED BY SUPERVISORS RESPONDING TO QUESTIONNAIRE

Percent	Functions
100	Attending meetings of professional organizations
97	Discussing educational philosophy or objectives with teachers
96	Holding group conferences to discuss common problems
96	Making classroom visits
95	Holding individual conferences with teachers on problems they propose
94	Discussing methods with teachers
89	Working on committees in professional organizations

(Continued on page 38)

TABLE 2—FUNCTIONS FREQUENTLY OR REGULARLY PERFORMED BY SUPERVISORS RESPONDING TO QUESTIONNAIRE—*(Continued)*

Percent	Functions
88	Evaluating and selecting books for pupil use
88	Leading teaching groups in formulation and development of a common philosophy of education
86	Helping teachers organize and develop source or teaching units
86	Giving suggestions or instructions on how to initiate or carry thru an instructional unit
85	Organizing and working with teacher groups in curriculum revision programs
82	Interpreting test data to teachers and helping them to use them for improvement in teaching
81	Evaluating and selecting books for teachers' libraries
79	Acting as consultant in local faculty group meetings
78	Working with curriculum consultants in analysis or development of curriculum program
73	Speaking to lay organizations
72	Speaking to parent study groups
71	Holding office in professional organizations
70	Interviewing parents or laymen regarding educational matters
69	Writing or developing curriculum materials
67	Preparing descriptions of educational philosophy or objectives with teachers
65	Preparing manuals or bulletins on teaching various subjects
65	Setting up courses of study, scope, and sequence plans
65	Developing pupil-accounting systems, such as cumulative record cards
64	Interviewing prospective teachers, employees
62	Setting up and administering program to evaluate school practices
62	Directing testing programs
54	Preparing source or teaching units for use of teachers
53	Organizing and/or directing worshops for local teachers in the local area
47	Previewing films, stillfilms, records, or recordings
46	Instructing teachers in the use of audio-visual aids
45	Preparing written reports of classroom visits for the superintendent
44	Writing articles on education or the activities of the school for the newspapers
42	Administering standard tests
39	Planning demonstration teaching
39	Organizing audio-visual materials
39	Working with a teacher to help her do demonstration teaching
37	Organizing and/or directing worktype teacher meetings
36	Distributing audio-visual materials
30	Organizing and/or directing workshops for teachers on university campuses
29	Writing for professional journals or magazines
26	Correcting tests
14	Writing or collaborating in writing of textbooks

Of the functions listed as being performed regularly or frequently by between 80 and 100 percent of questionnaire respondents, more than half involve the discussion of the theory and philosophy of teaching or are concerned with professional meetings. May it not be that the fault lies not so much in the performance of functions inconsistent with the theories advanced by supervisors, but in a general tendency to talk too much and do too little? Should supervisors spend more time organizing, directing, and participating in teacher workshops; making provision for teachers to see excellent demonstration teaching; and working with teacher groups in the revision or development of curriculum programs?

There Is Confusion Over Duties

Another major handicap to supervision, according to questionnaire respondents, is confusion concerning supervisory duties. The questionnaires list over forty-five supervisory functions. Not a few of the respondents indicated that they performed more than half of these frequently or regularly. The supervisors expanded this list of duties still further. It is no wonder that some supervisors, especially those in general elementary or secondary supervision, are confused. It is obviously impossible for any one individual to handle successfully such a wide variety of duties. The problem of selecting which activities result in the greatest good is serious in itself. Added to this, many supervisors are asked to perform various duties which are essentially administrative in nature. Tensions arise when such individuals, accustomed to handling certain administrative details, unwittingly assume more authority than they should, or when supervisors are given so many tasks not directly related to the instructional program that they are frustrated in attempts to effect improvement in the classrooms. Certainly there is need for a clear-cut statement of those functions which should be expected of various classes of supervisors, together with a precise differentiation between administrative and supervisory functions.

Some Fail To See Their Job Realistically

Principals in both secondary and elementary schools, according to questionnaire responses, felt that supervisors do not see educational problems realistically, and that they do not make sufficient efforts to understand administrative problems and points of view. Many supervisors, on the other hand, felt that their services are not used to the best advantage by administrators.

The supervisory group was even more critical of supervisors' failure to achieve a broad view of educational problems than were the other groups. Solutions they offered to the problem were:

1. More general supervision, or requiring all supervisors of special

subjects to have experiences designed to show them how to use specialized knowledges and interests to strengthen the total educational fabric

2. The placing of much stress upon good teamwork among the members of supervisory staffs

3. Clear definition of supervisory duties and functions and differentiation between administrative and supervisory functions

4. Closer contacts between supervisors and administrators in order to gain better understanding of each others' problems and points of view

5. Much more vigorous attempts than have been made so far by supervisors to make their services valuable.

Human Relationships Create Problems

In an article dealing with handicaps to improved instruction Alice Miel presents an interesting analysis of barriers to instruction compiled from data obtained from students in a course at Teachers College, Columbia University.[4] Slightly more than 17 percent of the items named as handicaps to improved instruction deal directly with the problems of supervision.

'One man rule,' 'needless red tape,' 'teacher feuds,' 'lack of good leadership—the small mind in the high place,' 'failure of the supervisors to use the thinking ability of their teachers for the benefit of the whole school,' 'lack of equipment essential for better learning on the part of the pupils'—these are only a few of the 440 items listed by a group of 50 students enrolled in the writer's course at Teachers College, Columbia University, when they were asked to name what seemed to them to be the most significant barriers to improved instruction in the schools they know best.

The greatest lack in supervisors' knowledge and understanding, in the opinion of the group, is in the field of human behavior. Special knowledge in this field should be part of the equipment of such officers, it is felt.

The tabulation . . . reveals the frequency with which individual items referred to in the foregoing discussion are named as barriers.

Barriers	Frequency of Mention
Materials, equipment, facilities	41
Teacher load	26
Inertia, lack of interest	24
Leadership	19
Teacher preparation	16
Lack of cooperation	14
Philosophy and goals	13
Community lack of understanding	13
Teachers' salaries	11
Community meddling and pressures	11
Fear of change	10
Politics	9
Teacher quarreling, jealousy	9
Lack of in-service education	7

---

[4] Miel, Alice. "Barriers to Improved Instruction." *Teachers College Record* 46: 434-44; April 1945.

ANALYZING OUR PROBLEMS 41

Barriers	Frequency of Mention
Teacher fear and insecurity	7
Inflexibility	7
Tradition	6
Supervisory inconsistency	6
Teachers' personal problems	6
Racial differences	6
Financial support	5
Teacher selection	5
Pupil load	5
Vision	5
Supervisory technics	5
Supervisory knowledge of human behavior	5
Professional ethics	5
Lack of recognition and incentives	5
Interruptions of classroom work	4
Administrative ability	4
General understanding of children	4
Religious differences	4
Teacher rating	3
Physical condition of pupils	3
Teacher health	3
Schedules	3
Standardized tests	3

There are several salient features of the problem of educational barriers. Altho conditions of work are mentioned with highest frequency, it is obvious that the solution to the problem of removing these and other barriers is almost entirely one of improving human relations in and around schools. Something is wrong with a picture which contains so little interest and drive, so much fear and insecurity, so much quarreling and misunderstanding, so much conflict and lack of cooperation, such unwholesome attitudes.

Somehow educational leaders must find ways of improving the quality of the motivations of all persons connected with schools. They must help groups to realize the significance of the job they have undertaken when they enter the teaching profession so that they will be able to set for themselves worthwhile and challenging goals. They must also help themselves to learn better ways of getting along with others so that groups may accomplish what individuals working at cross purposes may never do. Once people who are motivated by high purposes and skilled at working cooperatively set their minds to the task, many of the relatively mechanical barriers to progress can be dealt with effectively and with comparative ease.

How Is Supervision Being Provided?

How are state, city, and county departments of education organized to provide for supervision services? How are these services financed? What do superintendents consider to be the major functions of supervisors? In the foregoing section of this report the inability to pay for super-

Fig. 4
STATE MEDIAN LEVELS OF SUPPORT PER CLASSROOM UNIT
THE 48 STATES AND DISTRICT OF COLUMBIA
CURRENT EXPENDITURE PER CLASSROOM UNIT

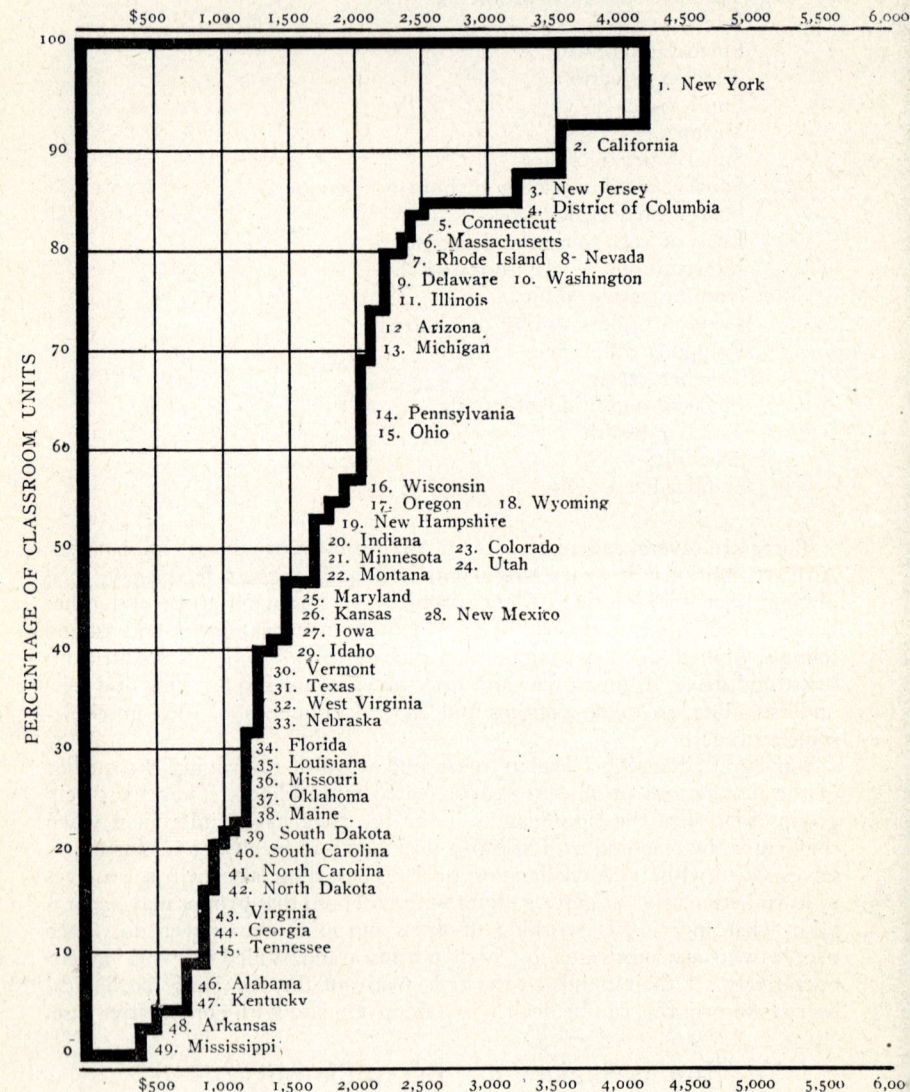

1. New York
2. California
3. New Jersey
4. District of Columbia
5. Connecticut
6. Massachusetts
7. Rhode Island
8. Nevada
9. Delaware
10. Washington
11. Illinois
12. Arizona
13. Michigan
14. Pennsylvania
15. Ohio
16. Wisconsin
17. Oregon
18. Wyoming
19. New Hampshire
20. Indiana
21. Minnesota
22. Montana
23. Colorado
24. Utah
25. Maryland
26. Kansas
27. Iowa
28. New Mexico
29. Idaho
30. Vermont
31. Texas
32. West Virginia
33. Nebraska
34. Florida
35. Louisiana
36. Missouri
37. Oklahoma
38. Maine
39. South Dakota
40. South Carolina
41. North Carolina
42. North Dakota
43. Virginia
44. Georgia
45. Tennessee
46. Alabama
47. Kentucky
48. Arkansas
49. Mississippi

ANALYZING OUR PROBLEMS 43

vision services was rated as one of the three greatest handicaps in the extension of such service. An examination of the basis of financial support of a program of public education reveals information pertinent to this problem.

A committee of educators representing the United States Office of Education, the National Education Association, the American Council of Education, the National Council of Chief State School Officers, and the Southern States Work Conference was shocked by its findings in a study of this problem. The following graph incorporates the significant data gathered in this study which was reported by John K. Norton and Daniel R. Davies.[5]

After making this careful analysis of state median levels of support per classroom in the forty-eight states and the District of Columbia, the committee concluded that "millions of children are either being denied all educational opportunity or the provision made for their schooling is so meager that their preparation for citizenship is wholly inadequate." A study of the current expenditure per classroom unit in New York contrasted with a similar study in Mississippi sharpens the gross inequalities that exist in the United States in the provision made for public education. Norton and Davies further conclude that "the states themselves are not going to be able to provide educational opportunity as long as the financing of education rests almost solely on the fiscal resources of the individual state."

To what source may states without adequate resources to finance a desirable program of public education go for support? Can provision be made other than thru the federal government?

State Programs Offer Many Ways of Working

Financial Support Is Planned For

In preparation of this yearbook the question was asked, "Will you describe briefly the state's responsibility for financing supervision?" Responses came from thirty state departments of education, and it is obvious that they were conditioned, in large measure, by the facts revealed in the foregoing discussion of inequalities of educational opportunity.

The state of Virginia, which Norton and Davies ranked forty-third in ability to provide adequate financial support for a program of public education, submitted a comprehensive statement which is quoted here.[6]

---

[5] Norton, John K., and Davies, D. R. "National Educational Inequality: Revealing the Facts in the Case." *Teachers College Record* 46: 353-59; March 1945.

[6] Virginia State Board of Education. *Regulations Governing Reimbursement from State Funds to Counties and Cities on Account of Supervisors of Instruction for White and Negro Elementary Schools, High Schools and of Directors of Instruction Employed for the School Year 1945-1946.* Richmond: the Board, April 1945. (Mimeo.)

44 LEADERSHIP THROUGH SUPERVISION

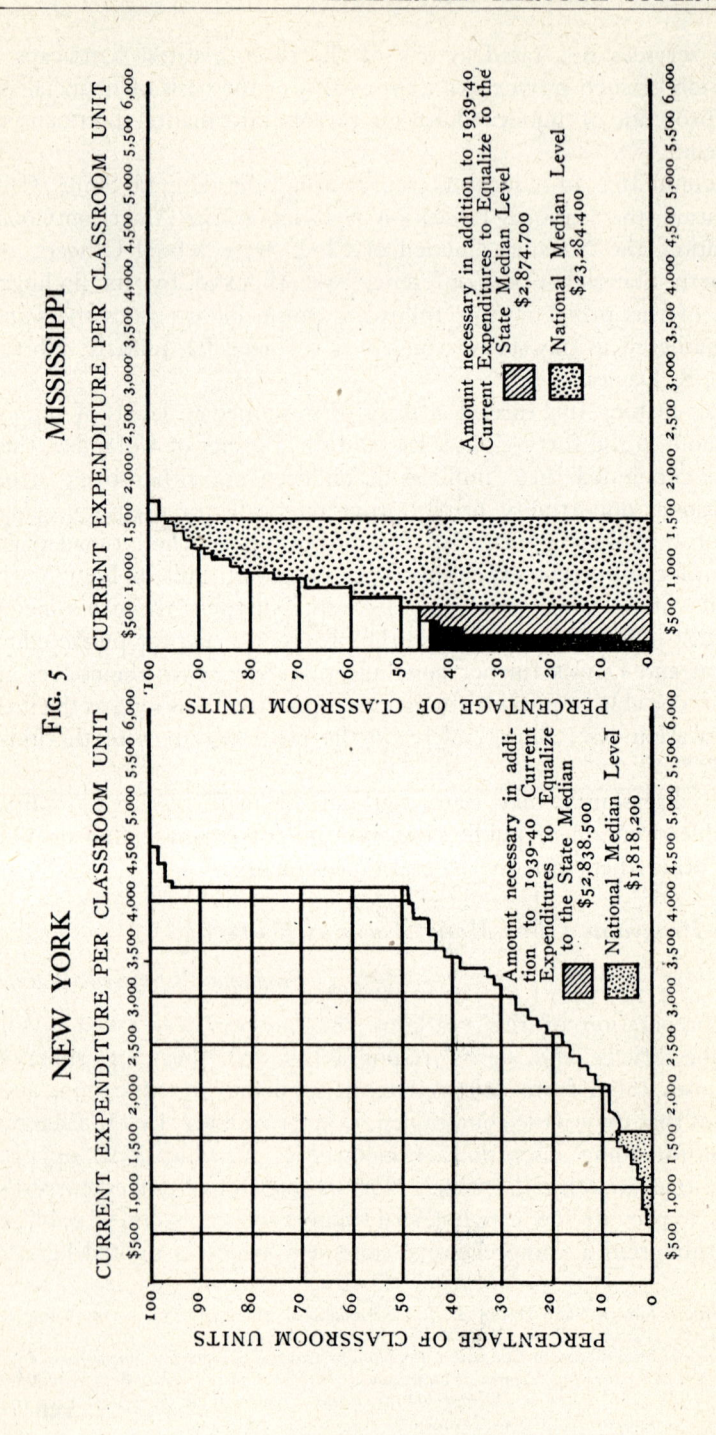

FIG. 5 MISSISSIPPI

CURRENT EXPENDITURE PER CLASSROOM UNIT

Amount necessary in addition to 1939-40 Current Expenditures to Equalize to the State Median Level $2,874,700
National Median Level $23,284,400

NEW YORK

CURRENT EXPENDITURE PER CLASSROOM UNIT

Amount necessary in addition to 1939-40 Current Expenditures to Equalize to the State Median $52,838,500
National Median Level $1,818,200

ANALYZING OUR PROBLEMS

1. Reimbursement from State funds will be made only on salaries of individuals employed for and doing *general* supervision of instruction, whether in the elementary schools, high schools, or both. No reimbursement will be made on salaries of individuals doing special supervision in the schools—such as supervisors of Art, Music, etc.

2. Reimbursement from State funds to counties and cities on account of salaries paid for general supervision of instruction will be made on the following basis:

   a. *Elementary Schools*—Two-thirds of the annual salary paid each elementary school supervisor not to exceed two-thirds of $2500.00, and not to exceed four supervisors for the White and Negro elementary schools of any school division. The distribution of supervisory personnel as between the White and Negro schools in the division will be based upon the recommendation of the division superintendent of schools, subject to the approval of the State Superintendent of Public Instruction. (Maximum State reimbursement per supervisor $1666.66.)

   b. *High Schools*—Two-thirds of the annual salary paid each high school supervisor not to exceed two-thirds of $2500.00, and not to exceed *one* high school supervisor for any county or city. (Maximum State reimbursement per supervisor $1666.66.)

   c. *General Supervisor*—In lieu of a high school supervisor or an elementary supervisor (a and b above) two-thirds of the annual salary paid a general supervisor not to exceed two-thirds of $2500.00, and not to exceed *one* general supervisor for any county or city. (Maximum State reimbursement per supervisor $1666.66.)

   d. *Director of Instruction*—In lieu of a high school supervisor or general supervisor (b and c above), two-thirds of the annual salary paid a Director of Instruction not to exceed two-thirds of $3000.00, and not to exceed *one* director for any county or city. (Maximum State reimbursement per director $2000.00.)

3. Reimbursement from State funds will be made only on the salary paid the supervisor. In addition to the salary of the supervisor, an allowance for travel expense proportionate to the amount of travel required of the supervisor should be made. This allowance must be paid in full from local school funds.

4. Reimbursement from State funds on the salaries of supervisors or directors of instruction is based on the assumption that the full time of such individuals will be given to the general supervision of instruction in the fields to which assigned; hence the right is reserved to make such reimbursement from State funds toward such salaries only to the extent of two-thirds of the time given to the general supervision of instruction, pro-rated on reimbursements as above set forth.

Recent legislation enacted in California concerned itself with equalizing the burden of supporting the program of education thruout the state. Ranked second by Norton and Davies in ability to finance education, California's provision for supervisory services should be more adequate than provision for similar services afforded by Virginia. Even in this state, however, inequalities exist and it is necessary to equalize the financing of public education.

In California the county elementary-school supervision fund is derived entirely from state apportionments, and is intended for use for the payment of salaries and expenses of supervision of instruction under the direction of the county superintendent of schools. Until recent legislation all moneys were to be used exclusively for the payment of salaries and necessary expenses of supervisors to supervise instruction in the elementary-school districts of the county having less than 300 units of average daily attendance during the next preceding school year. Provision, however, has been made for a county elementary-school supervision fund for schools of fewer than 900 units of average daily attendance. These moneys may also be used for the furnishing of such clerical help, supplies, and equipment to the supervisors as the county superintendent of schools deems necessary. In addition, the county superintendent may expend from the county elementary-school supervision fund such amounts as may be necessary for the preparation and coordination of courses of study.

County secondary-school supervision is also provided for in the *Education Code* of California. This fund shall be used by the county superintendent of schools in instances where unified school districts contract with the county superintendent to provide supervision of instruction and service in connection with preparation and coordination of courses of study for secondary schools.

Provision for supervision in the cities of California is made in accordance with the following section of the *Education Code*.[7]

> 4173. One additional teacher unit shall be allowed to each unified school district for each 300 units of average daily attendance in the aggregate in the elementary schools of the district during the next preceding school year. All moneys received by a school district under this section shall be expended exclusively for the salaries and necessary expenses of supervisors of instruction and for the preparation and coordination of courses of study as prescribed in Article 8 of this chapter.

In checking the questionnaire for this yearbook, the California State Department of Education stated that supervision services were not adequately provided for in the state as a whole. One of four reasons given was "lack of funds," just as was the case in the response from Virginia. After examining the ability of each of these states to support a program of public education it is obvious that lack of funds means something very different in each instance.

---

[7] *Education Code, State of California.* Sacramento: Bureau of Printing. (Documents Division) 1943.

State Financial Provisions Vary

Other replies concerning a state's responsibility for financing supervision indicate similarities with the two programs which have been detailed. The Alabama plan allows to counties teacher-units on the basis of the average daily attendance, and money is allocated to the counties on the basis of teacher units. Counties may use money for one or two teacher-units to employ a supervisor. In the study reported by Norton and Davies, Alabama ranks forty-sixth in its ability to support a program of public education.

The state of Georgia, which is given forty-fourth place in the study just mentioned, reports that counties employing instructional supervisors receive for supervision from the state: (a) teacher's salary for which the certificate held qualifies; (b) one-third salary as administrative funds; and (c) supplement of $400 or $500 (depending upon supervisor's certificate) provided it is matched locally. Idaho, twenty-ninth in ranking, states that so far the state does and must supply the limited supervisory finances. It adds, however, that there is need for supervisors sent out from normal schools and universities to follow up their graduates in addition to the services of the two supervisors sent out by the state department of education. Supervision services in Kentucky, which ranks forty-seventh in its ability to support an educational program, are financed by local boards. Mississippi, the state least able to finance education, reports that the state should provide consultative and advisory services at state expense and should assist local units in developing supervisory programs.

New Hampshire is unique in its provision for supervision. In its original program of statewide supervision the superintendent was accepted as a supervisor of instruction supplemented by subject supervisors on the state level. This state, which ranks nineteenth in the Norton and Davies report, contributes a base salary of $2000. Pennsylvania, fourteenth in ability to support education, pays the minimum (prescribed by law) salary of county superintendents, assistant county superintendents, and supervisors of special education. The state mandates the employment of superintendents in districts not under the county superintendent and reimburses for a portion of the salary. Additional supervisors may be employed. If employed the state pays a portion of the salary. If House Bill 568 is approved by the governor, the basic plan in Pennsylvania will be changed. State support will then be provided under an equalization plan providing a maximum of $1800 per teaching unit (thirty elementary pupils or twenty-two high-school pupils) on the basis of a local levy of five mills on the assessed valuation. After a period of two years the maximum state reimbursement per teaching unit will be $2000.

Wisconsin provides support for the nine supervisors in the state depart-

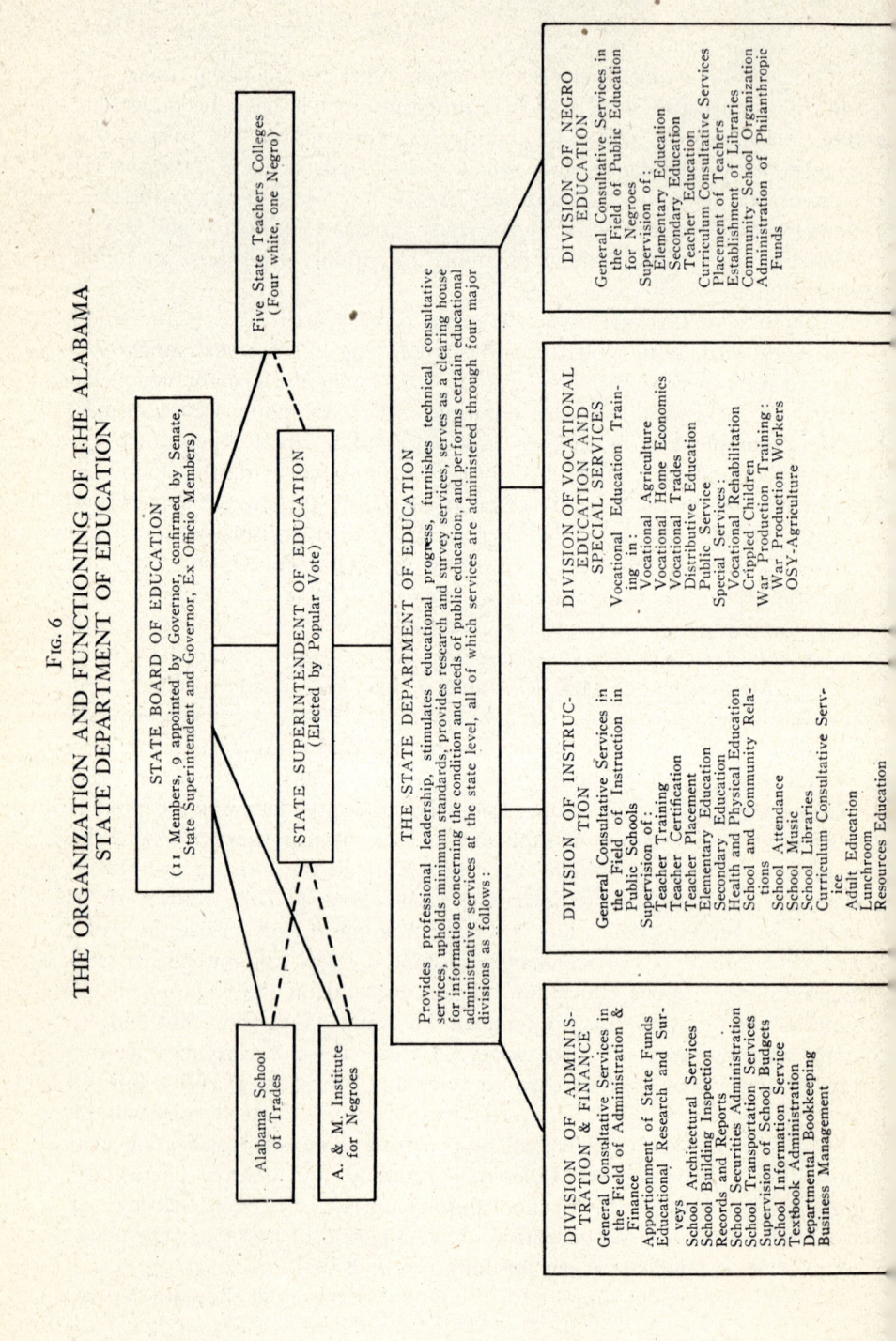

48 LEADERSHIP THROUGH SUPERVISION

Fig. 6

THE ORGANIZATION AND FUNCTIONING OF THE ALABAMA
STATE DEPARTMENT OF EDUCATION

STATE BOARD OF EDUCATION
(11 Members, 9 appointed by Governor, confirmed by Senate, State Superintendent and Governor, Ex Officio Members)

STATE SUPERINTENDENT OF EDUCATION
(Elected by Popular Vote)

Five State Teachers Colleges
(Four white, one Negro)

Alabama School of Trades

A. & M. Institute for Negroes

THE STATE DEPARTMENT OF EDUCATION

Provides professional leadership, stimulates educational progress, furnishes technical consultative services, upholds minimum standards, provides research and survey services, serves as a clearing house for information concerning the condition and needs of public education, and performs certain educational administrative services at the state level, all of which services are administered through four major divisions as follows:

DIVISION OF ADMINISTRATION & FINANCE
General Consultative Services in the Field of Administration & Finance
Apportionment of State Funds
Educational Research and Surveys
School Architectural Services
School Building Inspection
Records and Reports
School Securities Administration
School Transportation Services
Supervision of School Budgets
School Information Service
Textbook Administration
Departmental Bookkeeping
Business Management

DIVISION OF INSTRUCTION
General Consultative Services in the Field of Instruction in Public Schools
Supervision of:
 Teacher Training
 Teacher Certification
 Teacher Placement
 Elementary Education
 Secondary Education
 Health and Physical Education
 School and Community Relations
 School Attendance
 School Music
 School Libraries
 Curriculum Consultative Service
 Adult Education
 Lunchroom
 Resources Education

DIVISION OF VOCATIONAL EDUCATION AND SPECIAL SERVICES
Vocational Education Training in:
 Vocational Agriculture
 Vocational Home Economics
 Vocational Trades
 Distributive Education
 Public Service
Special Services:
 Vocational Rehabilitation
 Crippled Children
 War Production Training:
  War Production Workers
  OSY-Agriculture

DIVISION OF NEGRO EDUCATION
General Consultative Services in the Field of Public Education for Negroes
Supervision of:
 Elementary Education
 Secondary Education
 Teacher Education
 Curriculum Consultative Services
 Placement of Teachers
 Establishment of Libraries
 Community School Organization
 Administration of Philanthropic Funds

ment of education and also reimburses the several counties for rural supervision to the extent of one supervisor for every county having 120 elementary teachers and two supervisors for counties having more than 120 elementary teachers.

The encouraging factor in this view of the ability of states to finance a program of public education is that each one, within the limits of its resources, is making some provision for supervisory services.

Organization For the Job Is Important

How are state departments of education organized to provide for supervisory services? What is the relation of such a department to the smaller units in the states? Are they organized on the modern and democratic method or is the organization a traditional line and staff type?

The following diagram submitted by the Alabama State Department of Education presents an interesting study. As has been previously pointed out, Alabama ranks forty-sixth in the report by Norton and Davies, in terms of ability to support a program of public education. There is no indication, however, that the lack of financial resources has influenced the basic planning done in Alabama. The state superintendent of education reports that there is need for more supervision at both elementary and secondary levels and that such supervision should be of a general rather than a special nature.

Many Services Are Included

Thirty state departments of education responded to the question, "What do you consider to be the major function of supervisors employed in your department?" Their statements fall into the following categories:

1. To assist local leaders and teachers to improve the quality of instruction in the state
2. To provide professional leadership thru conference and group activity
3. To visit schools and check on teaching aids, methods, and technics
4. To interpret and administer the laws governing the program
5. To bring to superintendents, supervisors, and teachers tested educational principles and technics
6. To help evaluate local practices
7. To prepare curriculum materials
8. To assist governing boards of school districts to formulate intelligent policies of instruction
9. To guide and stimulate teachers toward educational growth
10. To develop the individual to live in a democracy.

Curriculum Building Is Part of Supervision

A review of the answers given by state departments of education to an inquiry concerning curriculum development is essential before an interpretation can be made of the supervision services. The question asked was,

"What major responsibilities do you expect supervisors in your department to assume for a statewide program of curriculum development?" Supervision and curriculum were treated in separate questions on the questionnaire in order that curriculum work going forward in any state might not be overlooked. The following ten major classifications cover the responsibilities expected of state supervisors for curriculum development:

    1. To assume leadership for the proper building of curriculum, and to advance ideas and execute plans to insure broader and more progressive programs of work
    2. To serve on the state steering committee in assisting in the preparation or reviewing of state curriculum bulletins
    3. To work with local curriculum groups, becoming a member of such groups and providing study bibliographies
    4. To serve as consultant in in-service courses for teachers
    5. To head curriculum projects carried on primarily in the summer workshops at state universities or colleges
    6. To organize and direct continuous curriculum study and development thruout the state
    7. To stimulate and provide leadership for professional growth
    8. To help coordinate the work of curriculum committees in the state, and to bring to these committees outstanding teachers who have a sane outlook and know the goals or objectives
    9. To develop the aims and objectives to be achieved in the state
   10. To check outcomes of all subjectmatter.

Mississippi again answered with a statement almost identical to that given by California. In essence both states said, "The major responsibility we expect supervisors in our department to assume for a statewide program of curriculum development is to organize and direct continuous curriculum study and to establish constantly improved practices." It is significant that the basic thinking concerning the importance of curriculum development is the same.

Wisconsin Plans a Five-Year Study

The state department of education in Wisconsin responded to the questionnaire by submitting a description of the five-year curriculum revision program which it is sponsoring in cooperation with the Wisconsin Education Association. The following statement is quoted from an article which describes the state curriculum staff and its relation to local programs.[8]

    The Wisconsin Cooperative Educational Planning Program is somewhat unique among the self-study and planning programs set up by and for

---

[8] Mackenzie, Gordon. "Wisconsin Cooperative Educational Planning Program." *Wisconsin Journal of Education* 77: 52-55; October 1944.

the schools of various states, in that all types of problems are being considered, and citizens of the state are carrying the leadership responsibility. The Wisconsin program is concerned with the total educational program and all conditions which influence its success. The committee organization will indicate this breadth of concern.

The chart on page 52 shows that the total program is under the direction of the Cooperative Planning Council, members of which were appointed by the Wisconsin Education Association and the state department of public instruction.[9] The arrows on the chart indicate that all recommendations involving the public schools of the state clear thru the coordinating committee of the state department of public instruction.
The purposes of the Wisconsin state program and the relation of the curriculum staff members and the supervisors of the state department of education to the program and to one another are quoted from the *Wisconsin Journal.*[10]

> Among the several purposes of the state curriculum program, two are of first importance: (1) the encouragement of continuous and long-time local programs of curriculum study, and (2) the development of curriculum guides for elementary and secondary schools. The preparation of curriculum guides is most valuable as a means for encouraging local study programs and widespread discussion.
> Recognition must be given to the fact that the most significant part of the state program is the local curriculum activity which takes place in the cities and counties throughout the state. Few, if any, desirable modifications will be made in the learning situation for boys and girls unless local groups and individual teachers study their problems. For this reason, much attention has been given to plans for assisting individual schools and committees on their curriculum planning.
>
> . . . .
>
> *Policies Governing the Work of Curriculum Staff Members.* To assist local school units in their curriculum study activities, a curriculum staff will be organized. Members of this staff group will be available on request to aid cities, counties, or individual schools to start curriculum study programs, or to reexamine some particular phase of their work. To suggest ways in which it is believed that staff members can be used most effectively, the Curriculum Guiding Committee has prepared a statement of policy. This has three parts, one is addressed to the curriculum staff member, the other to the local school unit wishing to have the services of the staff member, and the third to both groups. This statement is presented for the guidance and use of all concerned with the curriculum program.
> *Guides to Curriculum Staff Members.* In all relationships with school, faculty, or community groups, the curriculum staff member should be

---

[9] Wisconsin Cooperative Educational Planning Program. "Organization for Curriculum Planning." *Wisconsin Journal of Education* 77: 173-76; December 1944.
[10] Wisconsin Cooperative Educational Planning Program. "The State Curriculum Staff." *Wisconsin Journal of Education* 77: 317-19; March 1945.

FIG. 7
WISCONSIN COOPERATIVE EDUCATIONAL PLANNING
PROGRAM—I

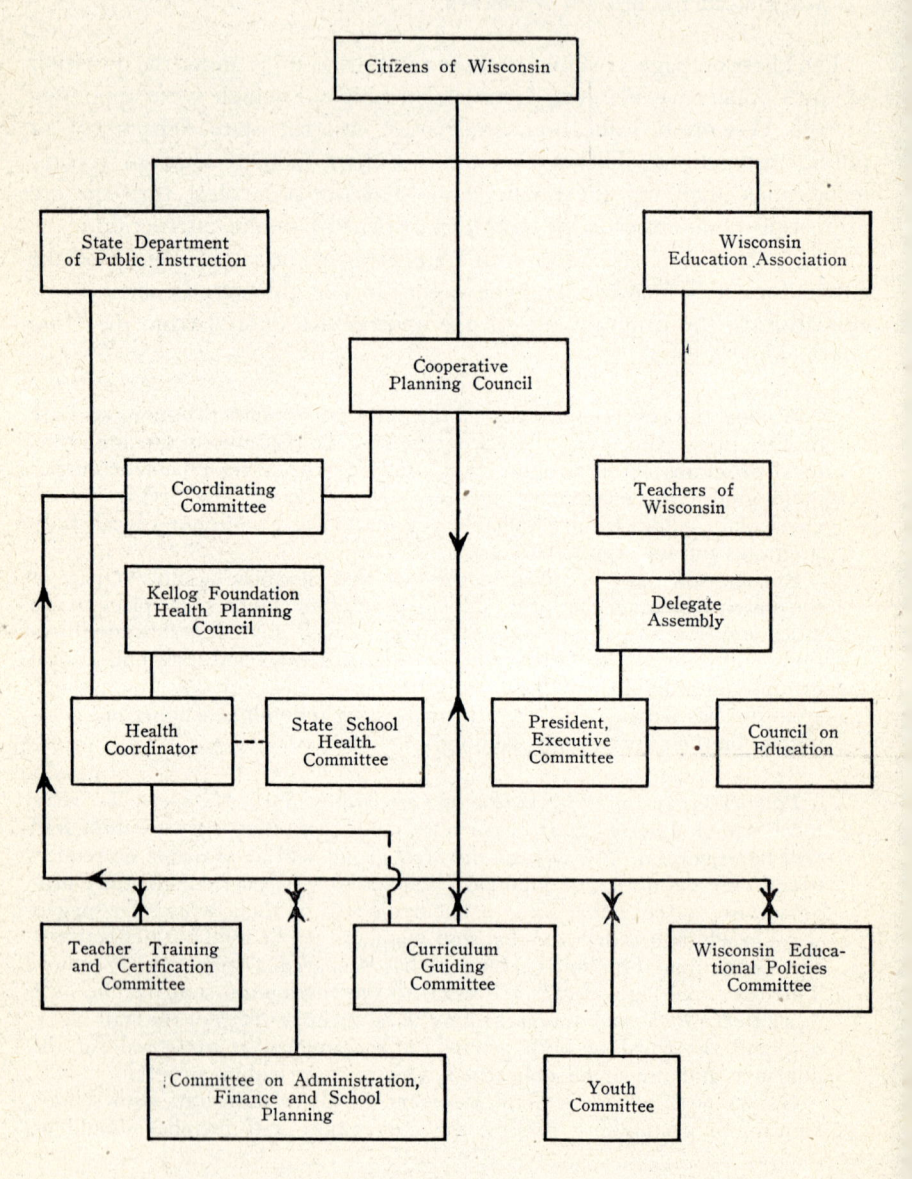

ANALYZING OUR PROBLEMS 53

regarded as a resource person whose background of experience, training and thinking, and whose personal characteristics, make him a valuable counselor to those who are working on curriculum problems. This concept of the curriculum staff member as a resource person and counselor leads to several suggestions as to procedure.

1. The curriculum staff member's first responsibility is to study the local situation and carefully analyze the problem on which help is requested.
2. The curriculum staff member can serve best as he becomes a member of a working group and can raise questions, make suggestions, and help evaluate plans and their execution. It is not his responsibility, however, to recommend specific solutions in either oral or written form.
3. The curriculum staff member can serve best if he is an adaptable person who encourages groups to work out variations from known practices, as well as promising original procedures of their own. His function is to stimulate group thinking rather than indoctrinate for his preconceived concept of the curriculum.
4. The curriculum staff member will work with and thru the local administrative officer.

In Figure 8 the proposals for the organization of curriculum activities are incorporated.[11]

A study of this proposal for the organization of curriculum activities reveals the close cooperation between the state department of public instruction and the teacher-training institutions in their efforts to improve the instructional program in the state of Wisconsin. Workshops are being planned in several institutions for three purposes.[12]

1. To assist individual teachers in planning their work and preparing units
2. To enable committees from individual cities and counties to work together under guidance, where instructional materials and other resources are available for their use
3. To facilitate the work of various statewide committees and to prepare bulletin materials.

Montana Tries a Cooperative Program

The state department of public instruction in Montana is taking leadership responsibility for the development of a cooperative program for secondary curriculum revision in the schools of that state. The agencies and individuals working cooperatively with the state department in the curriculum revision program are the Montana Education Association, Montana School Boards Association, Montana School Administrators, faculty members of the University of Montana, and teachers and admin-

---

[11] Wisconsin Cooperative Educational Planning Program. "Organization for Curriculum Planning." *Wisconsin Journal of Education* 77: 173-76; December 1944.
[12] Wisconsin Cooperative Educational Planning Program. "The State Curriculum Staff." *Wisconsin Journal of Education* 77: 317-19; March 1945.

Fig. 8
WISCONSIN COOPERATIVE CURRICULUM PLANNING PROGRAM—II

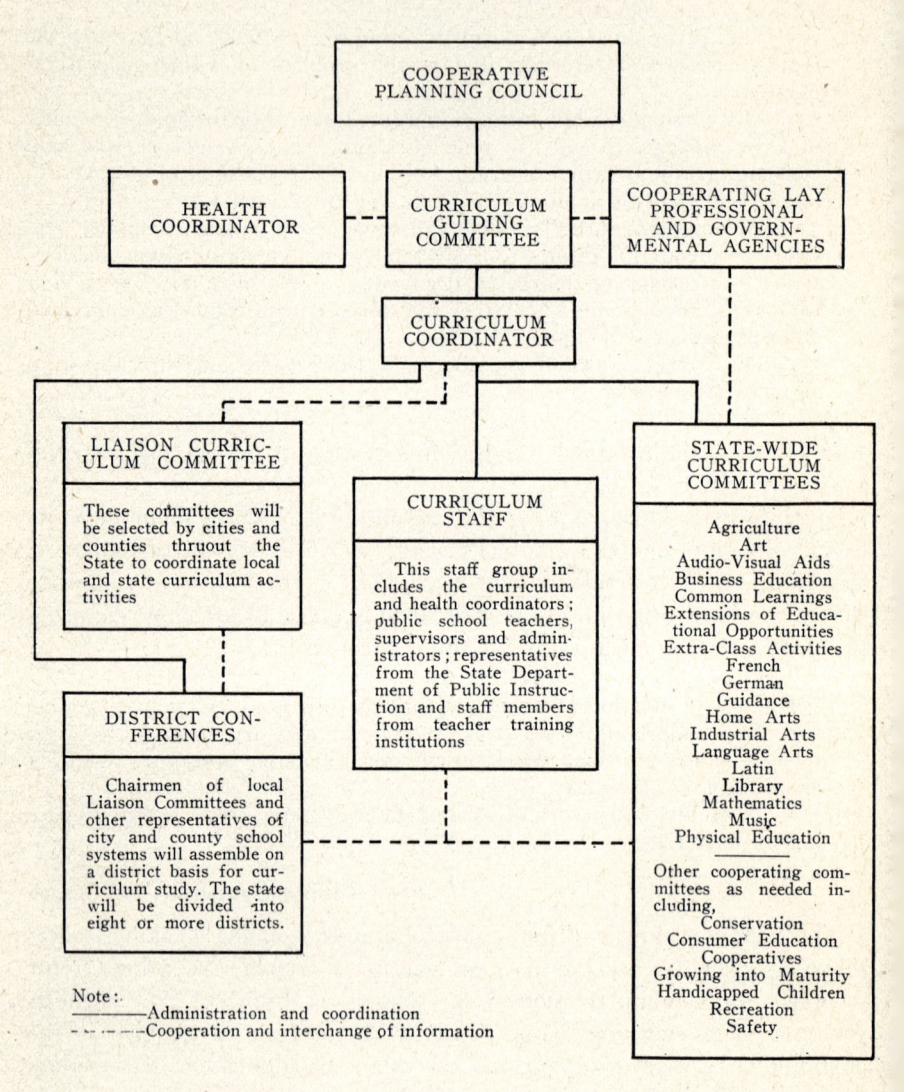

COOPERATIVE PLANNING COUNCIL

HEALTH COORDINATOR

CURRICULUM GUIDING COMMITTEE

COOPERATING LAY PROFESSIONAL AND GOVERNMENTAL AGENCIES

CURRICULUM COORDINATOR

LIAISON CURRICULUM COMMITTEE

These committees will be selected by cities and counties thruout the State to coordinate local and state curriculum activities

CURRICULUM STAFF

This staff group includes the curriculum and health coordinators; public school teachers, supervisors and administrators; representatives from the State Department of Public Instruction and staff members from teacher training institutions

DISTRICT CONFERENCES

Chairmen of local Liaison Committees and other representatives of city and county school systems will assemble on a district basis for curriculum study. The state will be divided into eight or more districts.

STATE-WIDE CURRICULUM COMMITTEES

Agriculture
Art
Audio-Visual Aids
Business Education
Common Learnings
Extensions of Educational Opportunities
Extra-Class Activities
French
German
Guidance
Home Arts
Industrial Arts
Language Arts
Latin
Library
Mathematics
Music
Physical Education

Other cooperating committees as needed including,
Conservation
Consumer Education
Cooperatives
Growing into Maturity
Handicapped Children
Recreation
Safety

Note:
——————Administration and coordination
- - - - - -Cooperation and interchange of information

istrators. In addition to these groups, the state of Montana tapped the resources of a professional group not yet mentioned in curriculum programs. The cooperation of the Montana branch of the Northwest Society for Supervision and Curriculum Development, a regional organization which is a part of Association for Supervision and Curriculum Development of the National Education Association, suggests to other state departments a source of leadership for curriculum revision programs.

From a study bulletin which the Montana State Department of Public Instruction prepared for school faculties, professional organizations, parent-teacher groups, school trustees, and laymen, the following excerpts were taken: [13]

> *Who Can Do the Job?* The job of revising the state course of study for high schools can be done best by the teachers and administrators of our public schools, representing every part of the state and all types of Montana communities. They are closest to the problems of youth and they are the ones who will put a new curriculum into practice.
>
> *Who Can Help?* The State Department of Public Instruction, charged by law with the responsibility for preparing and distributing the course of study of schools.
>
> A State Curriculum Steering Committee appointed to advise the State Department. The Committee consists of representatives from interested professional and lay groups.
>
> The Montana State University, through the setting up of a Curriculum Revision Center during the summers of 1945 and 1946.
>
> Outside curriculum consultants and specialists who have worked on similar programs in other states.
>
> School trustees and administrators by providing funds to send one or more representative to the Curriculum Revision Center.
>
> High school pupils by making suggestions for improvement.
>
> *How Can the Job be Done?* The answer lies in cooperative effort. This means:
>
> 1. Preliminary discussion this winter and spring by teachers and lay groups throughout the state.
> 2. Teachers working together at the MSU Curriculum Center in the summer of 1945 to produce first drafts of curriculum materials.
> 3. Teachers trying out these materials under classroom conditions during the school year 1945-46.
> 4. Revising these materials in the MSU Curriculum Center in 1946.
> 5. Provision for continually revising the materials and keeping them up to date.
>
> To carry out such a cooperative project will require:
>
> 1. A state curriculum steering committee to formulate revision policies and to advise the State Department of Public Instruction.

---

[13] Montana State Department of Public Instruction. *A Cooperative Program for Secondary Curriculum Revision in Montana Schools.* Bulletin No. 1. Helena: the Department, 1945.

2. An editorial board responsible for editing all materials before publication.

3. A well-organized handbook of procedure and guiding principles for use in preparing the details that will make up the completed curriculum.

4. Provision for contacts with students, teachers, and lay people from time to time for the purpose of criticism and evaluation.

5. A center for continuous curriculum development functioning through the University for the purpose of assisting school systems working on the adaptation of the state curriculum to local circumstances.

6. Supervision of the entire project by the State Department of Public Instruction.

7. Continuous evaluation and revision of the curriculum to keep it alive and useful.

The organizational chart for this secondary curriculum revision in Montana is shown on page 57.

These curriculum development programs, in a sampling of states, provide evidence of a close correlation between the supervisory and administrative functions listed by superintendents as being of major importance and the services actually rendered by those they employ as state supervisors. A careful analysis of the ten supervisory and ten curriculum functions considered significant by state superintendents reveals a considerable variety of leadership services expected of the staff of a state department of education.

In addition to the programs described, curriculum materials which have come out of the leadership work carried forward by supervisors in Alabama, California, Connecticut, Kansas, Maryland, Oregon, Texas, Virginia, and Washington were carefully reviewed. It is significant that in no instance did a state report that curriculum development was not a part of the supervisor's responsibility. There seemed to be little correlation between a state's ability to support a program of public education and the quality of curriculum thinking going forward in that state. Does that conclusion pose a problem for the states that are above the median in their ability to support a program of public education? Are those states providing the supervisory services they are financially able to support?

Counties and Cities Provide for Supervision

Financing Parallels State Plans

The manner in which a city, county, parish, district, or other subdivision of the state finances a program of supervision is indicated in the discussion of the state and national situation.

Groups Organize for Service

The responses given by county and city superintendents to the question

FIG. 9
Organization for
SECONDARY CURRICULUM REVISION
in Montana

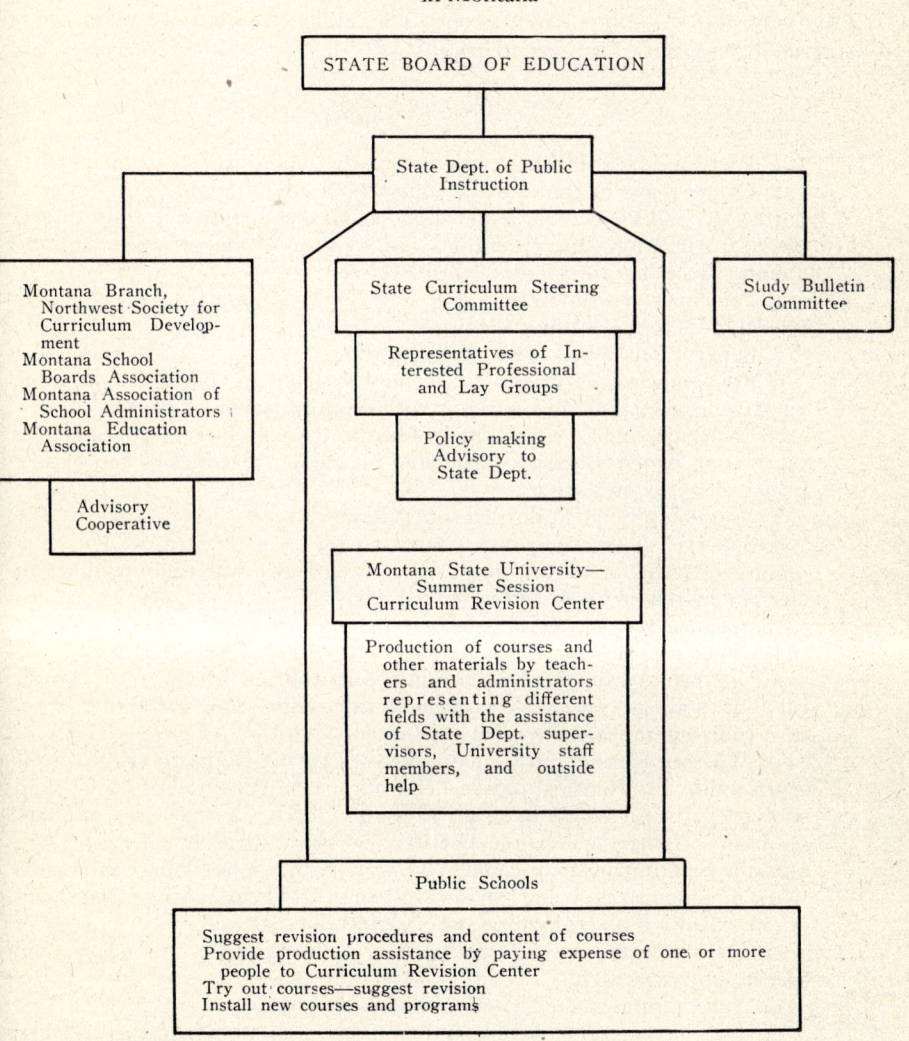

```
                    STATE BOARD OF EDUCATION
                              |
                    State Dept. of Public
                         Instruction
```

| Montana Branch, Northwest Society for Curriculum Development
Montana School Boards Association
Montana Association of School Administrators
Montana Education Association | State Curriculum Steering Committee | Study Bulletin Committee |

Representatives of Interested Professional and Lay Groups

Policy making Advisory to State Dept.

Advisory Cooperative

Montana State University—
Summer Session
Curriculum Revision Center

Production of courses and other materials by teachers and administrators representing different fields with the assistance of State Dept. supervisors, University staff members, and outside help.

Public Schools

Suggest revision procedures and content of courses
Provide production assistance by paying expense of one or more people to Curriculum Revision Center
Try out courses—suggest revision
Install new courses and programs

concerning supervision personnel provided in their school systems revealed many similarities. For purposes of this report responses from counties and cities will be separated, and only those statements which indicate some differences in provision of supervisory services will be included. The questionnaires in which it was not possible to deduce whether the superintendent represented a county or a city school system were not considered in regard to this particular item.

Supervisory Personnel For Cities

1. Part-time basis in cooperation with the university.
2. On the basis of traditional public-school organization.
3. A general elementary supervisor for Grades I thru VI; a health and physical education supervisor for Grades I thru VI; an art supervisor and a music supervisor for Grades I thru XII.
4. Principals are supervisors, but they can't do enough. Supervision in special fields is fine, but not adequate.
5. Supervision joined with administration.
6. Four supervisors in the city school system; art, physical education, vocational education, and one for vocal and instrumental music.
7. Each school has a principal. The principal's chief responsibility is supervision. Supervision is coordinated by regular meetings of supervising principals every two weeks.
8. The superintendent does all supervision.
9. Supervision services are provided on the basis of needs of the community in terms of health, music, art, physical education, household arts, elementary-school work, and industrial arts.
10. Elementary supervisor, secondary supervisor, and special subject supervisor.
11. Elementary supervision only in special subjects of art, music, physical education, and science. Two general supervisors—one for kindergarten thru fourth grade and the other for Grades V to IX.
12. The services of thirty-one supervisors are largely in the special fields —art, music, handwriting, physical education, etc. The director of the child study department works in all divisions, and there is a supervisor of counselors in secondary education. We have no broad division supervisors. An assistant superintendent in elementary and another in secondary education work in administrative and advisory capacities. We are working at present on an expansion or reorganization of supervisory services.
13. Departmental—kindergarten-primary, intermediate, secondary, and special subject areas.
14. Special subject supervisors available on call.
15. District superintendent in common school districts, and the principal in central school districts.
16. Special teachers.
17. Director of curriculum for kindergarten thru Grade XII, supervisor of handwriting for the elementary grades and the same person has charge of commercial studies in senior high schools with other duties as to the requisition and distribution of supplies and textbooks for the entire system, supervisor of kindergarten and Grades I to III, supervisor of mathematics

and science for Grades IV thru XII, supervisor of art for kindergarten thru twelfth grade, supervisor of industrial arts in junior and senior high schools, supervisor of language arts for Grades IV thru XII, supervisors of boys' physical education for kindergarten thru Grade XII, supervisor of girls' physical education for the same grade range, supervisor of home economics and cafeteria for the junior and senior high schools, supervisor of vocal and instrumental music for kindergarten and Grades I thru XII, and supervisor of pupil personnel. (In this instance four routine visits are made annually and a great many "on call" responses are answered.)

18. Our supervisory services are in the process of shifting from the formal type of supervision to the type of supervisory coordination which more nearly responds to the needs of teachers and classrooms.

Supervisory Personnel For Counties

1. One director of education and three general supervisors. The director serves the secondary as well as the elementary schools and that person together with two of the general supervisors spends a minimum of four week days in the classrooms of the entire rural area of the county. The third general supervisor, who is hired jointly by the county superintendent and a district superintendent, spends four days a week in a specified school and the remainder of the time in general supervision work with the other members of the county staff. In this county there is no division of subjects or territory.

2. Supervision services are provided to all schools having under three hundred children in average daily attendance and to all other schools, regardless of size, who request supervision.

3. On call from various teachers in conjunction with the regular meetings possible.

4. County superintendent supposedly visits all common school district teachers twice yearly.

5. A primary supervisor paid for by the county office.

6. One supervisor for 124 rural schools.

7. Supervision is done thru three or four teachers meetings during a year.

8. Two helping teachers and the superintendent provided by the state. Local districts, outside of cities, employ teaching or nonteaching principal. Three districts provide supervising principal.

9. The state provides supervisors in agriculture and home economics; also county superintendent with five assistants.

10. Rural supervision is provided for all schools of less than 300 A.D.A. The average load of a supervisor is forty-three teachers. They are on call and on regular schedule. Curriculum coordination or consultation service to schools over three hundred A.D.A. Average load 325 teachers and ten districts.

11. An elementary supervisor for nine towns is employed by the state.

12. Supervisory services are provided as an administrative and supervisory program to be carried on by a county superintendent who is elected by one group and advised by another group or board. The county supertendent must divide his time between supervision and many administrative duties.

13. One full-time director of instruction is employed. Another part-time person who serves as coordinator for the county program and college teacher training in a consultative capacity.

14. No supervisor at present.

An analysis of supervisory personnel in counties and cities seems to indicate an absence of any particular principle or basic guide in providing supervision. The majority of superintendents stated that their programs of supervision were based on the following four goals: (1) to make American public schools an effective means for maintaining and extending American democratic ideals (2) to help boys and girls understand and deal with personal and social problems which have meaning for them now, so that they may, as adults, be prepared to face issues which will necessarily arise (3) to develop individuals who will be able to live effectively in a world in which mechanical inventions and discoveries have made imperative the cooperative efforts of all races and nationalities in a highly interdependent world and (4) to work continuously with professional and lay groups that educational problems may be more clearly defined and dealt with, and that schools may better serve the public. Are supervisory services, therefore, provided in relation to the goals of education which were ranked high by superintendents? It may well be asked whether a school system which provides several special supervisors and no general supervisor gives first consideration to the goal ranked first by superintendents.

The study of the inability of the various states to support a program of public education offers adequate explanation of the dearth of supervisors in some rural areas. The expectation of supervisory services rendered and curriculum development helps given when one supervisor works with forty-three teachers and another supervisor is responsible for one hundred twenty-four teachers cannot be easily evaluated. There are city systems in which the established plan is for one supervisor to work with forty but not over fifty teachers and county systems in which thirty teachers represent the maximum load for a supervisor. These differences are as great as are the programs of education provided for children and youth in some areas of our country. Can adequate supervision be carried forward when the only contact with teachers is thru four regular meetings during the school year and no classroom visits? These are only a few of the questions which might be raised after studying this data. It is encouraging, however, that of the cities responding to the questionnaire, 50 percent stated that they had plans for the addition of supervisory personnel in the postwar period, and 60 percent of the counties indicated that similar plans had been made.

Figure 10 shows the relationship of a supervision staff to the total

ANALYZING OUR PROBLEMS 61

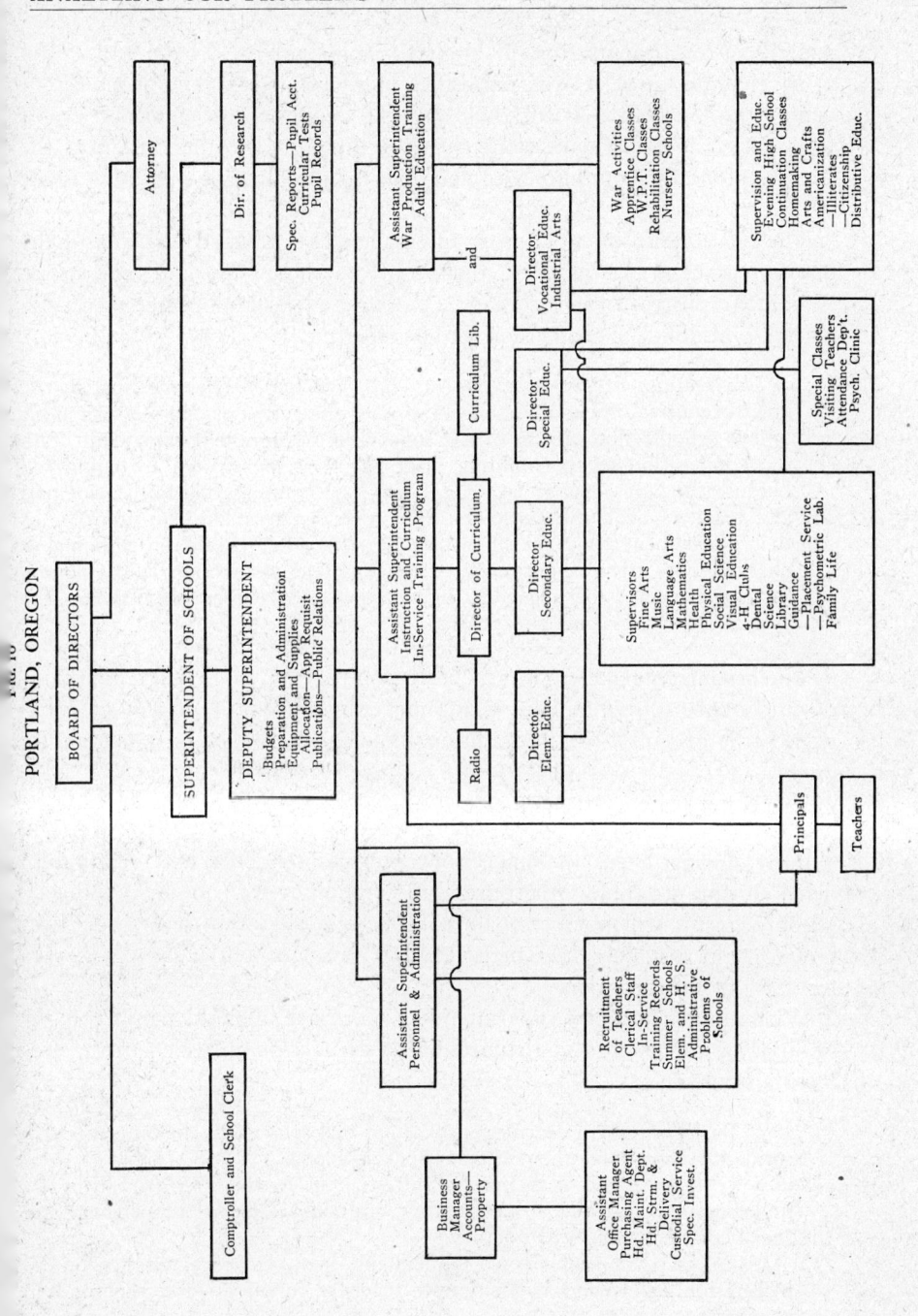

PORTLAND, OREGON

BOARD OF DIRECTORS

- Attorney
- Comptroller and School Clerk

SUPERINTENDENT OF SCHOOLS

- Dir. of Research
  - Spec. Reports—Pupil Acct.
  - Curricular Tests
  - Pupil Records

DEPUTY SUPERINTENDENT

- Budgets
- Preparation and Administration
- Equipment and Supplies
- Allocation—App. Requisit
- Publications—Public Relations

Assistant Superintendent — War Production Training — Adult Education

- Director, Vocational Educ. Industrial Arts
  - War Activities
  - Apprentice Classes
  - W.P.T. Classes
  - Rehabilitation Classes
  - Nursery Schools
- Supervision and Educ.
  - Evening High School
  - Continuation Classes
  - Homemaking
  - Arts and Crafts
  - Americanization
    —Illiterates
    —Citizenship
  - Distributive Educ.

Assistant Superintendent — Instruction and Curriculum — In-Service Training Program

- Director of Curriculum
  - Curriculum Lib.
  - Radio
- Director, Special Educ.
  - Special Classes
  - Visiting Teachers
  - Attendance Dept.
  - Psych. Clinic
- Director, Secondary Educ.
  - Supervisors
  - Fine Arts
  - Music
  - Language Arts
  - Mathematics
  - Health
  - Physical Education
  - Social Science
  - Visual Education
  - 4-H Clubs
  - Dental
  - Science
  - Library
  - Guidance
    —Placement Service
    —Psychometric Lab.
  - Family Life
- Director, Elem. Educ.

- Principals
- Teachers

Assistant Superintendent — Personnel & Administration

- Recruitment of Teachers
- Clerical Staff
- In-Service Training Records
- Summer Schools
- Elem. and H. S. Administrative Problems of Schools

Business Manager — Accounts—Property

- Assistant Office Manager
- Purchasing Agent
- Hd. Maint. Dept.
- Hd. Strm. & Delivery
- Custodial Service
- Spec. Invest.

administrative organization in a city school system. There have been some changes since it was published in March 1944. The planning of demonstration classes is all done by the directors of elementary and secondary education who work thru the director. In other instances the work is done by committees rather than by the director operating alone altho that person has supervision of all of the committees.

The relationship of supervisors and principals was listed on many of the questionnaires as an important concern of superintendents and supervisors. A monograph from El Paso, Texas, emphasizes the importance of a two-way responsibility if supervision is to be effective.[14]

> *The relation of the supervisor to the principal.*—The principal as the chief executive officer is responsible for all the activities and services in his or her school. The success of the supervisor's program is dependent upon the cooperation of the building principal. The supervisors are employed because the work of a given department is so complex that both principals and teachers need the assistance of a specialist to make the program of that department function smoothly. On the other hand, the principal is charged with the responsibility of unifying the instruction in his school. Supervision shall be regarded as a cooperative enterprise between the special supervisor and the principal.

The organizational chart for a county, on page 63, discloses the thinking of one county superintendent in administering a program of public education. Is the organization the traditional line and staff type or a democratic one?

Varied Tasks Fill Supervisors' Day

In reviewing types of supervisory services rendered and curriculum development programs in progress, the responses from county and city school systems will not be separated. The school system will be evident, however, in instances in which detail is given of curriculum materials resulting from a program.

What county and city superintendents conceive of as the major responsibilities of supervisors in their school systems is summarized in the following statements:

> 1. To improve the learning process in our schools by helping teachers to identify and solve their instructional problems
> 2. To aid teachers in helping children achieve maximum growth in the understandings, attitudes, information, and skills essential to personal and social competence in a democracy
> 3. To help all teachers to understand growth characteristics on all maturation levels and to help new teachers to understand the modern program

---

[14] El Paso Public Schools. *Rules and Manual for School Employees.* El Paso: the Board, 1944.

ANALYZING OUR PROBLEMS 63

Fig. 11
INTERRELATIONSHIPS OF ADMINISTRATIVE PERSONNEL
AND COMMITTEES

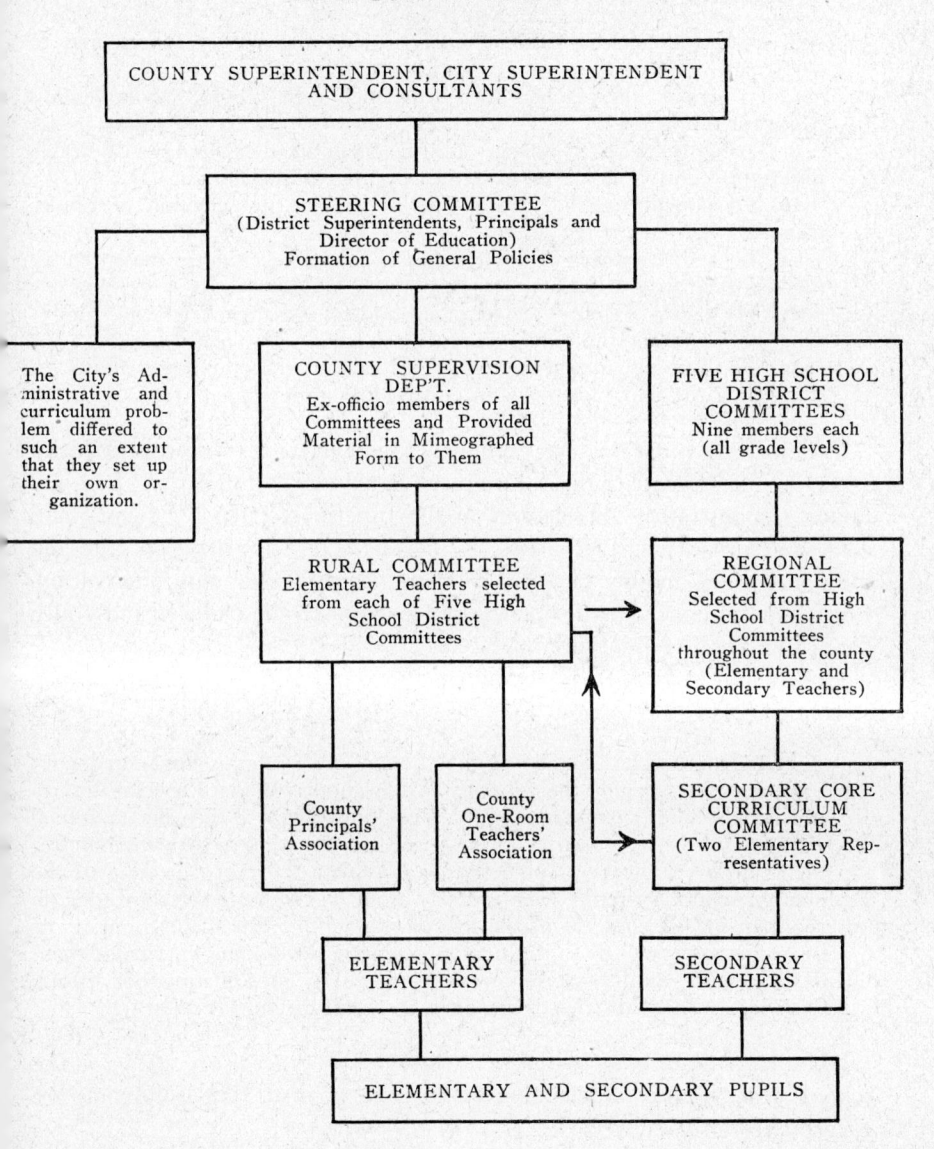

```
┌─────────────────────────────────────────┐
│ COUNTY SUPERINTENDENT, CITY SUPERINTENDENT│
│           AND CONSULTANTS               │
└─────────────────────────────────────────┘
                    │
    ┌───────────────────────────────────┐
    │        STEERING COMMITTEE         │
    │(District Superintendents, Principals and│
    │      Director of Education)       │
    │     Formation of General Policies │
    └───────────────────────────────────┘
```

| The City's Administrative and curriculum problem differed to such an extent that they set up their own organization. | COUNTY SUPERVISION DEP'T. Ex-officio members of all Committees and Provided Material in Mimeographed Form to Them | FIVE HIGH SCHOOL DISTRICT COMMITTEES Nine members each (all grade levels) |

RURAL COMMITTEE
Elementary Teachers selected from each of Five High School District Committees

REGIONAL COMMITTEE
Selected from High School District Committees throughout the county (Elementary and Secondary Teachers)

County Principals' Association

County One-Room Teachers' Association

SECONDARY CORE CURRICULUM COMMITTEE
(Two Elementary Representatives)

ELEMENTARY TEACHERS

SECONDARY TEACHERS

ELEMENTARY AND SECONDARY PUPILS

4. To encourage leadership and development of teachers in service
5. To increase the efficiency of the schools and try to keep the work as nearly uniform as possible thru the system
6. To keep people alert to the changes in educational procedures; help them to be good teachers who love to teach
7. To implement educational goals in working with teachers, and to participate in general in-service study programs
8. To awaken the teachers to a broadened view of the "whole" child's needs for tomorrow
9. To work with principals and teachers in developing a desirable philosophy and practices consistent with that philosophy
10. To coordinate the efforts of teachers in the selection of books, materials, testing, and teaching
11. To assist teachers in doing a better job of teaching as measured by modern evaluative criteria
12. To plan a system-wide program and to assist teachers with curriculum problems and individual student problems
13. To become a vital factor in leadership in community affairs to strengthen the part of citizens in educational leadership.

When these functions are examined together with those expressed by superintendents responsible for state programs, it is noted that there are fewer administrative implications in the functions stated by county and city superintendents. The distinguishing characteristics between state and local programs might, in large measure, account for this observation. Local superintendents and supervisors are closer to the children and youth for whom public schools are operated.

One school system, in reporting on the major function of supervisors, states that:[15]

> The county school office in the state of Washington is charged with only a minor part of the supervision of schools. We are specifically required to render supervision to third-class districts and to make an annual visit to each high school. We have furnished much more than the requirement; however, it is our objective to complete the reorganization of the county school system. Over the past four years we have succeeded in reorganizing 90 per cent of the school population. The major function of our office now will be in the field of research, developing curriculum, and dealing with administrative problems. We are coordinating our efforts with local school districts, regardless of classification.

A bulletin describing to teachers the county supervisory plan for the school year 1944-45 was submitted by one county. The following are excerpts from this source:[16]

> Planning is essential for best results in any undertaking. This is especially true for those undertakings that are designed to improve learning in our

---
[15] King County, Washington.
[16] Crawford County, Pennsylvania.

ANALYZING OUR PROBLEMS

schools. Such planning has now been completed for the activities of the supervisors of Crawford County, for the improvement of learning during the present school year. The achievement of the aims set forth in any plan depends upon the cooperation of those who are concerned in executing the plan. This cooperation can best be secured thru intelligent understanding of the aims.

I. Objectives (General)

A. To continue the development of a philosophy of education that: (a) conceives of its purpose as being the promotion of optimum child growth, and (b) meets the requirements of effective living in a democratic social order.

B. To continue making those changes in practices and procedures which appear to be necessary to make our practices square with our theories. (Major emphasis on this aspect of the general objectives during the year.)

II. Methods

A. Group teacher conferences—Three group conferences in each of the eight areas of the county will be held during the year. The enclosed schedule gives the time and place for each conference. General topics such as the following will be considered: Distinctive characteristics of a modern elementary school, and work on the problem of marking, of promotions, and reports to parents.

B. Individual and committee work—(Brief account given)

C. Classroom visitations. The aims in these visitations may be stated as follows:

1. Make teacher ratings in all cases where this is necessary (Temporary professional employees)
2. To assist in developing improved teaching technics, in securing more adequate materials, and more advantageous use of available materials
3. To survey all factors in the learning situation so that recommendations may be made to the teachers and the boards
4. To assist teachers in applying principles contained in bulletins listed in specific objectives

D. Bulletins. Bulletins will again be used in preparation for teacher conferences, to summarize results of conferences, and at other times when necessary.

E. Testing and guidance program (Explained)

F. Activities for improvement of materials (Explained)

G. Talks to PTA groups, commencements.

III. Evaluation. The effectiveness of the above supervisory program will be measured by the results achieved. The following specific conditions will be evidence of a worthwhile achievement:

A. Increased number of schools using adjustment devices in reading and other subject fields

B. Presence of a new county report card

C. Development of a set of principles governing promotions

D. Development of a marking system which evaluates a child's achievement in terms of his ability to achieve rather than in terms of the achievement of the other pupils in his group.

To know a year's supervisory program for an area, to know how it is to be carried forward, and to know the basis on which it is to be evaluated affords specific information not only for the people in the particular county but for supervisors in other areas as well. This Crawford County program is concisely but definitely stated. Are the criteria listed adequate for evaluating the general objectives which were to be emphasized during the year and which have such far-reaching significance?

There is considerable variation in the way in which supervisors carry forward an in-service training program, according to the reports by county and city superintendents. Some of the variations stated indicate highly desirable trends. It seems appropriate to indicate what supervisors themselves report concerning procedures which they employ frequently or regularly. In examining the following table it is well to remember that any procedure, altho it may be good in itself, may be misapplied or misdirected.

TABLE 3—SUPERVISION PROCEDURES USED BY RESPONDENTS TO SUPERVISION QUESTIONNAIRE

Percentage Using Procedures	Procedures	
85	Having a definite schedule of classroom visitation	
15	Having no definite schedule for classroom visitation	
	Frequency of visitation when there is no definite schedule	
	Once a month	32%
	Once or twice a month	16%
	Twice a year	12%
	Once every one or two years	8%
	Upon request only	8%
	Four times a year	4%
	Weekly to bi-monthly	4%
	Three or four times a semester	4%
	Every four to six weeks	4%
	Six out of fifty schools about every 2 weeks	4%
	Problem teachers two or three times a year	4%
84	Following each classroom visit by a conference with the teacher	
23	Following each classroom visit by leaving written recommendations	
70	Following each classroom visit by a combination of conference and written recommendations	
70	Having specified periods when teachers may make appointments to discuss school or classroom problems with supervisor	
83	Holding group meetings with teachers who have the same type of difficulties or problems, arranging to have present one or more teachers who have successfully dealt with the problems under discussion	
86	Helping teacher groups to preview audio-visual materials	

(Continued on page 67)

TABLE 3—SUPERVISION PROCEDURES USED BY RESPONDENTS TO SUPERVISION QUESTIONNAIRE—(*Continued*)

Percentage Using Procedures	Procedures
65	Helping teacher groups plan for use of audio-visual materials
86	Holding conferences with teachers on use of audio-visual materials and equipment
96	Using the results of a testing program for diagnosing pupil and school strengths and weaknesses
64	Using the results of a testing program as a partial basis for promotions
74	Using the results of a testing program in planning ability groupings
78	Using the results of a testing program as a means of deciding upon specific problems upon which a school or a school system needs to work

Questionnaire responses from supervisors indicate their concern as to the merit of scheduled visits in contrast to on-call visits. Doubtless there is no one answer. The on-call basis has many values. If a whole school system developed to a point where supervisors functioned effectively on that basis, the achievements in terms of the development of children and youth should be of a very superior quality, and certainly the human relationships could be sound. Beginning teachers, teachers who lack motivation, or teachers who are not familiar with supervision, usually respond to regularly scheduled visits even tho they may not have recognized their own problems. Another value in scheduling visits is that the supervisor plans carefully in order to insure adequate time for creative work with the artist teacher who might not attain the heights of success of which she is capable without regular professional stimulation from a

Supervisors Help Plan Curriculum

County and city superintendents were asked what responsibility their supervisors assumed for a program of curriculum development. Their responses fell into thirty categories. Only nine of these will be given. Most of the listings were grouped in the first three items below:

1. Acting as leader of teacher committee groups working on curriculum revision
2. Working out courses of study for grades and subjects supervised
3. Continuous direction of the development of materials
4. On a consultant basis
5. Leadership and guidance in curriculum programs
6. Group planning with superintendents and teachers
7. Curriculum improvement; initiating and directing
8. Cooperating with superintendent in revision of curriculums
9. Total responsibility for curriculum revision.

Does the item given second highest ranking coincide with the philosophy expressed by superintendents in stating their goals? (See page 60.) Perhaps a more specific question might be whether or not practice complements theory. One respondent stated that there was not enough responsibility for curriculum development expected of supervisors, another said there was very little expected, and a third stated that there was none.

Printed and mimeographed bulletins were submitted by several superintendents in which curriculum development and in-service training programs of the respective school systems were described. From a statement prepared by a superintendent of a large city a few pertinent items are quoted to give the trend of thinking in such a school system.[17]

> If curriculum planning in Philadelphia is to serve effectively in the improvement of teaching, it is necessary that the basic assumptions underlying this planning be widely understood and pretty generally accepted through the instructional personnel of our schools.
>
> *We presuppose a democratic way of working.*—The assumptions which are stated here and discussed have been formulated through extended conference with teachers, principals, supervisors, directors, and superintendents from among the personnel of the Philadelphia Public Schools. It is believed that they are assumptions which our schools are at this time ready to accept in principle and to adopt in practice. It is also important to note that these are assumptions which seem to be in accord with the democratic way of working together. That way is here viewed as one in which the total personnel works together cooperatively and intelligently in the formulation and realization of common ends. Further, the democratic way is here viewed as by far the most difficult way of life, imposing the sternest obligations for self-control both on the citizens of a truly democratic state, and on those among them who accept the risks and privileges of leadership.
>
> *City-wide plans are set up on this foundation.*—The assumptions that follow are at the present time used as guides in all activities that have to do with city-wide curriculum planning. They will continue to be so used until some revision seems appropriate. It follows, obviously, that our city-wide curriculum planning will be effective only to the extent that others— teachers, principals, department heads, supervisors, directors, and superintendents—work with these same assumptions in mind.
>
> The assumptions to which reference has been made are as follows:
>
> Assumption 1. Every teacher (used to include all educators), should be looked upon as a person capable of developing considerable ability to behave intelligently with reference to the particular teaching situation of which he is a part.
>
> Assumption 2. Intelligent behavior in a teaching situation means (1) that a teacher studies the interests and needs of the particular pupils of his class, or classes; (2) that he informs himself of the work of other teachers who have dealt with or will in the future deal with the pupils to whom he is assigned; (3) that he takes account of the neighborhood in which the

---

[17] Philadelphia Public Schools. *Basic Assumptions for Curriculum Planning in the Public Schools of Philadelphia.*

school is located; (4) that he acquaints himself with the full range of instructional materials and specialized services that are available to him; (5) that he seeks continuously to clarify and enrich his objectives; and finally, (6) that he continuously organizes and carries through a program that takes proper account of these elements in the teaching situation.

Assumption 3. Intelligent teaching is most readily achieved and maintained in a school that has developed the capacity to act unitedly, or as an organic unit.

Assumption 4. If individual schools are to develop the capacity to act as organic units, it is necessary that they be granted (and that they use wisely) a considerable degree of freedom.

Assumption 5. Courses of study, curriculum plans, teaching materials, and all activities designed to improve teaching should be developed in full harmony with the foregoing assumptions; that is, they should be such as to promote intelligent teaching (as conceived in Assumption 2) in schools possessing a considerable degree of freedom.

The functions of the department of instruction and curriculum in a Texas city reveal numerous, but closely related responsibilities, carried by the individuals in charge.[18]

> The assistant superintendent in charge of instruction and curriculum shall be in a capacity that is essentially professional and which is administrative only as directly connected with his professional and supervisory responsibilities. He shall act as chairman and leader of the supervisory staff and consultant to them in professional work and shall be directly responsible for junior and senior high-school instruction. It shall also be the duty of the assistant superintendent in charge of instruction and curriculum to direct the following: a study of the curriculum, its formation and revision; testing, measurements, and research for maintaining the best possible methods in teaching; supervision of teachers in the way of aid, guidance, and counselling; appraising teaching results; visits and inspection of classrooms from a professional standpoint; program of pupil counselling and guidance; child accounting; program of group meetings of teachers; visual education, teaching aids, and equipment; selection of textbooks; preparation and editing of the professional publications of the El Paso public schools; approval of requisitions directly connected with teaching service; public contacts and educational publicity for keeping people informed and promoting understanding of educational policies; and general critical supervision of all other phases of teaching activity, such as evening schools, special schools and classes, adult education work, and the teachers' library.

How curriculum committees should be formed is a problem raised by leaders responsible for curriculum programs. One answer is given in the following statement: [19]

---

[18] El Paso Public Schools. *Rules and Manual for School Employees.* El Paso: the Board, 1944.
[19] King County, Washington.

> There is an extensive curriculum development program proceeding in King County at the present time. The county office selected chairmen of committees in the various subject fields, such as social studies, science, etc. These chairmen in turn organized a vertical or steering committee, and a horizontal or development committee, both of which met regularly. The chairmen made progress reports at intervals to the office. When materials are fully developed, the county board of education and representatives from steering committees edit them, after which they are published by the county office.

The King County office took the leadership in organizing the original plan for in-service training of which the curriculum work is a part, and supervisors are charged with some responsibility for curriculum development. Since the first year of King County's program, school districts desiring in-service training directly contact the state department of public instruction and the program is arranged.

Supervisors in cities and counties in many states have been in key positions in terms of influencing curriculum thinking. The interrelationships of the administrative, consultative, and supervisory personnel are complex. The channels of working and clearance in one school system are shown in Figure 12.

It is pertinent to include a summary of the responses to one of the questions asked of supervisors, "How are your efforts coordinated with those of other supervisors in your school system?" Forty-three percent of the replies stated that coordination was done thru staff meetings in which the superintendent outlined policies and made assignments, 38 percent indicated that there was no definite plan of coordination used, 10 percent stated that coordination was thru assignments made by a director of education, 6 percent stated that there were no other supervisors in the school system, and only 3 percent reported that coordination took place thru group planning in staff meetings. (See Figure 13.)

How Can Supervision Be Improved?

Since there is general agreement among the groups represented in the questionnaire study as to the educational goals or aims that are most important, as well as the problems that are most pressing, it is surprising to note that there is considerable variance of opinion as to those areas in which advance in supervision is most needed.

Good Public Relations Are Called For

The area listed by the greatest number of supervisors as needing the most advance was the improvement of public relations toward education in general as well as toward supervision services specifically. Altho principals did not list this among the first five areas in which advance is

ANALYZING OUR PROBLEMS 71

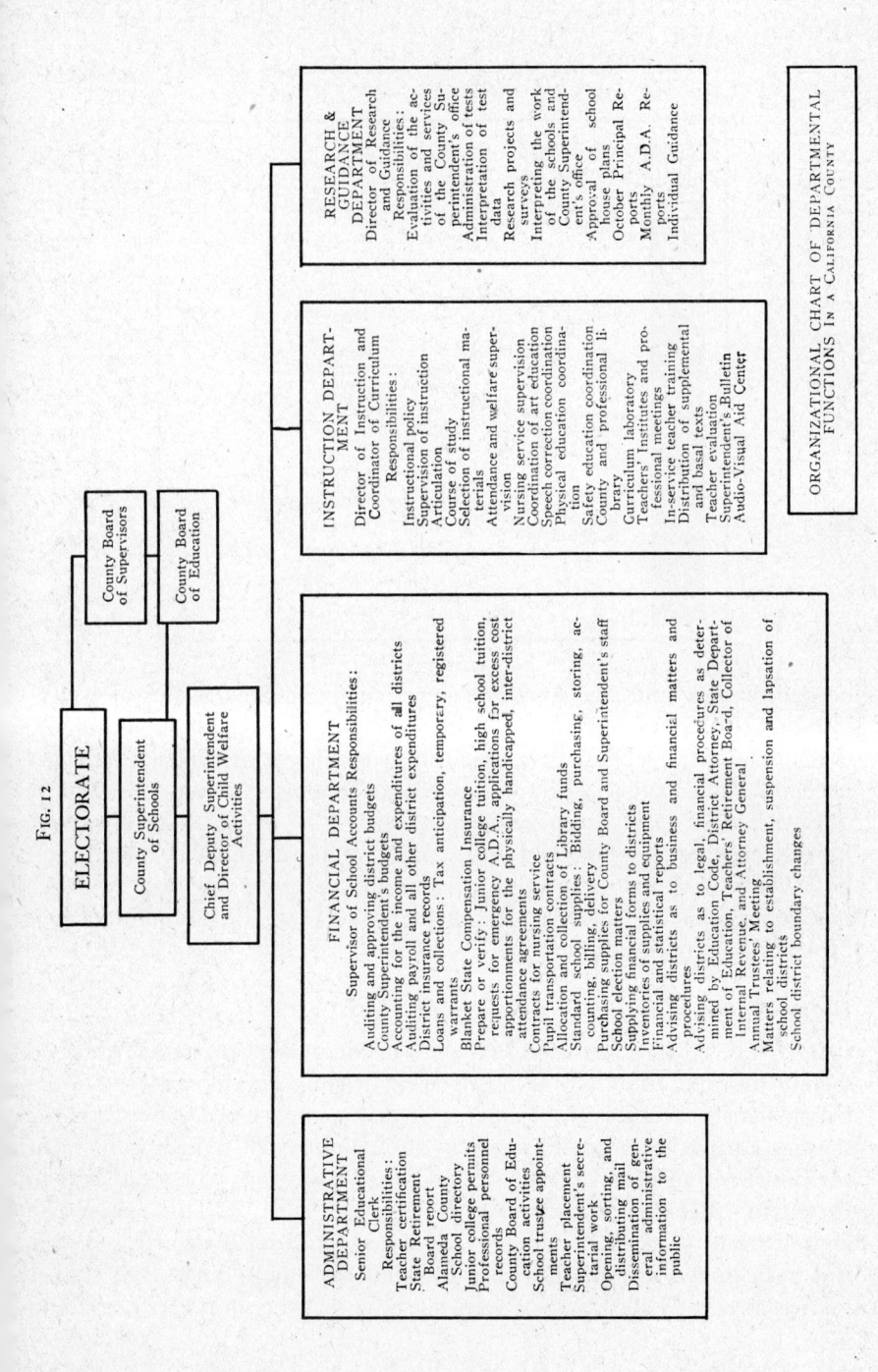

Fig. 12

ELECTORATE

- County Board of Supervisors
- County Board of Education

- County Superintendent of Schools
- Chief Deputy Superintendent and Director of Child Welfare Activities

ADMINISTRATIVE DEPARTMENT
Senior Educational Clerk
Responsibilities:
Teacher certification
State Retirement Board report
Alameda County School directory
Junior college permits
Professional personnel records
County Board of Education activities
School trustee appointments
Teacher placement
Superintendent's secretarial work
Opening, sorting, and distributing mail
Dissemination of general administrative information to the public

FINANCIAL DEPARTMENT
Supervisor of School Accounts Responsibilities:
Auditing and approving district budgets
County Superintendent's budgets
Accounting for the income and expenditures of all districts
Auditing payroll and all other district expenditures
District insurance records
Loans and collections: Tax anticipation, temporary, registered warrants
Blanket State Compensation Insurance
Prepare or verify: Junior college tuition, high school tuition, requests for emergency A.D.A., applications for excess cost apportionments for the physically handicapped, inter-district attendance agreements
Contracts for nursing service
Pupil transportation contracts
Allocation and collection of Library funds
Standard school supplies: Bidding, purchasing, storing, accounting, billing, delivery
Purchasing supplies for County Board and Superintendent's staff
School election matters
Supplying financial forms to districts
Inventories of supplies and equipment
Financial and statistical reports
Advising districts as to business and financial matters and procedures
Advising districts as to legal, financial procedures as determined by Education Code, District Attorney, State Department of Education, Teachers' Retirement Board, Collector of Internal Revenue, and Attorney General
Annual Trustees' Meeting
Matters relating to establishment, suspension and lapsation of school districts
School district boundary changes

INSTRUCTION DEPARTMENT
Director of Instruction and Coordinator of Curriculum
Responsibilities:
Instructional policy
Supervision of instruction
Articulation
Course of study
Selection of instructional materials
Attendance and welfare supervision
Nursing service supervision
Coordination of art education
Speech correction coordination
Physical education coordination
Safety education coordination
County and professional library
Curriculum laboratory
Teachers' Institutes and professional meetings
In-service teacher training
Distribution of supplemental and basal texts
Teacher evaluation
Superintendent's Bulletin
Audio-Visual Aid Center

RESEARCH & GUIDANCE DEPARTMENT
Director of Research and Guidance
Responsibilities:
Evaluation of the activities and services of the County Superintendent's office
Administration of tests
Interpretation of test data
Research projects and surveys
Interpreting the work of the schools and County Superintendent's office
Approval of school house plans
October Principal Reports
Monthly A.D.A. Reports
Individual Guidance

ORGANIZATIONAL CHART OF DEPARTMENTAL FUNCTIONS IN A CALIFORNIA COUNTY

FIG. 13
COORDINATION OF SUPERVISORY EFFORTS WITHIN EDUCATIONAL SYSTEMS REPRESENTED IN THE 1946 YEARBOOK QUESTIONNAIRES

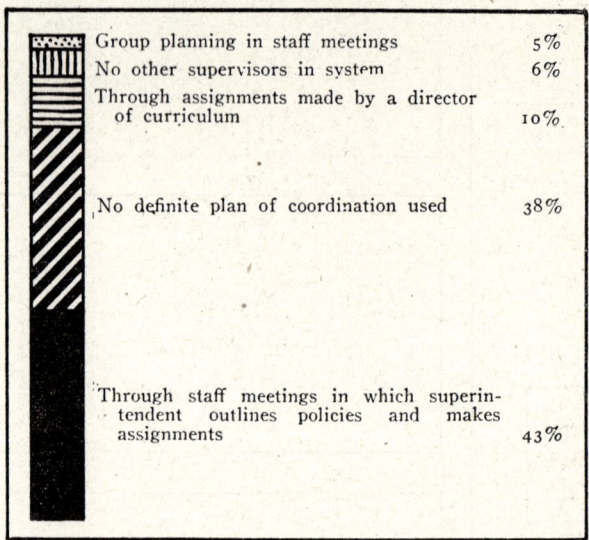

Group planning in staff meetings	5%
No other supervisors in system	6%
Through assignments made by a director of curriculum	10%
No definite plan of coordination used	38%
Through staff meetings in which superintendent outlines policies and makes assignments	43%

needed, county and city superintendents and state departments of education ranked it in fourth and fifth places respectively. It goes without saying that public interest must be aroused in order to get the financial support needed for adequate supervision services for schools. Use of graphs such as those reported by Norton and Davies should be a persuasive argument for establishing a sound basis for public support. Publicity campaigns, however, will be valueless unless they are backed by good, solid evidence that supervision services really contribute markedly to the improvement of American public education.

Better In-Service Programs Would Help

In-service education for all branches of educational personnel is placed second by supervisors on the list of areas needing development. State departments also feel this to be an area of major importance. It seems likely that for a period of years the problem of obtaining well-trained, competent personnel for all phases of educational work will grow worse rather than better. In order that schools may operate at all, it has already been necessary in many parts of the country to lower educational standards. While it is to be hoped that any lowering of standards is only temporary, studies such as a recent California one seem to show that the shortage of teaching

ANALYZING OUR PROBLEMS

personnel will increase in many areas for a number of years after the war, and then subside only gradually. Already in many localities pupils fresh from high school and older people who have not taught for years or who have had no teaching experience at all are employed in our schools. We owe such individuals a debt of gratitude, for without their services many American children would be deprived of any chance for education during the war years and those immediately following. We owe them and the children they teach more than gratitude, however.

Since teachers colleges cannot meet the teacher shortage with young and efficient, well-trained teachers, emergency teachers must be given all the help possible to upgrade their teaching. Excellent summer courses for war emergency teachers have been offered in many places thruout the country, but supervisors and state departments of education are convinced that vigorous programs of in-service training are also needed. State departments, with very few exceptions, insist that supervision services must be increased in order to cope with this problem. Most of these departments reported that they had increased their own supervision staffs within the last five-year period.

In-service growth is not to be thought of in terms of war emergency teachers only. The continuous in-service education of educational personnel is urgently needed in order to provide a strong vanguard of individuals who are professionally abreast of the times and who can help materially in the struggle to keep educational services from lessening in quality.

Curriculum Must Be Based on Child Needs

The third area in which supervision most needs advance, supervisors say, is in curriculum study and revision based upon child needs and upon a working knowledge of child growth and development. All groups responding to the questionnaires agree as to the importance of this area. The growing conviction among individuals engaged in all varieties of educational work is that the greatest improvement in education can come only thru increased knowledge and understanding of the nature and needs of pupils. This can be expected to have much influence on both preservice and in-service teacher-training programs.

Skills Need To Be Taught More Effectively

Supervisors place fourth in order of importance the development of better ways of teaching specific skills and knowledges, as well as the improvement of methods of supervision on various grade levels. Superintendents and principals place improved methods of teaching skills and abilities at the head of the list of areas needing development. Supervisors are especially concerned with the improvement of supervision in the primary grades, with improvement in school health programs, and with the development of strong reading readiness programs. Principals agree with supervisors that much development is needed in the area of primary supervision, of supervision on the high-school level, with improved coordination between the elementary and high schools. State superintendents believe that there is need for better supervision of the fine arts, and that supervisors should concentrate also upon developing improved reading and social studies programs for the schools.

Rethinking in Evaluation Is Necessary

Questionnaire responses give supervisors' rating of evaluation as fifth in order of importance of areas especially needing advance and development. This is another area recognized as of major significance by all groups of questionnaire respondents. There is general agreement that evaluation must be continuous, that it should be used diagnostically and as a means of improving school services rather than as a basis for grading or rating pupils, and that it should include the evaluation of school procedures and practices as well as new and approved methods of appraising pupil growth. A number of supervisors speak of the need for some form of guide or evaluation technic which they, as supervisors, can use in evaluating their own services.

Leadership Must Come From Cooperative Effort

Supervisors and state departments of education agree that the development of democratic methods of leadership is another area needing much study and work. One of the major problems recognized and dealt with previously in this chapter is confusion on the part of supervisors as to their functions and duties. It is clear that most of the individuals agree that the solution to this problem does not lie in authoritarian determination by administrative officers or by supervisors, but rather in cooperative group planning. Teachers, supervisors, administrators, interested laymen, and pupils should all have a share in carrying out the total educational program. The difficulty lies in the fact that each person has his own interpretation of just what is involved in democratic leadership, and even when a clear definition is agreed upon by a group, the problem of operating democratically still must be solved. Certainly, basic to the solution of this is much closer cooperation and understanding among those engaged in the various phases of the school program. Preservice and in-service education programs will need to concentrate upon a type of training specifically designed to develop teachers who are capable of democratic "followership" as well as leadership.

ANALYZING OUR PROBLEMS

Supervision Needs To Be General Rather than Specific

Many principals responding to the questionnaire feel that the most effective work can be done when supervision is not broken down into specialized subjectmatter fields. Just what kind of training and supervision program is the best for developing individuals who will have real competence in special subject fields and yet who will not allow subject interests to cloud their vision of broad basic problems of education? The answer to this question should absorb an increasing amount of the time and attention of consultants and educators, especially those responsible for teacher training and leadership.

Teaching Atypical Children Requires More Study

Improved methods of teaching atypical children is an area which questionnaire respondents also recognize as needing an increased amount of attention. After all, our children today are subjected to so many atypical experiences that it would be surprising if the number of children in need of educational and personality adjustments did not increase. A study of the individual responses of principals shows that, in speaking of the atypical child, they have in mind the gifted child as well as the child with educational or psychological problems. Even among so-called normal children, individual differences are so great that any plan that does not make provision for them is doomed to failure. If we truly believe, as we assert, that every child is entitled to education consistent with his potentialities, each child must be given equal consideration within the educational framework, whether he be a slow learner, the mythical average child, or the gifted child.

Adequate Tools for Working Must Be Available

All groups responding to questionnaires feel the need for development of improved methods of distributing and using various instructional aids, such as auditory-visual equipment; environmental resources; and professional books, journals and ephemeral materials. The widespread use of auditory-visual materials in both the Army and Navy instructional programs should accelerate their adoption and use in public schools. Forward-looking school systems thruout the country are well aware of this, and are already seeking to develop, collect, and instruct teachers in the effective use of a wide variety of recently developed materials and equipment. While many of these, in themselves, are excellent they are of value only when utilized by individuals able to use them and to understand their possibilities. In most of the states curriculum laboratories and professional libraries are now an established part of the educational system. The value of these agencies will increase in proportion only to the degree to which teachers who have access to them are helped to select and use materials with discrimination.

Supervision Needs Better Qualified People

City and county superintendents to whom questionnaires were sent make a plea for principals who are trained supervisors, and supervisors who are trained clinicians. They believe that improvement in the preparation of supervisors is essential, and suggest the use of a screening process of some type preceding education in order to insure that candidates for credentials will be temperamentally suited to leadership positions. Supervisors, superintendents believe, should be thoroly trained as consultants, should be aware of the latest developments in child guidance, and should be skilled in the various technics necessary to an effective guidance program.

State departments also are concerned with this problem. They speak for an increase of supervision both in rural and in urban areas, placing special emphasis upon the need for more and better supervision for rural schools, in order to assure rural children equal rights to sound educational procedures with children in urban areas.

4

A Look at Our Best

Having viewed the goals which educational leadership has set itself and the organization it has so far effected for the task, as well as the problems and obstacles it sees in its path, we turn now to another kind of question: Among all the practices now employed, which hold the greatest hope for success?

For an analysis of these most promising practices, we examine programs at national as well as local levels and turn to outstanding professional literature of the day. They provide us with clues to those areas in which supervision at present is operating on frontier lines.

What Do Responses Reveal As Current Practices of Promise?

One of the questions asked of supervisors and supervising principals was, "In your opinion what are the three most helpful and promising ways of working in public education?" Figure 1 summarizes the responses. *Democratic leadership in supervision,* the *establishment of effective community relationships,* and *group conferences* received the three highest ratings from the supervisory group. The group included individuals engaged in supervision of kindergarten, elementary and secondary schools, adult education, special subject fields, and supervision training in colleges and universities. Secondary and elementary principals responding to the same inquiry agreed in general with the supervisor group except that they believed that *individual conference* technics are more significant than the establishment of community relationships. Supervisors placed the same value upon workshops as principals place upon individual conferences.

Democratic Leadership Stems from Group Cooperation

An examination of the thinking which prompted these ratings will give added meaning to the terms. Supervisors believe that there is need for more leadership based on democratic group action in which each member

---

By Lelia Ann Taggart, *Director of Education, Santa Barbara County, California, and* Mary C. Evans, *General Supervisor, Santa Barbara County, California*

Fig. 1
THE FIVE SUPERVISORY PRACTICES RATED AS MOST PROMISING BY A SELECTED GROUP OF 175 SUPERVISORS AND PRINCIPALS

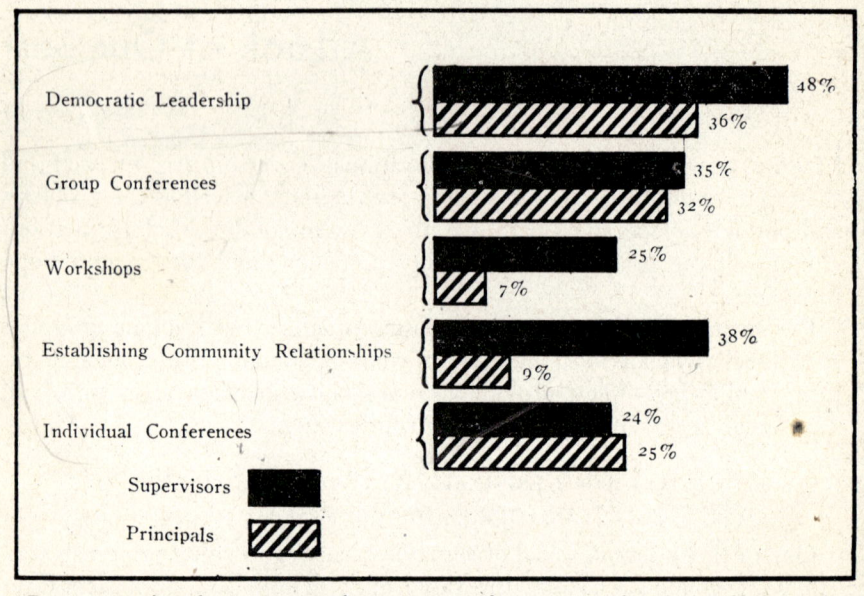

Practice	Supervisors	Principals
Democratic Leadership	48%	36%
Group Conferences	35%	32%
Workshops	25%	7%
Establishing Community Relationships	38%	9%
Individual Conferences	24%	25%

(Percentages given here represent the percentage of responses rating the specified practices as among the three most promising. Other practices listed as being of promise were: classroom visitations; curriculum development, the supervisor as a resource person, research and advanced study, in-service training, putting philosophy into practice, raising professional standards, working closely with administrators, defining the job, building teacher morale, demonstration teaching, coordination of supervisory services, and working closely with principals.)

belongs and participates to the limit of his capacity. Individual responses show that the qualities both supervisors and principals feel to be inherent in democratic leadership are cooperation, sympathetic understanding, provision for freedom of action and ideas, encouragement in experimentation, and a spirit of willingness on the part of all persons concerned to adjust or subordinate personal judgments to those determined by the group. To some respondents democratic leadership means simply "giving the teachers more 'say'!" On the other hand, there is general recognition that teachers as well as those responsible for teacher leadership have definite responsibilities for making democratic processes work in all phases of the educational program. Also cited is the administrators' responsibility for instituting procedures and policies that make truly democratic educational leadership possible. Democratic leadership, supervisors say, is characterized by "greater decentralization of authority and responsibility, making the supervisor a leader by virtue of leadership qualifications rather than authority." In other words, in respect to supervisory services specifically, the consensus is that supervisors should not be teachers of teachers, but leaders of teachers.

Education Is a Community Enterprise

Both supervisors and principals represented in the questionnaire responses feel that the establishment of community and school relationships is of great importance and that supervisors have very definite functions in this respect. Respondents make it clear that in speaking of community participation they have in mind a reciprocal relationship. They believe that education may be improved by using lay members and community organizations in the formation of school plans and procedures, and that the school, in turn, should extend its influence to the improvement of many phases of community life.

Some respondents give as their motive for emphasis upon community relationships the obtaining of more adequate financial support for education. A far larger number believe, however, that the community can make other contributions to public education which are at least as valuable as "paying the bills." They feel that supervisors should be active in projects of community concern, and that every effort should be made to encourage community participation on the part of both teachers and pupils. They believe that participation in community affairs provides children with the best possible training in functional citizenship.

Suggestions for achieving satisfactory school and community relationships proposed by respondents are: (1) working with key persons in the community (2) working with teachers in making an analysis of community resources, needs, and problems (3) studying educational problems from the angle of the social worker, the anthropologist, and the social scientist, using their combined thinking to initiate community self-improvement programs (4) inviting people from other fields—social service, health, and local governmental agencies—as well as interested laymen to share in educational planning and policy-making (5) encouraging laymen to join with teacher committees in curriculum revision studies (6) making contacts with the public thru community clubs and organizations to interpret the educational program (7) active participation on the part of supervisors in a wide variety of community projects and activities (8) working as an integral part of a coordinating council of social agencies and (9) instituting a planned publicity program to interpret the educational program to the public.

Certainly, since situations vary widely, no community would find all of these approaches equally effective. Too many public relations programs in the past have relied heavily upon campaigns to present accounts of school activities to the newspaper-reading public. In contrast to this type of one-sided activity, a wholesome trend, easily discernible in the questionnaire responses is toward combined lay and professional study of educational and community problems. In addition, the school still retains the responsibility of making a coordinated effort to acquaint the general public with basic issues facing education today. One obvious and very significant role of educational leaders in such programs is that of collecting and making available the kinds of necessary data and evidence difficult for individuals without professional training in public education to obtain or interpret.

Just what proportion of the supervisor's time should be spent in helping to cement school and community efforts? The answer to this question also necessarily varies with each situation. In many systems where supervision staffs are small, concentration on those supervisory functions which are of the greatest benefit to the total educational program is essential. It is well to remember that improvement of educational methods which results in evident gains to boys and girls in the classrooms is a powerful force in arousing public support of the schools. One of the newer instructional practices found beneficial in many systems is that of enlarging the classroom to include the expanding community. New methods and changed instructional approaches are difficult for many teachers to deal with, but they are inevitable in a rapidly changing social order. If a major duty of supervisors is to help teachers succeed, may it not be that the supervisors' best contribution to the improvement of school and community relationships is that of counselor, guide, consultant, resource person, and friend to the classroom teachers under their supervision?

Conferences Play a Major Role

Group and *individual* conferences are also valued highly by questionnaire respondents. Much emphasis is placed on the opportunity the individual conference affords the supervisor for gaining a real understanding of each teacher and her problems. Most of the principals and many supervisors believe that a conference following each classroom observation is almost an essential. But there is a growing trend toward another type of conference, that arranged at the teacher's request to deal with a problem proposed by her. Several respondents emphasized the importance of supervisors' learning to "know each teacher as a person." Well-planned individual conferences provide an opportunity for this. One warning is voiced, however. As one response put it, "Have more individual conferences—but *short* ones." Just what the length of the individual conference should be and what should be the number of items covered at any one time will vary with individuals and situations, of course, but careful consideration should be given to determining what specific conference technics are most effective. Might it not be wise for supervisors to consider carefully the fine balance between the professional and the personal which is necessary if conferences are to help supervisors and teachers know each other as people? Is it not necessary also that the type of conference held and the balance maintained between personal and professional emphases be considered relative to the individual personalities of the supervisors and teachers involved?

Principals, supervisors, and teachers all place group conferences higher on the scale than individual conferences. In a study involving eight New York schools, group conferences were cited as very helpful by almost three-fourths of the two hundred teachers consulted.[1] May it not be that one reason for the appeal the group conference has for teachers is that it gives them opportunity to learn about new theories, methods, and technics without undergoing the embarrassment of revealing ignorance of them in a classroom observation or an individual conference? And may we also conclude that teachers recognize the truism that "two heads are better than one."

Local Workshops Deal in Concrete Problems

Teacher workshops, or workshops in which the total educational staff of a school or system participates, are rated third in importance by supervisors. The workshop conducted in a local area for local teachers is given preference over that conducted on a college or university campus, altho both types are considered valuable. Typical supervisory functions in relation to any workshop situation include defining the purposes of the workshop, planning a thoroly coordinated program of activities, seeing that an adequate supply of pertinent and worthwhile materials are available, channeling teachers into activities best suited to their tastes and capabilities, evaluating results, and keeping accurate records to use in planning subsequent workshop experiences. Workshops have little value unless they result in tangible evidences of changed teacher behavior. This can only occur when careful planning has been done and when a sincere effort has been made to meet those problems which seem most pressing to each participant. The role of the supervisor is seen here, not as an instructor, but as a coordinator, consultant, and guide.

Practices of Promise Are Many and Varied

One to 22 percent of questionnaire respondents listed other practices as being of significant value. They follow in order of the importance assigned them: (1) in-service training programs (2) classroom visitations (3) curriculum development programs (4) the supervisor as a resource person (5) advanced study and research (6) helping school staffs to estab-

---

[1] Antell, Henry, "Teachers Appraise Supervision." *Journal of Educational Research* 38:606-11; April 1945.

lish and implement educational goals (7) raising professional standards (8) building teacher morale (9) demonstration lessons (10) coordination of supervisory services and (11) "selling" supervision to teachers and administrators. Principals seem to be more aware than supervisors of the importance of raising professional standards, of establishing satisfactory human relationships, and of supervisors' assuming responsibility for making teachers and administrators aware of the fact that supervision can be valuable. Supervisors, in evaluating themselves, might do well to examine the more objective point of view of principals toward supervision services.

How Has a National Organization Helped To Chart the Road Ahead?

Organized on a nationwide basis, with its roots in local communities, the Association for Supervision and Curriculum Development, a department of the National Education Association, is engaged in a variety of activities. Any discussion of these activities and ways of working has little meaning without an understanding of the principles by which the group operates. For it is only as the activities which the Association supports serve as means of promoting better educational experiences for children and youth that they can be justified. The Association at present operates on the following platform:

We believe that modern schools can do their jobs ONLY IF . . .

- —pupils, teachers, and administrators grow in understanding what life is all about.
- —everyone has a chance to test for himself what is important and what isn't.
- —youngsters learn by making choices and seeing how they work.
- —youngsters have a chance to think and talk about our social structure and decide how it may be improved.
- —what happens in the school is determined by what boys and girls need individually and in groups, now and tomorrow.
- —the curriculum—what boys and girls do in school—has meaning and significance for the youngsters.
- —all community agencies, including our homes and schools, work together for better education.
- —there is mutual respect and confidence as we work together to improve our schools.
- —school programs are continually being weighed and improved in the light of tested ways of working.
- —parents and citizens are helped to understand what their youngsters need to learn and how it can be taught.
- —state and federal aid goes to communities which cannot pay for good schools.

Since the important function of the Association is to stimulate better supervisory practices in the interest of developing better schools, it is important to consider how it implements the realization of its program. Strong working committees, a regional organization, and a program of publications are among the most promising means thru which the organization works. Basic to all activities is the conviction that efforts of regional and national character are of significance only as they emanate from and affect the quality of educational opportunity in local situations.

Committees Work in Significant Areas

As some of the major problems confronting supervisors were isolated, group action was seen as an ideal means of attacking them. In order to facilitate action, several committees were organized. This committee work on which the Association relies heavily is essentially group action. Basic principles of group action to which committees subscribe are very similar to those stated in a recent publication:

> The first principle that stands forth is that *the goal of the group should be action.* . . .
> The second principle, related to the first, is that *the membership of a working group should consist of those who have a common function and are consequently in a position to test in action conclusions that may be reached.* . . .
> Third is the principle that *common purposes—the elements that serve to tie individuals together—should be constantly borne in mind.* . . .
> This leads to the statement of a fourth principle,—namely that *group coordination of smaller group activities is essential*, that it is critically important that there should exist what is often called a central planning committee.* . . .
> One of the temptations from which every group suffers is that of imposing its collective—often bare—majority will too readily upon the individual. The fifth principle may consequently be stated that *there should be a constant effort to discover and release the powers of all individual persons.* . . .
> A sixth principle is that in group planning and action *rational methods should be meticulously followed.* . . .
> This brings us to a seventh principle, namely that a *dynamic attitude should be developed.* . . .

In-Service Education Merits Attention

Since 1943 a study on *in-service teacher education* has been going forward which involves supervisors and teachers in various parts of the nation. The core committee of this study has stated that its purposes are: (a) to stimulate more effective supervisor-teacher effort on the solution of problems that are faced by individual teachers and (b) to serve as a clearinghouse for reports from supervisors and teachers as to effective ways of overcoming obstacles. The field committee members were chosen from those with supervisory responsibilities in education and were representative of all sections of the country as well as of rural areas, villages, and small and large cities. Each supervisor selected as a field committee member was asked to cooperate with two or three teachers of his local staff in working on problems of the teachers' own choosing. The teachers were asked by the supervisor to keep informal records such as diaries, log books, and anecdotal recordings. The supervisor's report was kept independently, and both reports were sent to the core committee. Beginning in September 1944, it was anticipated that a two-year period would be the minimum time for a supervisor and his teachers to work together before recognizable evidence of the effectiveness of procedures would be available. The committee reports its progress and findings from time to time thru conferences and Association publications.

A Study of Basic Education Gets Under Way

Another leadership activity of the Association is the sponsorship of a study of basic education in secondary schools. After a plan for the study was outlined, a proposal for implementing the study drawn up by the Northwest Society was approved with the following suggestions:

1. That a certain portion of the school program should be set aside in each school taking part in the study for the consideration of common interests, needs, and concerns of young people.
2. That it is not essential whether we talk of core curriculum, general education, basic education, or some other term. Such a study will stand or fall upon the types and varieties of experiences children will have.
3. That changes in the nature of basic education should be dependent upon two factors:
    a. Growth in our understanding of the problems that face us
    b. Changes in the nature of society itself.
4. That groups in proximity to field committee members should be encouraged to develop similar studies.
5. That administrators should be encouraged to bring teachers into the planning of the experiment and should realize that school time is essential for such planning.
6. That within a building the problems should be attacked on a whole-school basis. Programs go forward only as total faculty will sanction.
7. That thru pupil-teacher planning in setting up objectives, providing for classroom experiences, and evaluating growth comes opportunity for optimum development (curriculum planned by both).

In 1945 it was recommended by the chairman of the core committee that this study, which has far-reaching implications for the improvement of education provided for youth, be broadened to include a twelve-year range of school experiences. Proceedings and findings of this undertaking are being made available thru the publications of the various school systems participating as well as thru the Association. Preliminary progress reports which merit careful consideration have already appeared in Washington and Oregon.

Beginning Supervisors Get Help in Local Situations

Florida, Tennessee, and Virginia report that supervision practices in those states have already been influenced by a third Association project which embodies the principles of group action. In each state a small group of beginning supervisors had, as a special consultant, a field worker of the state department of education. Ideas were exchanged and resources pooled thru group meetings with supervisors who served in nearby school systems. Utilizing the findings of this study in one state, a handbook for supervisors on *Ways of Working as a Supervisor in Florida* has developed. In this instance we have evidence of activities of nationwide scope and backing resulting, not in a conventional printed report, but in action at a local level.

Committees Deal with Many Problems

Other Association groups are studying additional problems with supervisory implications. Extended school services for children of school age, interpreting children thru lay periodicals, recruitment of teachers, a city and its children, and a ten year study of teacher development are among the other problems receiving attention. In most instances a national core committee makes the initial proposal, assumes coordinating responsibility, provides leadership and stimulation during the undertaking, and directs its attention to a variety of activities on local levels.

Publications Provide Channels for Working

The Association employs several channels thru which information is disseminated to supervisor-leaders at regular intervals. Other publications are developed as a result of particular research and of committee work of the type discussed in the preceding paragraphs. A publications committee directs its attention to regular evaluation of all publications with a view toward continual improvement. Regular publications by the Association are the annual yearbooks and *Educational Leadership*, the Association journal. *Building America*, a publication designed for pupil use, is sponsored by the Association. Pamphlet publications available from the Association include consideration of films interpreting children and youth; discipline for children in today's world; education in the armed forces; publications in elementary education; and evaluation of recent city, state, and county curriculum bulletins.

Regional Activity Is Facilitated Thru Organization

Another means of disseminating findings of significance to the supervisor-leader and of stimulating additional study of supervisory problem is thru the Association's Committee of Twelve. This committee was organized to include all forty-eight states and the District of Columbia.

Most of the regions have engaged in some phase of planning, and several have held successful regional conferences and undertaken activities proposed by the department. In instances in which objectives and outcomes of the regional group are similar to those of a state department of education working thru its legal representatives, close cooperation is desirable.

Thru the activities stimulated by the regional organization, the national association is further enabled to move toward a "grass-roots approach" to supervisory problems. What publications are unable to do, first-hand contacts often accomplish. Thus supervision *purposes* conceived on a nationwide scale and *ways of working* to attain these purposes achieve dynamics as regions, states, and local school systems identify their own problems and attack them at the source. The functions and promising ways of working discussed from this national viewpoint correlate closely with those reported by local school systems. This is not surprising since the Association "is the man in the local school system."

WHAT NEW WAYS OF WORKING DO REGIONAL PROGRAMS REVEAL?

A trend which is increasing in popularity, and which indicates great promise in the studies submitted, is the cooperative action of a group of states in working on a problem which has elements of concern for several states. A number of educational groups have been experimenting with a variety of approaches based on the regional concept.

What's Tried with Youth Has Possibilities for Teachers

Based on the premise that there probably has never been a time when the need for effective leadership of teachers in service was greater, a subcommittee of the North Central Association of Colleges and Secondary Schools was appointed to study the problem of educating teachers in service. In initiating its work this committee made an investigation of the technics commonly employed in education in our secondary schools and noted that they were not those listed as most promising in surveys. Its next step is one that should have suggestion for educators concerned with in-service training thruout the country. Teachers in the selected schools were asked to record in anecdotal form the procedures they considered of greatest promise for educating teachers in service. They were requested to make their judgments in the light of the results in their respective schools. The following technics were most frequently mentioned: [2]

1. Having teachers organize themselves into committees to study problems
2. Having teachers, rather than the principal or department heads, plan faculty meetings
3. Providing an adequate professional library in a room used exclusively by teachers and fitted as a comfortable, home-like, browsing room
4. Having teacher panels discuss recent articles in periodical literature
5. Giving special financial awards for participation in cooperative attacks upon school problems
6. Encouraging an evaluation of the school by use of such devices as the application of the criteria of the Cooperative Study of Secondary School Standards
7. Organizing a well-planned, cooperative attack on problems of curriculum development
8. Holding forums where teachers, pupils, parents, and board members could discuss their common problems
9. Attending summer schools, more particularly summer workshops
10. Visiting other teachers.

. . . .

These data appear to indicate that *frequent use of cooperative techniques* seems to be the better procedure to remove the obstacle known as "poor professional attitude of teachers"; to increase the attention paid to research, educational literature, and a study of the learning process; to increase the attention paid to study of the local community; to encourage experimentation; and to promote activity in the area of curriculum development.

. . . .

Technics which are supervisory and inspectorial and which originate with administrators and supervisors and which are individualistic rather than cooperative in character are considered of doubtful value, but they are most frequently used. Technics which involve teacher participation in planning and policy making, which involve teacher participation in all phases of the program of in-service education, which encourage teacher initiation of action as well as planning are considered most valuable, but these technics are the least used.

Do not the ten procedures or technics most frequently listed by the teachers in this study give directives to all personnel charged with supervisory responsibilities? Progress reports of this subcommittee on in-service training of teachers merit careful study by secondary administrators, department heads, coordinators, and supervisors. Weber concludes that,

---

[2] Weber, C. A., "A Summary of the Findings of the Sub-Committee on In-Service Education of the North Central Association of Colleges and Secondary Schools," *Journal of Educational Research* 36:694-706; May 1943.

"apparently, the task confronting the educator is to cast aside the fetters of traditional devices and let the teachers share in planning, policy making, procedures, and evaluation."[3]

Cooperative School Experimentation Employs Regional Ways of Working

A unique feature of the Horace Mann-Lincoln Institute for School Experimentation is that it includes school systems in various parts of the United States. It has features in common with regional programs in that group planning by representatives from all school systems is an important part of the experimentation. During the summer of 1945 a central workshop was held at Teachers College, Columbia University, to provide opportunity for collaboration between the Institute staff and representatives of the associated schools. Teachers, administrators, supervisors, and consultants shared in the planning and worked cooperatively on the problems of concern to their respective school systems, or to the total group.

The schools included in the study became associated thru invitation by the Institute staff. Representatives from this staff visited the various schools in a system "to discover the common problems in which several might collaborate, and the problems which would provide individual schools or school systems with projects peculiar to their local conditions."[4] When need for a service is indicated, special consultants from Teachers College, Columbia University and other institutions are called in to work in the local situation.

Progress reports of this cooperative school experimentation will be made available thru the Bureau of Publications at Teachers College. Procedures and practices should have great value to elementary- and secondary-school supervisors. As a way of planning, this study should offer suggestions to institutions of higher education.

The South Pioneers in Regional Study

A study which provides elementary-school supervisors with an opportunity to evaluate the services they are rendering is sponsored by the Southern States Work Conference. The states already cooperating in this study are Alabama, Georgia, Kentucky, South Carolina, and Tennessee.

> Objectives of the study are: (1) compilation of points of view regarding the purposes and functions of the elementary school in a community, (2) gathering and use of factual data, currently available, that serve to help interpret the elementary-school situation in the respective states, (3) initiating programs of action that will cause teachers, school leaders, and lay

---
[3] *Ibid.*
[4] Harap, Henry, editor. "Front Lines in Education," *Educational Leadership* 2:175-78; January 1945.

citizens to evaluate critically present conditions and practices in elementary schools and communities and to evolve plans that will result in a more effective education, (4) preparation of case studies of school and community activities that reflect varying qualities of work and give insight into local conditions.

The conference believes that the rehabilitation of the South depends on the development of an effective educational program, particularly in the elementary school. "For, it is here and here only that all the children of all of the people can be reached, and it is here that children are most amenable to change."[5]

In this work conference, supervisors of counties, states, and cities are cooperating with other leaders on a steering committee whose responsibility is the direction and coordination of the work of the total group. State committees will:[6]

... (1) provide for the gathering of factual materials, (2) give guidance to local groups in the collection of data relating to classroom practices, community participation, and statistical information, which may be used at the 1946 work conference, (3) contribute to the 1946 conference point of view as to purposes and functions of the elementary schools in the community.

It is obvious that there is an absence of complacency with "what is" when key educators, including the supervisor-leader, recognize the necessity for critically evaluating their functions in the interest of developing better programs of education. Previously untapped resources are utilized to achieve desired goals.

Values determine supervisory practices in programs such as these three of regional nature. Commenting on the soundness of employing cooperative group work as a means of developing a fine instructional program, Corey states that in working with teachers:[7]

A ... method ... that contributes to a sense of well being and security and results ... in much more rapid and more permanent progress involves concentrating upon those things that the teacher already does well and of which she is proud and then helping her realize that in the degree that all of the teaching practices are consistent with her best ones she is professionally superior.

. . . .

The principal or superintendent or supervisor who insists upon functioning as a 'leader' rather than a 'director' recognizes the importance of having those with whom he works secure and adventuresome and familiar with and responsible for the entire educational program. He recognizes that the

---

[5] Spotlight. "South to Study Elementary Education," *School Executive* 64:32; August 1945.
[6] *Ibid.*
[7] Corey, Stephen M. "The Importance of People—Teachers ARE People," *Educational Leadership* 1:491-93; May 1944.

sum total of the ideas of all of the teachers as they think about education is a more impressive and fruitful aggregate than the sum total of the ideas of a few administrators.

Such a leader's chief concern is in improving the schools. He cares very little for a reputation as the fellow who has all of the inspiration and is aggressive in putting them into practice. Because this latter role, however, is the one most people think a successful school administrator or supervisor must play, the leader will find the going rough. He will be tempted again and again to *tell* people what to do because the alternative takes time and requires patience.

Altogether apart from any sentimental notions about democracy, the chief difficulty when teachers are told what to do is that the directions cannot ever be sufficiently explicit because teaching by its very nature requires much individual initiative and resourcefulness. A second difficulty is that the followers of directions are chronically unable to accept personal responsibility for the success of the activity. A third difficulty is that people who are constantly following administrative directives lose something as persons. They tend like cogs in a machine or automatons on an assembly line—to become things rather than people.

How Are States Weighing the Values of Present Programs?

Today many states are engaged in evaluating education programs from kindergarten thru the senior high school or in studying critically educational provisions at specific levels. Institutions of higher learning are evaluating the provision they are making for preservice and in-service training of supervisors and teachers. The trend toward more carefully planned cooperation between the latter institutions and public-school systems is a significant one. *Long-term planning* is an important feature of many state programs. Their accounts show that in a number of instances efforts toward improvement of instruction affect supervision directly.

A Findings Committee Goes to Work in North Carolina

Supervisors in North Carolina, thru the state meeting of the Department of Supervision and Curriculum Development, expressed a desire to know what kind of instructional leadership city and county administrators preferred. They selected a findings committee to confer with the administrators in this matter for two reasons: [8]

> That members of the Department of Supervisors and Curriculum might have additional bases for evaluating their present procedures.
> A selected list of types of service that superintendents would desire could be valuable information for future supervisory groups.

---

[8] North Carolina Education Association. *Report of Findings Committee of the N.C.E.A., Supervisors' Department, Raleigh:* State Department of Public Instruction, April 1944. (Mimeo.)

A LOOK AT OUR BEST 91

One hundred and twenty-four administrators representing seventy-four counties and fifty cities replied to the questionnaire. It is with the findings on the first question that the yearbook committee has particular concern. Administrators were asked, "Will you list the types of service that you would want in your administrative unit from an instructional leader, provided you had that service?" The twelve items most frequently listed are reported by the findings committee without interpretation.

1. Supervision or improvement of instruction: 18
   a. Constructive professional and ethical supervision of classroom activities   7
   b. Cooperative supervision   40
2. Aid in selection and use of materials of:
   Instruction   2
   Library   1
   Textbooks   28
3. To foster in-service growth of teachers   13
   Visiting   1
   Conferences   7
   Selecting materials   1
   Finding strengths and developing them   2
   Forming classes   3
   Giving advice   2
   Giving encouragement   2
   Planning meetings   3
4. Selection and building of effective curriculum   19
5. Coordinating the work of the system   15
6. Special help with beginning teachers   12
7. Improved use of tests and testing follow-up   10
8. Pupil progress
   a. Proper gradation and promotion system thru tests and otherwise
      (1) Special attention to accelerated pupil   4
      (2) special attention to borderline cases   3
      (3) slow mentality   3
9. Evaluation in order to improve weak spots   9
10. Improvement of county teachers' meetings   7
11. Someone who can go to the aid of teachers when they feel they need help   6
12. Assist in the best selection and placement of teachers   5
    (discharging)   2

Thirty-three other types of services were listed by from one to five respondents. "Cooperative supervision" which was listed by forty of the administrative units implies some of the same characteristics as "democratic leadership in supervision" which was listed first by secondary and elementary principals and supervisors who replied to the yearbook questionnaire. The area that this questionnaire covers included 33 counties and 15 city administrative units containing 7 one-teacher schools, 49 two- and three-teacher schools, 64 four- to six-teacher schools making a total of 327 schools and 2862 teachers.

With a view of indicating possible approaches to state departments, other questions asked of these administrative units in North Carolina follow:[9]

> Titles of helper
> 1. Do you object to the name "supervisor"?
> 2. Would you like one of the following names better?
>   a. Director of instruction   d. Helping teacher
>   b. Director of curriculum   e. ―――――――
>   c. Supervising teacher   f. ―――――――
>
> Do you think that you have a person in your administrative unit who is now prepared or with some additional training could be well qualified for the type of work you desire in your unit or another unit in the state desiring this service?

It is obvious that this step taken in North Carolina is a positive approach to establishing mutual understandings concerning desirable supervision services. It indicates a realistic facing of the problem and a high professional attitude on the part of the supervisors seeking to improve their work. It should result in giving new vitality to supervision.

California Sees a Need for Better Supervision

Less attention seems to be given in literature to the evaluation of supervision purposes and procedures on the kindergarten-primary level than on any other level of the public-school program. A survey conducted in 1943 concerning the California situation contributes some items of importance to this level of supervision.

This study designed to ascertain trends in kindergarten-primary supervision was based upon reports from cities or counties with a population of five thousand or more and covered the period of time 1930-1943. The questionnaire which was used as a basis for the study was sent to 108 county school superintendents and sixty-two city superintendents. Both traditional and modern practices of supervision were included in the checklist. The large percentage of responses to questionnaires indicated that administrators were keenly interested in the problem of kindergarten-primary supervision. In order to secure more detailed information on some situations, conferences were held with supervisors and superintendents. Curriculum materials were also reviewed. The findings which are particularly significant for this report are quoted as follows:[10]

―――――――

[9] *Ibid.*
[10] Wood, El Doris. A Summary of a Study Made of Kindergarten-Primary Supervision in California Public School Systems Covering the Period of 1930-1943. California: (Mimeo.)

There appeared to be a trend toward increase in the time definitely apportioned by supervisors for classroom visitation in both city and county systems. These visits seemed to be more often planned with the teacher in recent years.

According to the data, the use of rating scales for evaluation of teachers' work seemed to be discouraged when used by the supervisor. When used by the teacher as a self-checking aid, the rating scales were more acceptable.

Trends seemed to be toward more democratic methods of curriculum development with emphasis placed upon democratic attitudes, beliefs, and procedures in supervisory services. The tendency appeared to be toward more teacher-participation in the development of the curriculum.

In the judgments of all the superintendents and supervisors reporting, the following five activities ranked highest in importance as services rendered by the supervisor:

1. Holding individual conferences with the teacher
2. Visiting classrooms for observation and evaluation
3. Taking leadership in curriculum development
4. Demonstrating technics and methods
5a. Conducting workshops for in-service growth of teachers
5b. Providing specialized resources upon which teachers may draw for meeting their classroom needs.

The number of teachers' requests for guidance were found to have increased over former years.

A high percent of all the superintendents and supervisors reporting indicated that the following activities are now engaged in by supervisors:

1. Attending professional meetings for their own growth
2. Holding individual conferences with teachers
3. Visiting classroom for observation and evaluation
4. Working with teachers in the classrooms
5. Demonstrating technics and methods
6. Taking leadership in curriculum development
7. Encouraging teacher participation in educational organization
8. Helping in the organization of groups and committees
9. Preparing bulletins for teachers' use
10. Providing specialized resources upon which teachers may draw to meet the needs of their classroom work.

The following supervisory activities were given high ranking by supervisors, but were not so ranked by superintendents:

1. Observing how plans carry over
2. Conducting workshops for in-service growth of teachers
3. Comparing results of the work of the system in order to aid individual schools and thereby benefiting the system as a whole.

SOME RECOMMENDATIONS GROWING OUT OF THE STUDY:

1. There is need for better understanding of the meaning and function of supervision as a coordinating service consisting of the combined and related efforts and abilities of all persons engaged in the education of children.
2. The personnel in the supervision of the kindergarten-primary grades need to be completely certificated in the work of this level in addition to

any general elementary or secondary certification which they hold. This would help to insure practical training and experience in the field of early childhood development, and help to lay a basis for better understanding of the needs of the child in his later school years.

3. A suggestion is offered for more coordination of the creative efforts of teachers, which might well be used for a stimulating program for the benefit of the entire school system.

4. Just as faith in human nature and regard for the worth of human intelligence and power in cooperative effort is basic to democracy, so is it recommended for the foundation for educational organization and supervision.

An important field for further study in California was opened by these findings. What would account for the different evaluation given by superintendents and supervisors as to the three most promising ways of working? While cities reported a slight increase in the number of kindergarten-primary supervisors employed, counties reported a slight decrease altho their total supervisory staffs had been increased. It would seem that not all superintendents have been convinced of the value of supervision services on the kindergarten-primary level. That may be due in part to the fact that only 10 percent of the supervisors reported that they hold kindergarten-primary teaching credentials and are supervising those grades under a general elementary credential. Since recent legislative action has made kindergartens a part of the public-school system in California, it is to be expected that more thoughtful attention will be given to the selection of leadership for this educational level.

Georgia Takes the Lead in Education for Supervisors

In Georgia, the state department of education, the university, and the state teachers colleges are cooperating in sponsoring a program of supervisory education. It is the belief of the leaders in this state that teachers who wish to become supervisors need a particular kind of training. Thru the program in Georgia, there is a close correlation of the preparatory period and the first actual supervisory experience. During this time they work closely with an experienced supervisor; the period of observation and participation varying with individual growth needs. Arrangements are made for these new supervisors to have contact with the functioning of social institutions which gives them an understanding of broader human values and far-reaching social situations.

The director of the education of supervisors at the University of Georgia reports that these student-supervisors agree that the following competencies are especially important for success in supervision:[11]

---

[11] Franseth, Jane. "Educating Supervisors," *School Executive* 64:50-51; February 1945.

(1) Personal qualities must be attractive. The supervisor must be kind, understanding, tactful, pleasant, and socially intelligent. (2) Superior skill is important in such areas as: teaching, helping teachers to understand child growth and development, helping teachers to understand good principles in teaching, working with children and adults cooperatively toward important ends, and in the use of such tools as written and oral English. (3) Superior knowledge in the fields as the following is important: Curriculum and methods, sociology as it is related to rural communities, human behavior especially as it is related to child growth and development, elementary science, arts and crafts, social science with special emphasis on present world affairs, and philosophy as it is related to democracy and education.

A Supervisory Program Is Enlarged in Kentucky

Leaders on both the elementary- and secondary-school levels in Kentucky are giving direct attention to the improvement of supervision. The increased number of emergency teachers being employed in the elementary schools in Kentucky led the state department of education to set up a workshop for the specific purpose of training helping teachers who were chosen from among the best teachers in the system. As a result of this intensive work, the number of supervisors employed increased in 1945-46 from 20 in the entire state to 78 helping teachers and supervisors in 44 counties and 12 in 9 large cities. The cooperation of all of the educational groups in the state in establishing this well-coordinated plan for in-service education offers convincing evidence to other states confronted with this same problem. Some of the yearbook questionnaires indicated that supervisors found that they could not work effectively with the numbers of teachers to which they had been accustomed because teachers with emergency credentials composed more than 50 percent of the group and required much more of the supervisor's time. This was particularly evident in county systems. Detailed plans and procedures developed in Kentucky should comprise a valuable contribution to the literature.

Curriculum Study in Washington Deals with Supervision

The statewide program of curriculum study and in-service training in Washington has many implications for supervision. Progress reports produced by this system should prove of interest to those who have the responsibility of employing supervisors as well as to supervisors themselves. The following excerpts are quoted from an article by the Curriculum Director in the State Office of Public Instruction.[12]

The records of American education show that ever since the improvement of instruction became one of the foremost concerns of the schools

---

[12] Anderson. Vernon E. "In-Service Education for an Entire State," *California Journal of Secondary Education* 19:219-23; May 1944.

outstanding school systems have provided some organized form of in-service training for teachers. These schools have added supervisors and directors of instruction and curriculum to their staffs, have conducted planned supervisory and curriculum improvement programs with teacher participation in planning and execution, have sponsored professional reading clubs, extension classes, and conferences, have participated in special studies and used the service of consultants. Generally, however, the schools which have provided special services have been limited in number.

Among the conclusions the following is particularly pertinent to this report.[13]

> Schools in which some organized type of supervisory or curriculum program is being conducted receive more benefit from the program than where there is no continuous study of local professional problems.

Since findings of this type have already been reached, it is significant for supervisors elsewhere to know what procedures and technics have been employed and which of these have proved most fruitful. Anderson states that since the program is entirely experimental in nature, the plan of operation must be kept flexible. He reports, however, that "most popular with teachers and administrators have been the individual school conference and visitation plan, whereby the instructors are scheduled to work in a school system for a period of from one to several days."[14]

In these state programs, as well as in twenty others that the yearbook committee had an opportunity to review, there seems to be an emphasis on helping teachers help themselves. There was evidence of opportunity for teachers, supervisors, and administrators to plan together. In the majority of programs studied consultants from universities or teacher-training institutions were members of these groups. Democratic ways of working were respected. When leadership of the type indicated in this section of the yearbook is assumed by state departments of education, county and city school systems within those states are motivated to evaluate and reorient supervision purposes and procedures in the interest of improving the instructional program.

WHAT WAYS OF WORKING ARE TAKING HOLD IN COUNTY PROGRAMS?

It is obvious that in instances in which state leaders are alert, the ideas conceived by them permeate counties and cities. Educational experimentation in local areas in its turn contributes to state programs. Otherwise there could be no state program, since the real leadership emanates from the local school system. A study of supervisory activities in counties reveals

---

[13] *Ibid.*
[14] *Ibid.*

many similarities with those considered desirable on a statewide basis. The chief difference lies in the initiatory source of the program. A glance at areas of emphases in various counties indicates the part supervision plays in preservice and in-service education programs.

County	Program Emphasis
Montgomery County, Maryland	Reorganization of program—in-service training [15]
	Child growth [16]
Sandoval County, New Mexico	Rural-school supervision—maintenance program [17]
Warren County, New Jersey	Workshops—good fellowship among teachers, supervisors, and parents [18]
Cherokee County, Alabama	Cooperation of school people with all county agencies [19]
	What union between school and community involves [20]
Chesterfield County, Virginia	The supervisory visit [21]
Carroll County, Georgia	Community planning [22]
Van Buren County, Michigan	Cooperative community enterprise [23]
Colquitt County, Georgia	Evaluation [24]
	Workshops and supervision [25]
Fayette County, Alabama	Supervisory program [26]
Vigo County, Indiana	Conference program [27]
Los Angeles County, California	Cooperation among schools in county [28]
Norfolk County, Virginia	Utilizing community resources [29]

---

[15] Montgomery County, Maryland, Public Schools. "The Present Crisis—The Technique of Planning," *Professional Yearbook*. September 1944. (Mimeo.)

[16] Broome, Edwin W. "Planning for Growth," *Childhood Education* 21:64-73; October 1944.

[17] Logan, Ruth P. "The Continuance and Maintenance of a Rural School Program for Supervision," *American School Board Journal* 110:29-30, 76; April 1945.

[18] Weber, Julia. "How Workshops Grow," *Educational Leadership* 3:10-12; October 1945.

[19] Smith, Estelle S. "The Rural Routes," *Educational Leadership* 2:149-51; January 1945.

[20] National Education Association, Department of Supervisors and Directors of Instruction. "The Cherokee County Cooperative Program," *Leadership at Work*. Washington, D. C.: the Department, 1943. p. 169-76.

[21] Coleman, Elsie. "The Supervisory Visit," *Educational Leadership* 2:164-67; January 1945.

[22] West Georgia College. *A College and a County*. Genola: University System of Georgia, August 1942. Vol. IX, No. 4.

[23] Van Buren County Schools. *Schools Awake*. Paw Paw: the Commissioner, February 1942.

[24] Troyer, Maurice E., and Pace, C. Robert. "Evaluation in an Ongoing Program," *Evaluation in Teacher Education*. Washington, D. C.: American Council on Education, 1944. p. 283-305.

[25] Prall, Charles E., and Cushman, Leslie C. "A Countywide Study of Community Problems," *Teacher Education in Service*. Washington, D. C.: American Council on Education, 1944. p. 387-435.

[26] National Education Association, Department of Supervisors and Directors of Instruction. "Fayette County Supervisory Program," *Leadership at Work*. Washington, D. C.: the Department, 1943. p. 176-83.

[27] National Education Association, Department of Supervisors and Directors of Instruction. "Vigo County Conference Program," *Leadership at Work*. Washington, D. C.: the Department, 1943. p. 184-86.

[28] Prall, Charles E., and Cushman, Leslie C. "An Articulation Study in Los Angeles County," *Teacher Education in Service*. Washington, D. C.: American Council on Education, 1944. p. 365-86.

[29] Carper, M. L. "Out of School Teachers," *Educational Leadership*. 1:350-53; March 1944.

Among statements submitted, a promising trend was indicated in terms of careful planning to coordinate the services of supervisors within a county system. In some programs counties and cities are cooperating in an examination of their educational plans and in defining the major purposes of supervision. Geographically close school systems are jointly planning curriculum development work. By pooling their finances for this purpose, they are able to bring a greater number of resource persons from universities and colleges to work with the local educational personnel. The majority of county programs studied revealed that ways of working were being determined only after values or purposes were established. It seems appropriate to close this section with the challenge by Aubrey Williams, "What is right for rural schools must wait upon an educational leadership which places the welfare of the people above organizational and jurisdictional prerogative."[30]

How Do Cities Supervise?

A great deal of specific information concerning the work of the supervisor-leader in city school systems is available in recent literature. Only one of the programs will be cited, while reference to the literature will be made in a limited number of instances.

New York Teachers Appraise Supervision

The research on supervision which was done by Henry Antell has already been referred to in this yearbook. It is significant to supervisors for two major reasons. In the first place it represents a type of investigation that could be employed to advantage in other city school systems; in the second place it reveals how teachers regard the supervision practices used in a particular city. Relative to the latter point certain trends are noted.[31]

> In analyzing the teacher appraisal of these practices it is well to list in order of preference, those which at least 50 percent of the teachers find very helpful. They follow:
> 1. Availability of professional library in school—86%
> 2. The supervisor acts as a consultant or technical adviser—81%
> 3. Demonstration lessons—74%
> 4. Grade conferences to discuss common problems—73%
> 5. Visiting an outstanding school—73%
> 6. Participation in the formulation of school policies—70%
> 7. Individual conference with supervisor—67%
> 8. Intervisitation—67%
> 9. An after-school conference at which there is open discussion of a topic of vital interest to the group—65%

---

[30] Williams, Aubrey. "Rural Education, Does it Adequately Meet the Needs of Rural Youth and Rural Communities," *Progressive Education* 22:30-33; January 1945.

[31] Antell, Henry. "Teachers Appraise Supervision," *Journal of Educational Research* 38:606-11; April 1945.

10. In-service courses or workshops—63%
11. Participation in course-of-study making—56%
12. Teachers' interest committee in the school—51%

It is noteworthy that in all the first ten items except number six, the teachers are chiefly interested in having made available to them resources materials for their own improvement. Thus they find very helpful a professional library, a supervisor who thinks of his job as one of advice and consultation, other teachers who may demonstrate some commendable teacher abilities, a conference of their colleagues where they may discuss their probems, visiting a school at which they may observe some outstanding technics, an opportunity to confer with the supervisor, intervisitation, a general afternoon discussion session, and courses or workshops. In all of these practices the teacher is intent upon discussing her problems and in finding possible solutions to them. They are resources she would like to use to improve her competence. Apparently, a supervisory practice which is of this nature, is very apt to be welcomed by teachers as very helpful.

Other Cities Make Contributions

Some of the ways of working which were considered most promising by questionnaire respondents are evidenced in the supervision practices discussed in each of the city educational programs listed here. The yearbook committee regrets that a comprehensive list could not have been given rather than such a highly selective one.

City	Program Emphasis
Long Beach, California	Supervision—secondary [32]
Newton, Massachusetts	Planning committee [33]
Denver, Colorado	Policies council [34]
Parker District, South Carolina	Comprehensive program of child study [35]
Des Moines, Iowa	Planning body in a complex situation [36]
Hyde Park, New York	Supervising principal [37]
Portland, Oregon	Workshops [38]
New York, New York	Educational program [39]

[32] Klopp, W. J. "Supervision Under War Conditions," *California Journal of Secondary Education.* 20:67-68; February 1945.

[33] Prall, Charles E., and Cushman, Leslie C. "A Planning Committee That Educated Itself," *Teacher Education in Service.* Washington, D. C.: American Council on Education, 1944. p. 34-57.

[34] Prall, Charles E., and Cushman, Leslie C. "A Policies Council of Varied Undertakings," *Teacher Education in Service.* Washington, D. C.: American Council on Education, 1944. p. 106-24.

[35] Prall, Charles E., and Cushman, Leslie C. "The Parker District Prior to 1940," *Teacher Education in Service.* Washington, D. C.: American Council on Education, 1944. p. 151-61.

[36] Prall, Charles E., and Cushman, Leslie C. "The Planning Body in a More Complex Situation," *Teacher Education in Service.* Washington, D. C.: American Council on Education, 1944. p. 72-91.

[37] Juckett, Edwin A. "Workshop Adventure in Democratic Administration," *American School Board Journal.* 109:35-37; October 1944.

[38] Anderson, Vernon E., and Long, Walt A. "A School System Builds Its Own Workshop," *Educational Leadership* 2:209-11; February 1945.

[39] New York Public Schools. *All the Children.* New York: the Board, 1943.

In many instances these programs seem to be an outgrowth of broader studies stimulated by county, state, and national enterprises. Teachers, supervisors, principals, and superintendents have been fired with a zeal to promote democratic living in the classrooms of America. Teacher leadership is being encouraged by supervisors who recognize that teachers are people. Altho there is some variation in the thinking expressed by educators as to what might be considered the *five* most promising ways of working if supervisors are going to meet their responsibility in public education, all of the ways suggested are diametrically opposed to practices handed from the top down. As groups work together, a common philosophy destined to realize the American Dream may emerge from the individual studies now going forward thruout the nation.

How Has Professional Literature Enriched the Concept?

Since questionnaire responses from supervisors indicated careful study of a wide range of professional literature, it seemed significant to canvass that source for national trends. Consequently, an extensive survey of recent educational literature was made to determine the promising ways of working described with greatest frequency.[40] Writings by university and college presidents and instructors, deans of schools of education, consultants to outstanding school systems and administrators of city and rural schools were included in the material studied.

In rating practices of promise these educators emphasized the classroom observation; next in order were teacher conferences and teacher excursions. This judgment may appear to be in opposition to the number one questionnaire response of supervisors and principals who considered democratic leadership the most promising way of working. The apparent discrepancy, however, raises a question as to whether or not there may be confusion as to what constitutes democratic procedure in supervision. Might it not be that the classroom observation is a process thru which the supervisor-leader has the responsibility to function democratically?

Observation Is Essential to Democratic Procedure

To some students in the field, there is certainly no conflict between the demands of supervisors and principals for democratic procedures and the opinions found in a study of the literature concerning the value of classroom observations.[41]

Observation, in order to be of value, must be carefully planned. The purposes for observation should be set up jointly by the teacher and the

---

[40] Taken from a study made and reported for this yearbook by Esther Cahill, Cincinnati Public Schools, Cincinnati, Ohio, August 1945.

[41] The sections on observation and conferences are taken from beliefs expressed by Florence Stratemeyer, Teachers College, Columbia University.

supervisor. This joint planning may be done either on a person-to-person basis or thru written communications. The supervisor needs to have a memorandum of the ways in which the teacher feels that he can be of most help. If the purpose of the observation is agreed upon, and the date of the visit is announced, a wholesome learning situation of mutual benefit should result. Unless the supervisor is informed of the problems with which he is to be confronted in advance of his visit, it cannot be assumed that he will be in a position to render the most effective service. It is his responsibility to know a wide variety of materials, but he cannot have these materials at hand unless he has had opportunity to prepare for a specific request. When the supervisor knows of the definite problems faced by the individual teacher and principal he is enabled to bring to these people a variety of means of attacking the problems. Consecutive visitation must be provided for, when needed.

The thesis of this position is that the supervisor exercises democratic leadership in the manner in which he conducts the classroom observation. The two cannot be separated. The supervisor cannot exert democratic leadership except in attacking a problem with which a teacher has concern. It is recognized that the problems of teachers vary according to the areas in which they work and the individuals with whom they are concerned. It is essential for supervisors to know something of the individual child in the classroom and of the environment in which he lives and works. The principal and the teacher know these problems because their lives are centered in the community with the children. Teachers will be helped more effectively if they provide the supervisor with a basic understanding of their local problems in order that he may plan specifically for a definite situation.

Conferences Center in the Individual or the Group

As a promising way of working, conferences have been given a ranking of significance by each of the groups consulted. In the questionnaire responses, principals and supervisors rated group conferences second in importance. Individual conferences were given third place by the principals and fifth place by the supervisors. In a survey made in New York, three-fourths of the teachers questioned rated group conferences as being very helpful.[42] In the study of professional literature, individual and group conferences were not separated. Conferencing as a way of working received second highest rating in this study. In this connection, it is pertinent to inquire whether there is any significant difference in the technic utilized in conducting a group or an individual conference? Since conferencing is

---

[42] Antell, Henry. "Teachers Appraise Supervision," *Journal of Educational Research* 38:606-11; April 1945.

a way of working popularly employed by educators, it is important to consider ways of ensuring its effectiveness.

There are numerous types of conferences necessary for a variety of purposes. All of them, however, have certain basic characteristics in common. A conference may be of two people, of three people, or of a small group of people having a common interest. Good conferencing implies that each person is thinking for himself. A conference that is one-sided is no more satisfying than a teacher-pupil situation that is one-sided. Discussions should be directed toward the matter at hand and the leader should not permit the time to be monopolized by one or two vocal individuals. Interaction is essential, and general issues should be embodied in concrete cases. As the conference proceeds the supervisor should know at what intervals to summarize the thinking. As a result of discussion, generalizations should be formulated and basic understandings should emerge. The conclusions reached at the end of the period should be clear cut and the proposals for next steps should be reviewed.

Individual conferences for the purpose of evaluating teaching are a must, since an observation is of no value unless its conclusions are shared with the people who are vitally concerned. With conferences as with observations, common purposes should be understood by all persons. The person who asks for the conference, whether he is a teacher, a principal, or a supervisor is the one who should make the purpose known. If it is to be a teaching-learning situation, careful preparation is essential. Each person involved must prepare for a teaching-learning situation; likewise all persons concerned must prepare for a conference. On the whole spontaneous combustion conferences are of doubtful value.

A carefully-planned, well-thought-thru, fifteen-minute conference permits supervisors to plan time for each teacher observed. This time factor is particularly significant in rural areas where distances between schools are great. Whenever possible, conferences should be held in the classrooms where the records of the children are kept or in the library or laboratory where materials are readily available for reference by the supervisor. Supervisors should help teachers evaluate experiences in terms of principles. A teacher should not go away with a pattern but with some basic principle that will help her to meet not only the immediate problem but also others with which she may be confronted. The basic technics in conducting a good conference are the same whether it is a conference involving just the teacher and the supervisor or several people working on a common problem.

The following statement summarizes thinking expressed concerning group conferences in a preponderance of the professional literature studied.[43]

---

[43] Davis, Robert A. "The Learning Conference: The Blending of Research with Teaching Experience." *Journal of Educational Research* 37:146-49; October 1943.

The conference is not a substitute for classroom visitation and individual conferences. Nor is it a substitute for systematic training in teacher-training institutions. Neither can the consultants, regardless of the breadth of their training and interest, advise with respect to all problems suggested by teachers. Then, too, to make provision for the varied needs and interests of all groups would require more consultants than are generally available. . . .

Systematic criteria have not as yet been formulated for evaluating the results of the conference as judged by modification in teaching practice. The conference, at its best, may assist in bringing the teacher's professional knowledge up to date and affecting some change in his attitude. Its real contribution must be judged by the extent to which it has the effect of improving the quality of his teaching. The use of question forms devised to elicit voluntary expressions of opinion indicate that teachers welcome the opportunity to discuss with their colleagues and consultants their teaching and learning problems; they seem to be stimulated to advance professional study, and in some instances they try out improved technics in their own classrooms.

Teachers Go On Excursions

Teacher excursions were cited as a third promising way of working in the study of educational literature. Questionnaire respondents included this item in their listing but did not give it as high a ranking as was revealed in the literature. In the New York study 63 percent of the teachers stated that in-service training was valuable.[44] It is deduced that teacher excursions were considered as one means of providing such training.

In the following quotation, an elementary-school principal points up the significance of knowing the community.[45]

> A study of the community has educative possibilities, because *it concerns all age levels;* it concerns all groups; it offers a challenge to unsolved civic, economic, social, and political problems; it provides leadership development; it makes school-community relationships more effective; it enables teachers to select experiences which will interpret life to the students and lead to richer and more significant future experiences; it utilizes nonhuman resources which are at hand—topography, soil, climate; it provides opportunities for first-hand experiences with human resources.

In educational planning, it is imperative that the teacher be concerned with the interaction between the whole child and his total environment. Since we "learn what we live," no short cut can be offered the teacher which will ensure her an understanding of the community in which she works. Just as teachers have found that the excursion is one of the most

---

[44] Antell, Henry. "Teachers Appraise Supervision," *Journal of Educational Research* 38:606-11; April 1945.
[45] Poulsen, Esther R. *A Guide for Utilizing Community Resources in Santa Barbara County Schools.* Stanford University, California: Leland Stanford Junior University, 1940. 139p. (Master's thesis.)

dynamic means of presenting concepts to children, educators reporting in the literature feel that the teacher excursion is a vital factor in providing in-service training for teachers.

An excursion should be carefully planned and its purposes should be such that the teachers are eager for the experience. It should be planned as an enriching experience for the participants and should emphasize the possibilities for educative experiences to be had in a particular community as well as in adjoining communities. A committee composed of teachers, principals, and supervisors may select the types of excursions that will be most meaningful for them. The delegated member of such a committee will need to plan the details involved in taking a given excursion, contact the industrial or other leaders affected and make final arrangements.

Some school systems have provided means thru which each teacher plans to participate in an excursion. A bulletin explains the educational purposes and affords information concerning the industry or institution to be visited. Teachers have reported that they had been helped in developing their own understandings by having such material for ready reference while taking the excursion. The inclusion of diagrams or charts was highly commended. A carefully planned but informal discussion following the excursion promotes an exchange of experiences and impressions and serves to clarify concepts. Rural supervisors reporting on the questionnaire stated that they have sometimes followed the excursion with another bulletin highlighting the observations or findings. This practice provides teachers with a valid source of material about the area in which they work.

Rural supervisors in a county in Maryland have developed an excellent bulletin for teacher use on the technics for planning, conducting, and evaluating an excursion.[46] They have also included specific suggestions for follow-up teaching in relation to pupil excursions.

Workshop Technics Need Examination

Present professional literature is replete with accounts of workshops carried on in local and state situations, on college campuses or within the confines of an individual community. It is appropriate in this respect to direct attention to recent and objective evaluation of the present trends apparent in the use of workshops.[47]

> The *real promise of school system workshops* is in the field of group thinking and joint planning . . . these programs promote looking at the situation as a whole, seeing the implications and ramifications of individual

---

[46] Cheezum, Mary L. *Handbook for Audio-Visual Aids.* 1945. (Unpublished.)
[47] Prall, Charles E., and Cushman, Leslie C. *Teacher Education in Service.* Washington, D. C.: American Council on Education, 1944. p. 238-40.

efforts; they foster the exchange of ideas unhampered by considerations of rank and position; they cultivate thinking on such topics as understanding children in their complex growth, using the resources of the community, discovering the importance of creative self-expression, and seeing human nature in larger perspective; and they bring numbers of people together to work on different aspects of what comes increasingly to be seen as one shared task. It is because workshops have served so effectively in this way hitherto that we are alarmed about the tendencies revealed in the attendance records. A further development that gives us pause is the reduction that appears to be taking place all the time in the number of people who share in making the preliminary plans. The amount of time spent in orienting the workshop staff has also been greatly shortened from summer to summer, in certain cities. Various shortcomings are appearing in organizational matters such as methods of recruiting persons to attend and cultivating the interest of potential leaders. Progress has been made, on the other hand, in finding ways of improving the reports and diversifying the program. But materials that have been prepared by workshop sections have not always been used to advantage afterwards, and time pressures have been allowed to take their toll of follow-up procedures.

. . . joint thinking cannot come into full flower at a workshop and then be ignored in the daily life of the school system. This despite the undisputed fact that a higher standard of performance can be, and often is, attained at a workshop than the regular routine of the school year allows. But unless the creative planning that lies at the heart of workshop activity has its counterpart in the association of principals and classroom teachers in individual schools, in the deliberations of committees and working groups, in the administrative councils, in classrooms, between teachers and pupils, and ultimately in the joint enterprise of educators and citizens, there is scant hope that the program will survive. The alternatives seem to us to be as follows: either group thinking on a creative level will become increasingly characteristic of our school systems in all their functioning, or the summer workshop will pass from the scene and be remembered simply as another of those promising developments that went awry because of the tendency to preserve the shell and ignore the essence of the movement.

. . . the public schools of America must face the problem of how they are to inaugurate changes in their procedures and curricular practice. No informed person will claim that our schools can remain static. Much of the impending change will be socially induced and classroom teachers, principals, supervisors are likely to be vitally affected—for that matter, so are superintendents and officers of the general staff. School systems have it within their power to plan for what is ahead in considerable measure, and may both guide some of its direction and help individuals to work much of it in their stride. The value of summer *workshops* in a continuous program with such ends in mind should be clear from what we have been saying; they *are instruments to be used for two closely related purposes—preparation for change and security while breaking with tradition.* If they are not used properly for such purposes, the time will soon come when they *may not* be used at all.

Workshop activities in local school systems might well be evaluated by the criteria in this quotation. Is there widespread evidence of too many short cuts being taken in organizational matters? As has been said earlier in this chapter, *purposes* must determine effective ways of working. If the workshop has become a shell, may it not be because the way of working has been determined before the purposes were clear? When the process becomes the item of first consideration any practice which seemed to have promise will lose its dynamics.

Literature Points to New Kinds of Leadership

Professional literature deals not only in present practices but also indicates the leadership role ahead for supervisors. The premise on which one recent article stands is that a major public-school responsibility lies in the field of adult education. That this level of education should be a part of the total educational program is the argument advanced.[48] Selection and training of supervisory personnel for this work is certainly an area of important consideration for all school systems.

Another individual asks that leadership be developed in actual curriculum planning. She states that teachers should be helped to analyze and interpret the behavior of youngsters, and that methods cannot be treated apart from what they are supposed to accomplish. Supervisors already employed have had too little training in curriculum construction and in studying children. They need to learn how to think thru and plan around curriculum problems in order to avoid promoting a specific curriculum organization for any and all problems and with any and all groups. They also need to develop insight into the curriculum as a whole because their training as supervisors in given fields often make them uncongenial to seeing values in other areas and they promote their own fields to the detriment of the whole program. This is particularly apt to happen in the secondary school.

One state department of education reports that for a period of years they have held an annual summer conference for the training of supervisors in service. In this particular instance the state department cooperates with one of the state universities in providing this specific training. The state elementary supervisor assumes leadership responsibility for the organizational planning, and during the work sessions she evaluates the supervisor-teacher conference for the benefit of the entire group. Many of the needs referred to in the preceding paragraph are considered in these conferences on elementary-school supervision.

---

[48] Kendall, Glenn. "Adult Education and the Total Educational Program," *School Executive* 64:59-60; January 1945.

The leadership role ahead for secondary schools is well expressed by the following from a recent article: [49]

> The type of high school pictured in *Education for all American Youth* and in a parallel publication, *Planning for American Youth*, raises a question regarding the conventional basis of high school organization in which subject-teaching departments are the chief elements. If the school, to be effective, must subordinate departmental teaching to the purposes of secondary education to the extent implied in these publications, justification for the prominence given to departmentalization in the school's organization in the future is required. A close study of the effects of these publications on school organization suggests that a more forthright acceptance of basic purposes as determinants of high school organization is demanded. Accordingly, it is here proposed that postwar high schools should be purpose organized. . . .
>
> *How Purpose Organization Would Change High Schools*
>
> If our high schools in general were to begin to unify their organization around the major purposes for youth education, we might expect to find more schools in which some of the following changes were being made. This is not meant to be an inclusive list, but will suggest the kind of institutional structure that might develop.
>
> 1. Under the immediate supervision of the principal would be four or five "coordinators," each representing a major purpose of secondary education which the school intended to stress. Three among the four or five who would be commonly used would doubtless be coordinators of citizenship, health and physical fitness, and life work.
>
> Others, such as use of leisure and homemaking would be added as the emphasis to be given merited it or, if not, they could be assigned to one of these three.
>
> Most schools would have four or five such coordinators to coordinate the work of the present departments around the achievements of the school's major purposes. Where schools now have from eight to sixteen department heads these would be retained as needed, but under the general direction of coordinators. In time it might be found unnecessary to retain all department heads. One in the field of communication, for example, might replace two or three of the present type of department head. Schools which have no department heads would operate directly under the coordinators.
>
> . . . These suggestions with reference to the coordinators are not intended to imply that there would be no assistant principal or special workers in guidance, for example.
>
> 2. The coordinator and/or coordinating committee would each study the school's work to see that everything possible was being done to achieve the major purposes of the school. . . .
>
> 5. The registration of students for a new year would be under the supervision of the coordinators. . . .

---

[49] French, Will. "The Postwar High School Should be Purpose-Organized," *Teachers College Record* 46:403-12; April 1945.

7. When the school's educational program is in the direct charge of coordinators who are responsible for their achievement of major purposes through that program, we may expect each of them to be concerned about evaluating pupil growth in terms of the purpose for which he as coordinator is responsible.

8. A trend toward purpose-organization of secondary schools will modify programs for the education of teachers. The current emphasis upon purposes in education is already beginning to modify these programs in some of the teacher-education centers. As schools become purpose-organized, this trend will be accentuated. However, with new teacher intake slowing down as it has recently and as it will again in the postwar period, the chief high-pressure area in teacher education shifts to in-service education. When a school moves toward purpose-organization, it automatically creates a different teacher-education situation for its faculty. The chief centers of group work by teachers become those created by the presence of coordinators in the school. Their leadership in terms of purpose poses different problems for study by differently organized groups. The main group meetings of teachers would be of those working under the general direction of each of the coordinators. The present type of departmental meeting would play a more minor role. Interdepartmental committees for study of problems concerned with purpose-achievement, for revision of courses of study and for other types of professional activity and study called for by the purpose-organization of the school would create a different setting for in-service education as well as a different content for it. It therefore seems certain that one of the most valuable by-products of a shift from process to purpose would be a stimulated and modified program of in-service education for teachers. . . .

If the school's real job is to do all it can through education to make youth healthy and physically fit; to make them good young citizens in every sense of the word; to make them self-supporting and efficient producers and consumers in the home, shop, factory, office, classroom, mind, and on the farm; to help them develop special interest and abilities; and to enable them to participate in and enjoy wholesome forms of leisure activities, then the school had better organize itself with an eye to the accomplishment of these very things. The complete achievement of these purposes requires many modifications in our nineteenth century high school, but none of these changes will be as quickly effected as is possible unless the school administrators redesign the school into a purpose-organized institution. Function should determine design.

Another recent study states the belief that "administration and supervision are coordinate, correlative, complementary functions having their common purpose the provision of means and conditions favorable to teaching and learning."[50] .... Supervision has many of the characteristics of creative teaching. It is a practical art based upon a philosophy of

---

[50] Brunstetter, Max R. "Principles of Democratic Supervision," *Teachers College Record* 44: 374-75; February 1943. (Doctoral study by John Alexander Rorer, Ph. D. Teachers College, Columbia University, Contributions to Education, No. 858.)

human values. This study lists the purposes of democratic supervision as: promotion of pupil growth, helping teachers create an environment favorable to teaching and learning, promotion of teacher growth, improvement of teaching and learning, coordination and integration of educational effort, and carrying out educational policies cooperatively arrived at.

In discussing the organization demanded by democratic supervision this investigation states that there should be an absence of an inflexible, hierarchial system of relationships between the superior and inferior officers. The superintendent should exercise leadership to gain full cooperation and participation of the staff and community in formulating, effecting, and evaluating educational policy. Leadership is a shared responsibility of all staff members. Democratic supervision should be able to adapt itself to the needs of each supervisory-teaching-learning situation. It operates from the bottom up rather than from the top down. Operation is determined by the needs of the learning situation rather than by administrative organization. The conclusion is made that the work of the supervisor in a democratic organization is organized neither by subjects nor grades, but by large centers of interest designed to integrate learning and provide for continuous pupil progress. In terms of supervisory technics planning, executing, and evaluating should be continuous and simultaneous. There should be wide participation of supervisors, teachers, pupils, and community members at all stages and to the greatest feasible extent.

A county monograph states that, "all teachers, supervisors, and administrators should make every effort to free themselves from prejudices and tendencies to discriminate against any minority group." Another critical issue discussed in this monograph is "the reorientation to the profession of former teachers now serving in the armed forces or war work."[51] Supervisor-leaders need to equip themselves to meet this problem effectively in the immediate period ahead. This same report places emphasis on the need for coordination, not only among the supervisory personnel within a school system but with professional association activities, curriculum construction programs, teacher-training institutions, and other group enterprises in order to facilitate professional growth of in-service teachers.

Another responsibility of supervisor, and one on which too little emphasis has been placed, is stimulating each teacher to think thru and write down his own philosophy of education. Significant in this respect is the *great*, and by the same token the *grave*, leadership role ahead in keeping in the forefront of educational thinking the role of education in developing international understanding thru an organization which will foster educational interchange between nations.

---

[51] San Diego, Office of County Superintendent of Schools. *Critical Issues in Administration and Curriculum With Recommendations for Education in the Postwar Period.* San Diego: the Office, December 1944.

What Is the Leadership Role Ahead for the Supervisor?

Responses of groups of supervisors; teachers; city, county, and state superintendents reveal that they, too, see in the future an important leadership role for supervisors. But, there exist, among the groups divergent opinions as to what the most significant leadership role of the supervisor is. The most striking fact, as shown by the accompanying graph is that the superintendents have, apparently, more clear-cut opinions of what constitute the most valuable potential contributions of supervision than do either the supervisors themselves or the teacher group. Do supervisors generally see their opportunities for service with a sufficient degree of objectivity? It may be that the very number of duties required of supervisors makes it difficult for them to see their broader and more inclusive roles.

It should be kept in mind that the opinions graphed represent only a sampling from each of the four educational fields. Altho almost one thousand questionnaires were mailed, some were not returned and other recipients did not respond to all of the questions. One hundred and sixty supervisors, twenty-two state superintendents, forty-eight city and county superintendents, and forty-two teachers responded to this question. The numerical representation of the last three groups is admittedly small, and therefore their responses cannot be taken as conclusive evidence. Since the individuals questioned were drawn from all areas of the country, however, their collective opinions may be considered as at least indicative of the thinking of many educators thruout the nation. Actual responses made to the question of supervision's future role are given here to show the caliber of thinking of questionnaire respondents on each of the ten supervisory roles considered most significant.

Supervisors Have Civic Responsibilities

Nineteen percent of the supervisors responding to the questionnaire felt that their best contributions could be made in the area of community relationships. City and county superintendents saw this function as of even greater importance, while teachers and state superintendents placed slightly less weight upon it. Sixty-three percent of those who listed this as the most important leadership role showed by their responses they did not believe that merely publicizing the school's activities was the answer.

Classroom teachers, general elementary supervisors, college professors, members of state departments of education, and county and city superintendents saw civic leadership as a responsibility of supervision and pointed to increasing cooperation between professional and lay groups in order to plan for an educational program to meet specific community needs.

A LOOK AT OUR BEST   111

FIG. 2
THE MOST SIGNIFICANT LEADERSHIP ROLE AHEAD FOR
SUPERVISION AS SEEN BY SELECTED GROUPS OF
EDUCATIONAL PERSONNEL

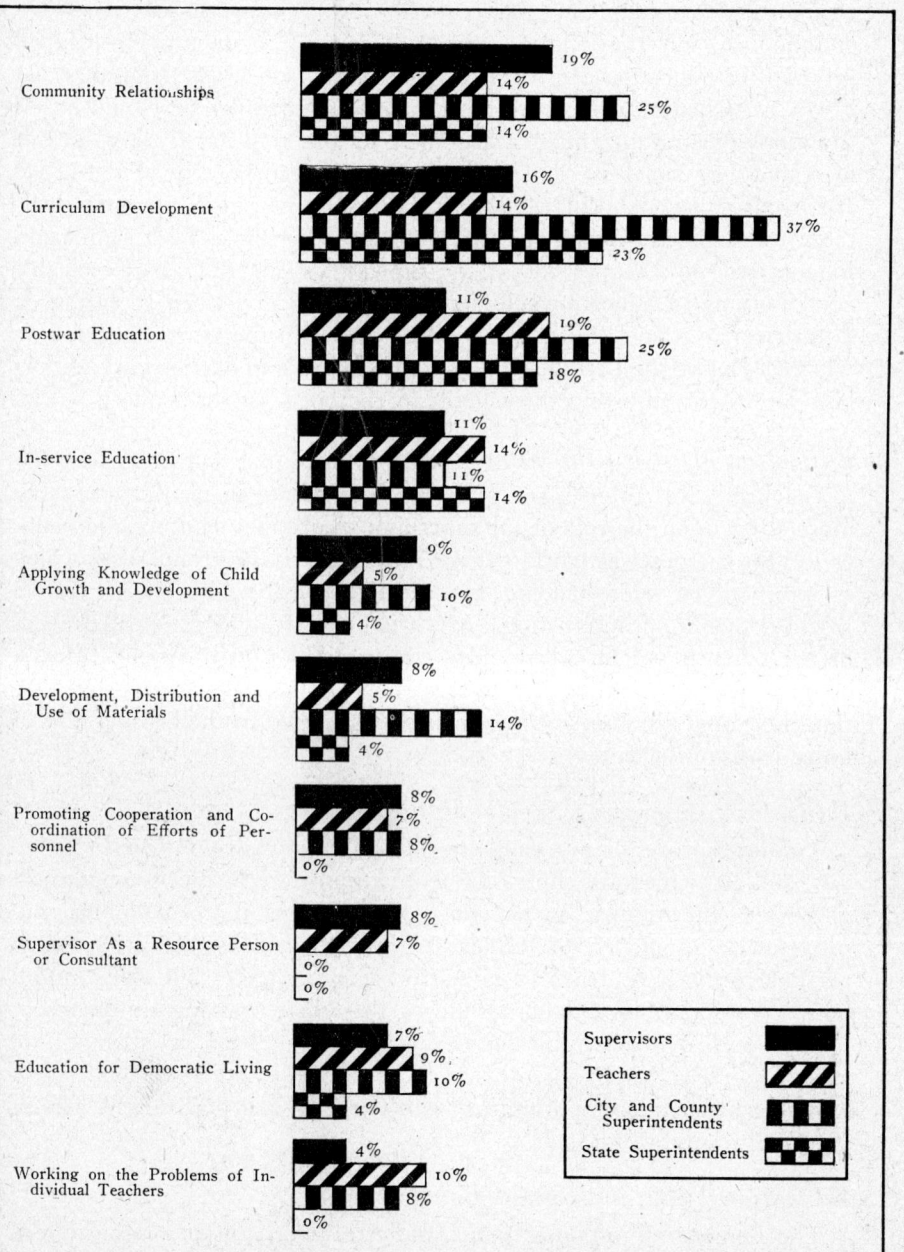

Community Relationships
- 19%
- 14%
- 25%
- 14%

Curriculum Development
- 16%
- 14%
- 37%
- 23%

Postwar Education
- 11%
- 19%
- 25%
- 18%

In-service Education
- 11%
- 14%
- 11%
- 14%

Applying Knowledge of Child Growth and Development
- 9%
- 5%
- 10%
- 4%

Development, Distribution and Use of Materials
- 8%
- 5%
- 14%
- 4%

Promoting Cooperation and Co-ordination of Efforts of Personnel
- 8%
- 7%
- 8%
- 0%

Supervisor As a Resource Person or Consultant
- 8%
- 7%
- 0%
- 0%

Education for Democratic Living
- 7%
- 9%
- 10%
- 4%

Working on the Problems of Individual Teachers
- 4%
- 10%
- 8%
- 0%

Legend:
- Supervisors
- Teachers
- City and County Superintendents
- State Superintendents

(This graph represents the opinions of 250 individuals working as supervisors, teachers, city and county superintendents and state superintendents. Every part of the country is represented in the study. The teachers included were enrolled in a supervision course during the 1945 summer session at Teachers College, Columbia University.)

Superintendents Emphasize Curriculum Development

A supervising principal in a midwestern elementary school who sees the responsibility for curriculum development resting in part on supervisory shoulders said, "Supervisors should lead in instituting a framework of school organization within which a meaningful, cooperatively planned program of education can be developed; one which has meaning because it is a participating experience both during the learning years and in life situations. Make subjectmatter mastery only one tool in the development of a thoroly wholesome personality." Thirty-seven percent of the urban and rural superintendents and 23 percent of the state superintendents rated the supervisor's role in curriculum development as most significant. In contrast only 16 percent of the supervisors saw their most valuable contributions to educational leadership in this area. When such a wide difference in rating exists, it may be well for supervisors to question whether or not they are placing enough emphasis upon this very important means for adjusting the schools to the needs of the modern world.

Education Must Fit the Times

Teachers, city, county, and state superintendents all placed noticeably more stress upon the role of the supervisor in planning and initiating education for the postwar world than did the supervisory group. Terms such as international understanding, problems of social and economic value, world cooperation, international education charter, and anticipated needs of the postwar world, are found in the responses on this item. In their comparatively low rating in this area supervisors need to seriously question their own vision in keeping their sights leveled to the broader educational issues of the day.

Educators Agree on In-Service Education

A college professor in a southern university, a classroom teacher in the east, and an elementary supervisor from a midwestern state characterized in-service education as an experience which aims for instructional improvement; stimulation of teachers to help themselves; and attention to personal growth of teachers in self-confidence, leadership traits, and a sense of responsibility. It is significant that there was less difference of opinion as to the relative value of in-service education as an important supervision area than of any other. Teachers were in agreement with supervisors regarding the importance of this function and both of the administrative groups rated it high.

Education Deals in Human Beings

The number of responses which indicate a recognition of the importance of the application of the latest findings on child growth and development was not large. Between 4 and 10 percent saw in this area a major leadership responsibility of supervisors in the days ahead. However, those who did emphasize it placed a knowledge of how children grow and develop as basic to the planning of an educational program concerned with providing for the needs of children and youth.

The Concept of Material's Use Is a Broad One

Fourteen percent of city and county superintendents believed that the development, distribution and use of instructional materials, particularly of auditory-visual materials, should absorb a major portion of the supervisor's time and attention in the future. Eight percent of the supervisors held the same opinion. A primary teacher in the South made an interesting comment which stated the function briefly and figuratively when she said, "Supervisors should be bringers-together of people with materials."

Improvement in Cooperative Action Is Possible

When educators asked for more cooperative action, they referred to cooperation between members of the profession as well as between lay and professional groups. One county superintendent said, "The supervisor should be a cooperator, a leader of groups working together." A teacher in the same state asks for more cooperation and collaboration "between those who are in a position of telling others what and how to teach and those who actually do the teaching." Eight percent of supervisors and of rural and urban superintendents and 7 percent of the teachers saw the coordination of the work of various groups engaged in education as a role of major importance for supervision.

The Supervisor Serves as a Consultant

A similar percentage of supervisors and teachers saw the supervisor serving best in a consultant or resource capacity. Said one individual in this respect, "Implied in this function is the role of these persons in encouraging group action, emphasizing democratic procedures, and otherwise motivating interest in working as a profession." An elementary supervisor as she considered this phase of the supervisory task saw it as more than a twenty-four hour job.

Democratic Living Gives Reality to Ideals

A role directly related to education for our times is that of education for democratic living. Ten percent of city and county superintendents saw this as a major leadership function of supervisors. Nine percent of the teachers, 7 percent of the supervisors, and 4 percent of the state departments of education placed this role first. There was general agreement that understandings in this area resulted only in proportion to actual experience in democratic living and relationships.

Teachers Ask for Help on Individual Problems

In proportion to their representation, more than twice as many teachers expressed the belief that a major contribution of supervision should be working with individual teachers on their problems. Administrators tended to agree with teachers in this respect. The differences are significant enough to raise the question of whether or not the greatest gain to education may not, after all, come thru services to the individual classroom teacher who carries the bulk of the responsibility for the success or failure of the classroom program.

Other Supervisory Roles Are Significant

The list of leadership roles given for supervision is an endless one—supporting equalization in educational opportunity, promoting guidance programs, working with principals, organizing study groups, making administrators conscious of their professional instructional responsibilities, trying to coordinate in a diplomatic fashion conflicting philosophies of education, getting and keeping efficient educational personnel, concentrating on a program for returning veterans, educating parents, or raising professional standards. To go on with the list would be convincing evidence that supervision is more than a twenty-four hour job. The encouraging aspect in the total program is that among the total number of schools carrying on supervisory programs one finds an evidence here and another there of goals already in action on our educational frontiers.

5

Tomorrow's Assignment

ON WHAT SHALL A SUPERVISOR SPEND HIMSELF? That, in essence, has been the question behind the two chapters just read. To the reader, comparing deviating percentages in the judgments of one group and another, reviewing the tremendous problems that block the path of full performance, the answer may have seemed obscure. But if he will relax, and contemplate those chapters as a whole, he will see that a picture of the supervisor's true work has been emerging in startling clarity.

It is a picture too full of detail to be susceptible of concise summary here. And it is too powerful to need the reinforcement of a general summarization. Yet, because each of us in his daily round of duties shapes his actions largely according to a mental image of his place and function—an image held, perhaps, only unconsciously—it may be well, while these chapters are fresh in our minds, to merge them with our common-sense perceptions of the nature of supervision and draw out a few generalizations.

To the supervisor who is eager to search out a standard of performance and willing to measure himself by it, two basic questions are profitable:

> What *is* supervision?
> What is a supervisor *for?*

No simple ten-word definition emerges from the questionnaire study in answer to either of these questions. In fact, among the selected group represented by the study no two superintendents, principals, teachers, or supervisors have shown precisely the same mental image of supervision. And yet among educators at large there will be many who have ready answers. A first answer likely to be given is that the supervisor is an expert who tells teachers the answers to their problems, who tells them how to do this or that skilfully.

By FRED T. WILHELMS, *Associate Director, Consumer Education Study of the National Association of Secondary-School Principals, Washington, D. C.*

Is the Supervisor Merely an Expert Technician?

Those who are more advanced in their thinking reject this answer—reject it, at least, if it is to be the *complete* answer—on several grounds: It does not square with the laws of learning; there are too many things which teachers—like the children they teach—cannot genuinely learn merely by being told. These things demand experiencing and real learning activities if they are to become a part of a changed teacher. It implies a qualitative difference in the expertness of supervisors and teachers which does not generally exist—sets the supervisor up as a know-it-all, degrades the teacher into a mere apprentice. Worse still, it does not tap for the school as a whole the real expertnesses possessed only by this or that teacher. But, primarily we reject this meager conception of supervision because its premise is paternalistic, authoritarian, out of tune with a democratic educational theory which sees teachers as robust, able individuals capable of learning on their own and contributing mightily to educational progress.

Just the same, let us not forget that there is something—a great deal, in fact—in this conception of supervision. Speed and ease in learning to do effectively the particular skills of everyday teaching are valid and important goals of supervision. There *are* things which teachers, young teachers especially, can learn quickly and smoothly thru a simple telling or demonstration by a supervisor who is older, more generally experienced, or more skillful in some particular. It is probable that these things tend to be chiefly in the little tricks of the classroom trade, but that does not make them unimportant.

When the supervisor, in such a case, can literally *give* the teacher the answer he wants, he is performing a service of great value. It is a service teachers value highly. The supervisor who can point out precisely the reference that will supply a wanted fact, who can enrich group living by suggesting the organization of a classroom library, or who can demonstrate how to develop a file of visual aids is a resource person not to be sneered at, even if he can give nothing more lofty than these types of services. All too many teachers are forced to pump daily at the dry wells of supervisors who can expatiate grandly upon professional progress or the atomic age, but who simply do not know the fundamentals of the teacher's job.

This conception of supervision, at its best, is based upon an image of the teacher reinforced at every side by resource persons more expert than himself in some particular, ready to serve him when that particular becomes his problem. It is a useful conception, so far as it goes, and one which must not be lost in the drive toward higher levels of supervision.

Even at its best, however, it poses one problem which the questionnaire responses have shown to be significant: the resource persons, instead of being welded into a solid line of reinforcements, all too often become separate, if not rival, forces, pulling and hauling at the teacher from every angle. The teacher comes out weary and feeling "supervised to death," eager chiefly to be let alone. As a consequence there is today a discernable trend toward coordination of supervisory efforts and a tendency to call for a larger proportion of general supervision—sacrificing, perhaps, something of specific expertness to gain greater attention to the teacher as a person.

Can He Rely on Inspiration Alone?

There is another conception of supervision, something like the view of the athletic coach (heard most often in a losing season) that his job is not so much to teach football as to build men. Analogously, the supervisor sees himself as one who inspires his teachers, lifts them above themselves, reinvigorates their flagging spirits.

Again, there is in this view a distressing assumption of a qualitative difference between supervisors and teachers—a difference objective observation will scarcely always reveal. It presupposes that supervisors are *inspiring* people, gazing down upon the little worries of ordinary men from the serenity of their Olympian heights. It presupposes that teachers are *uninspired*, harassed and driven by their work, incapable of high vision from heights of their own. In cold fact, many a supervisor is himself driven and harassed, drawing what strength and serenity he can from his superior teachers. And, again, there is a paternalism that rings a false note in a democratic school staff which conceives its teachers as men and women of dignity and strength.

But the greatest danger in this concept of supervision as inspiration lies in its potentialities for self-deception. All of us like to think ourselves inspired and inspiring; not all of us are. The supervisor who comes away from a "simply thrilling" meeting may be the only one there to have caught the thrill. Without his knowing it, he may have been thrilled only by the chance his dominance gave to express himself, to coin a felicitous phrase, to bathe his ego in applause. The teachers may have found it dull; they may feel that they were butchered to make a Roman holiday—even tho, from fear or from hope of some small gain, they contributed to the opinion that all was wonderful and clapped their hands in seeming rapture. The supervisor who, having read in some book of the heartening qualities of a warm smile, henceforth goes "smiling thru"—albeit a bit vacuously—no matter what the difficulties, does not necessarily solve any fundamental problems. All may be very cheerful during his visit, while the skeletons are carefully confined in their proper closets, but the teacher is none the better off when he leaves. In his casual brushing back of problems someone *wants* to face and solve, he may even be adding to discouragement.

And yet, this conception of supervision, too, is essential and important.

Not all of supervision, by any means, is science. Much of it is—and must always remain—art, to be accomplished only in that indefinable realm where human soul meets human soul.

That one function of supervision is to inspire is not mere fine philosophy. It is practical fact established over and over again in everyday practice. There must be thousands of educators who entered the field indifferently, only to catch the fire of vision as they saw their task thru the eyes of some glowing enthusiast. More important, there are thousands who esteemed themselves ordinary until they saw their real potentialities mirrored in the eyes of a perceptive leader. And every day many a discouraged teacher's mind is lifted over the hurdles of petty worries as he is led to remember or to see anew the great, inspiring goals for which he is spending himself.

Undeniably, it is a function of supervision to inspire, to lift men above themselves—or, better, help them rise to their true selves. To this task, as essential equipment, the supervisor must bring a genuinely seeing eye. He must have the eye to perceive men's troubles and the roots of these troubles, but above all, his must be an enthusiastic eye to discern their undiscovered capacities. Without this eye, the supervisor is a small figure. He who has it must have with it two things more: courage, not to ignore difficulties, but to face them fearlessly and intelligently; and steadfast friendship, keyed to unremitting loyalty in the pinches.

To Recapitulate

These are two basic concepts of supervision which come to men almost intuitively—that the supervisor shall be an expert supplying solutions to problems and that he shall be a builder of men. They are not enough to guide a supervisor adequately as he plans how to spend his energy. But each is in its way essential, and a superstructure of supervision not based solidly upon them is doomed to crash.

How Can Supervision Truly Fulfil Its Purpose?

For many years, now, professionally trained men and women have devoted their whole lives to supervision. It is only natural that they have gone beyond the intuitively grasped, common-sense concepts just described. For they have had time to cut and try many patterns of supervision, to experiment boldly, and watch the results objectively. Furthermore, the progressing intellectualization of the democratic philosophy of life has given them new tools for reflective thinking about supervision.

It is not surprising then that the best pioneers in supervision should have explored new concepts. Even so, it is surprising that we should find so definite a consensus among all the authorities consulted in this yearbook study. What that consensus is, the reader will have sensed before now: *That the supervisor is an organizer of opportunity, and that good supervision is the facilitation of opportunities.*

Opportunity for *whom?* For teachers, primarily. For tho supervisors deal with administrators and with the lay public, let us not be so polite in our zeal to be democratic as to balk at admitting that where there is the supervis*or*, there also must be the supervis*ed*. The basic objective of supervision is, after all, the improvement of instruction.

Opportunity for *what?* The answer to this question might be elaborated endlessly. But it can be cut down to two essentials:

1. Opportunity for teachers to learn what they need and want to learn.
2. Opportunity for teachers to play their full part in policy-making.

How Are Opportunities for Learning Provided?

Three assumptions lie behind the recognition that it is good to arrange many direct learning opportunities for teachers:

1. That teachers are professionally zealous persons with a strongly felt need for increased mastery of their work.
2. That teachers are intelligent persons, well able to attack learning problems swiftly and soundly when they have recognized the need and when they have the opportunity.
3. That with reference to the sorts of matters which constitute teachers' most common and important problems, there is no substitute for direct learning by each teacher. No outside person—no supervisor, however skilled—can supply the answers ready-made and achieve the desired change within the individual teacher.

The media or opportunities for direct learning will be of many sorts, and it is not our function here to describe them. For some matters a teacher will need only access to a good library with time to use it, plus perhaps enough guidance to save her from wasting time in preliminary explorations. In other cases, her need may be primarily to see something—to see another skilled teacher doing well something she herself has not dared to try or feels she does inadequately, or to see how a modern factory works. One of her needs is almost certain to be first-hand acquaintance with the salient institutions of her own community; another, the chance to hear experts on matters of concern to her—whether about education in particular or of the culture in which we exist. Certainly she needs opportunity to express herself and thus clarify her own thinking, in writing or in the give-and-take of the conference table. There will be no substitute for actual doing in the arts and crafts or in the development of some small unit of curriculum.

But what the opportunities shall be or how they shall be arranged is not so much our question here as how the supervisor shall conceive his function. What is important, in this conception of supervision, is that he go directly to teachers to find out what their problems and their desires for learning are, helping them to become aware of needs they do not yet sense, to whatever degree his perceptions of those needs may be better than their own. What is even more important is that when the teachers' problems have been identified and their urge to learn is strong, he devote his energies, not primarily to telling or teaching the answers, but rather to setting up situations in which they can learn for themselves.

In all this we do not mean that the arranging of opportunities to learn shall be made wholly by the supervisor for the teachers. That might simply be a higher form of paternalism. Certainly the teachers should participate in deciding what is to be provided, and can play an active part in the making of the necessary arrangements. But there is involved a kind of activity that can be carried on best by someone who stands close to the center of an administrative unit; there is time-consuming detail to be attended to; and there is a need for correlation of the efforts of scattered teachers. All these factors justify a large measure of initiative on the part of the supervisory staff.

How Can All Contribute to Policy-Making?

A certain proportion of educational policy-making traditionally has been administrative; that is to say, it has been primarily a function of boards of education, superintendents, and principals, as administrators. Without attempting any fine distinction, we can say that it has been concerned with such questions as what buildings shall be built and how they shall be maintained, what salaries and other moneys shall be provided, and what courses of study shall be offered. It is desirable that policy-making on such matters be democratic, especially with reference to the will of the supporting community. But in the main these policies constitute a framework within which supervisor and teacher operate and are not their direct concern.

What has not always been seen clearly is that within this chiefly physical and financial framework there is a tremendous amount of functional policy-making to be done. To institute a commercial curriculum within a high school is only to open up a thousand questions as to what shall constitute that curriculum. Even to draw up a seemingly detailed outline of the junior business training course is still to leave a thousand choices of content and objective and method to the teacher.

The important determinants of what goes on within the schoolroom—the real results of the whole school's efforts—are the philosophy of purpose, the mode of treatment of the students, the content of the curriculum, and the tools used in the task. On none of these has any school system, whether willing or not to give the teacher freedom, ever been able to do more than go a short way up the road with her, then give her her head to choose her own path. In simple fact—and inevitably—teachers have been our primary makers of curriculum and choosers of philosophy, as these things actually affect the child in action. They are the ones, in the main, who have selected or devised educational methods and tools. That they often have done so casually, not seldom unconsciously, and sometimes even furtively, does not gainsay the fact that they have done it.

Supervision now sees the institutionalizing of this casual policy-making as one of its greatest functions—probably its most important—single opportunity. Besides the basic reason that this is the democratic way, there are four compelling reasons:

 1. If teachers are willy-nilly the *de facto* policy-makers in important phases of the school's work, then teachers must be brought together to come to common decisions, or the school cannot have a coherent, unified philosophy and basic method.
 2. There is no other body of educators who can supply the same experience and expertness on functional details as that possessed by teachers, taken as a whole.
 3. Teachers, having consciously shared in democratic policy-making, are likely to show understanding, loyalty, and energy in carrying out the policies once they are made—a guarantee which cannot be given in anything like the same measure to any policy handed down from above.
 4. The teachers will themselves learn and improve tremendously in the process, not only in skill but even more in breadth of philosophy and interests, as well as in vigor and enthusiasm.

Again, there are various media or administrative methods for conducting cooperative teacher-planning. It is not our function in this chapter to explore them. Without question, participation in curriculum-making stands at the head of the list. As a phase of school policy-making it both stands close to the center of the teacher's interest and, when well conceived, it involves all the important problems. For this purpose the informal summer workshop seems unexcelled. But other, less striking methods, utilized continuously over longer periods, may be equally effective.

The important thing here, let us repeat, is not the detail of method, but how the supervisor conceives his function. Tho he need be no silent, voiceless partner in the enterprise, his chief function is to set up, or better to help the whole staff set up, the situation in which the teachers can most successfully work.

This is the thing which he can do, and which scattered teachers cannot easily do. This is, therefore, his *raison d'etre* as a specialized official. He can find and put in touch with one another teachers with similar problems, abilities, and desires. He can make arrangements to have time cleared for group work. He can care for the development of libraries containing visual and auditory aids as well as printed materials. He can wangle facilities for a central workroom. He can secure expert personnel and other necessities for a workshop at home or in some university.

For the sake of simplicity and realism, we have chosen to speak thruout this section as tho the relationship of supervisor and staff had to do only with problems within a single school. Not so. The school is a great moving force in a torn and worried world. It may be, without exaggeration, the last great hope of this nation, once called "the last great hope of humanity." The million or more men and women in American education bear a terrible responsibility, which they must analyze with intelligence and honesty and attack with unity and courage. Supervisors are leaders in this, too. We believe that the kind of supervision which we have sketched holds the greatest hope for meeting the responsibility which go with that leadership.

What Is the Distinctive Role of Supervision?

Thruout this yearbook we have portrayed a supervision which is *leadership*. But we have fought at every step any smug assumption that that leadership is due to a qualitative superiority of supervisors over other members of the staff. For a first requisite of good supervision is a deep humility and the attitude of a willing servant.

Supervision, a greatly extended supervision, is essential simply because in the organization of America's educational force it has a unique part to play. It is a role which would still be essential if every teacher in every school were already a truly superior person; only, then, it could bring its work to a tremendously increased fruition. It is a role which can be taken only by trained, professional men and women standing just outside the classroom, yet deeply familiar with many classrooms; men and women who deal nonadministratively in warm, human relationships with many teachers. Their greatest task is to serve those teachers—and in serving them, to upbuild the schools—by helping them to see clearly themselves, the profession, and the society in which they work, by removing every block, and by opening the way to the achievement of every teacher's greatest hopes and aspirations.

If You Are Concerned

with developing better schools, you are invited to become a member of the Association for Supervision and Curriculum Development. Members include supervisors, directors of instruction, superintendents, curriculum coordinators, professors of education, teachers, principals, department heads, leaders of youth groups, and other persons with similar professional interests.

Beliefs

The Association for Supervision and Curriculum Development, believes that modern schools can do their jobs only if . . .
—pupils, teachers, and administrators grow in understanding what life is all about.
—everyone has a chance to test for himself what is important and what isn't.
—youngsters learn by making choices and seeing how they work.
—youngsters have a chance to think and talk about our social structure and decide how it may be improved.
—what happens in the school is determined by what boys and girls need individually and in groups, now and tomorrow.
—the curriculum—what boys and girls do in school—has meaning and significance for the youngsters.
—all community agencies, including our homes and schools, work together for better education.
—there is mutual respect and confidence as we work together to improve our schools.
—school programs are continually being weighed and improved in the light of tested ways of working.
—parents and citizens are helped to understand what their youngsters need to learn and how it can be taught.
—state and federal aid goes to communities which cannot pay for good schools.

Membership

The annual dues of $4 entitle you to a subscription to EDUCATIONAL LEADERSHIP—the official ASCD Journal—a copy of the current yearbook, and all other privileges of membership. (Membership dues for persons whose salaries are less than $1200 a year are $2.) Write to:

Association for Supervision and Curriculum Development, NEA
1201 Sixteenth Street, N.W., Washington 6, D.C.

EDUCATIONAL LEADERSHIP

Educational Leadership is the monthly publication of the Association for Supervision and Curriculum Development. Those responsible for the publication during the 1945-46 publication year include:

PUBLICATIONS COMMITTEE

J. Paul Leonard, *chairman*, Pres., San Francisco St. Coll., Calif.
Vernon E. Anderson, Dir. of Curr., Portland, Ore.
C. L. Cushman, Assoc. Supt., Philadelphia, Pa.
Henry Harap, Assoc. Dir., Div. of Surveys and Field Studies, George Peabody College, Nashville, Tenn.
Dora S. Skipper, Asst. Prof. of Ed., F.S.C.W., Tallahassee, Fla.
Hollis L. Caswell, *ex officio*, President, Association for Supervision and Curriculum Development, NEA.

Editor
Gertrude Hankamp
Executive Secretary, Association for Supervision and Curriculum Development, NEA

Assistant Editor	*Circulation*	*Advertising*
Louise C. McCue	Elinor Cahill	Eleanor Warbritton

ADVISORY EDITORS

Corrie W. Allen, Assoc. Prof., U. of Texas, Austin, Tex.
William H. Bristow, Asst. Dir., Bur. of Ref., Res., and Stat., Bd. of Ed., Brooklyn, N. Y.
Jennie Campbell, Dir. Elem. Ed., Dept. Pub. Instr., Salt Lake City, Utah
Mary Henderson, Elem. Prin., Washington, D. C.
Baxter Hobgood, Assoc. Prof., Middle Tenn. St. Coll., Murfreesboro, Tenn.
Hal G. Lewis, Prin., P. K. Yonge Lab. Sch., U. of Florida, Gainesville, Fla.
E. T. McSwain, Prof. of Ed., Northwestern U., Evanston, Ill.
Mary Alice Mitchell, Dir. Elem. Ed., Newton, Mass.
Helen F. Olson, Head, English Dept., Broadway High Sch., Seattle, Wash.
D. C. Rucker, Curr. Dir., Bd. of Ed., Springfield, Mo.
Frederick L. Trott, Curr. Supv., Tulare Co., Visalia, Calif.

ASCD PUBLICATIONS

ASCD has available a variety of publications. These range from the regular yearbook of the Association to pamphlets and mimeographed bulletins of a bibliographical nature.

Publication	Price
AMERICANS ALL	$2.00
BIBLIOGRAPHY ON ELEMENTARY EDUCATION	.25
BUILDING AMERICA, $2.25 a year; bound volumes	3.95
A CHALLENGE TO SECONDARY EDUCATION	2.25
THE CHANGING CURRICULUM	2.25
THE COMMUNITY SCHOOL	2.50
CONSUMER EDUCATION	2.50
COOPERATION: PRINCIPLES AND PRACTICES	2.00
CURRENT PROBLEMS OF SUPERVISORS	1.00
DISCIPLINE FOR TODAY'S CHILDREN AND YOUTH	.50
EDUCATION IN THE ARMED SERVICES	.50
AN EVALUATION OF MODERN EDUCATION	2.50
EVALUATION OF SUPERVISION	1.00
FAMILY LIVING AND OUR SCHOOLS	2.75
FILMS INTERPRETING CHILDREN AND YOUTH	.15
GROUP PLANNING IN EDUCATION	2.00
INTELLIGENCE IN A CHANGING UNIVERSE	.50
INTEGRATION: ITS MEANING AND APPLICATION	2.25
LEADERSHIP AT WORK	2.00
SCIENTIFIC METHOD IN SUPERVISORY PROGRAMS	1.00
TEACHING AND LEARNING MATERIALS	.10
TOWARD A NEW CURRICULUM	2.00
UNITY THROUGH UNDERSTANDING	.25
WE, THE CHILDREN	.25

Ready in the Spring, 1946

BIBLIOGRAPHY ON SECONDARY EDUCATION	.25
LEADERSHIP THROUGH SUPERVISION	2.00

Discount on quantity orders: 2-9 copies, 10%; 10-99 copies, 25%; 100 or more, 33⅓%.

Order from: Association for Supervision and Curriculum Development
National Education Association
1201 Sixteenth Street, N. W., Washington 6, D. C.

ASCD BOARD OF DIRECTORS

Executive Committee, 1945-1946

President, HOLLIS L. CASWELL, Dir., Div. of Instr., Tchrs. Coll., Col. U., N. Y.
First Vice-President, GORDON N. MACKENZIE, Dir., Inst. for Sch. Exp., Tchrs. Coll., Col. U., N. Y.
Second Vice-President, GLADYS L. POTTER, Supv. of Elem. Ed., Long Beach, Calif.
Field Secretary, JAMES F. HOSIC, 1521 Highland Road, Winter Park, Fla.
EDGAR M. DRAPER, Prof. of Ed., U. of Washington, Seattle.
R. LEE THOMAS, Supv. of Elem. Schs., State Dept. of Ed., Nashville, Tenn.
JENNIE WAHLERT, Elem. Prin., St. Louis, Mo.

Board of Directors

Members of the Executive Committee, *ex officio*

MEMBERS ELECTED AT LARGE

VERNON ANDERSON, Dir. of Curr., Portland, Ore. (1949)
WALTER A. ANDERSON, Asst. Supt. of Schs., Minneapolis, Minn. (1947)
STEPHEN M. COREY, Prof. of Ed., U. of Chicago, Ill. (1948)
BESS GOODYKOONTZ, Asst. Comm., U. S. Office of Ed., Wash., D. C. (1948)
PAUL R. HANNA, Prof. of Ed., Stanford U., Calif. (1948)
E. T. MCSWAIN, Prof. of Ed., Northwestern U., Evanston, Ill. (1948)
ALICE MIEL, Asst. Prof. of Ed., Tchrs. Coll., Col. U., N. Y. (1947)
PAUL MISNER, Supt. of Schs., Glencoe, Ill. (1949)
MAYCIE SOUTHALL, Prof. of Elem. Ed., George Peabody Coll., Nashville, Tenn. (1946)
LELIA ANN TAGGART, Dir. of Ed., Santa Barbara County, Calif. (1947)
ETHEL S. WARD, Dir. of Supv., Alameda County, California (1949)
GILBERT S. WILLEY, Asst. Supt. in charge of Elem. Ed., Denver, Colo. (1949)
PAUL WITTY, Prof. of Ed., Northwestern U., Evanston, Ill. (1949)
WILLIAM E. YOUNG, Dir., Div. of Elem. Ed., State Ed. Dept., Albany, N. Y. (1947)
RUTH CUNNINGHAM, *ex officio*, Asst. Prof. of Ed., Tchrs. Coll., Col. U., N. Y. (1946)

STATE REPRESENTATIVES TO THE BOARD

Alabama—ELOISE C. KEEBLER, Elem. Supv., Talladega
California—ROXIE E. ALEXANDER, Dir. of Elem. Ed., Vallejo; LEONARD GRINDSTAFF, Dir. of Ed. Materials, Santa Barbara; CORINNE A. SEEDS, Asst. Prof. of Ed., U. C. L. A.
Georgia—ISABEL LUMSDEN, Supv., Stephens County Schools, Toccoa
Illinois—MARION JORDAN, Supt., Cicero
Indiana—HANNAH LINDAHL, Supv. Elem. Ed., Mishawaka
Kentucky—MARY I. COLE, Assoc. Prof. Ed., Western Kentucky Tchrs. Coll., Bowling Green; NAOMI C. WILHOIT, St. Supv. Elem. Ed., Frankfort
Louisiana—MAGGIE HAWS, Supv. of Schs., Bastrop
Minnesota—MAE IVEY, Elem. Supv., Albert Lea
New York—WILLIAM T. MELCHIOR, Prof. of Ednl. Supvn., Syracuse University; FRED B. PAINTER, Asst. Supt., Ithaca
Ohio—MARY A. HADDOW, Dir. of Elem. Curr., Youngstown
Pennsylvania—CATHERINE E. GEARY, Dir. of Elem. Ed. and Curr., Chester
Tennessee—EULA A. JOHNSTON, Elem. Supv., Chattanooga
Virginia—MARIE E. ALEXANDER, Supv. of Elem. Ed., Hampton; D. C. BEERY, Supt., Staunton
Northwest Region (Washington, Oregon, Montana, Idaho)—L. L. CARLSON, Supt., Lewiston, Idaho; WALTER E. SNYDER, Curr. Dir., Salem, Ore.

Executive Secretary

GERTRUDE HANKAMP, 1201 Sixteenth Street, N. W., Washington 6, D. C.

List of Members

The Association of Supervisors and Directors of Instruction

For the year 1945-46

(Corrected to Dec. 31, 1945)

ALABAMA

Barnes, Derlie, Elementary Supervisor, Box 950, Andalusia
Belser, Danylu, Professor of Elementary Education, University of Alabama, Box 1476, University
Bentley, Florence, Supervisor, Crenshaw County Elementary Schools, Brantley
Bristow, Mrs. John T., Supervisor, Elementary Grades, 301 S. Lawrence St., Montgomery
Campbell, Kayron, Elementary Supervisor, Box 284, Columbiana
Clark, K. J., Assistant Superintendent, Barton Building, Mobile 15
Comer, Louise, 807 Olive St., Florence
Dilworth, Bernice, Elementary Supervisor, Box 453, Guntersville
Driskell, Vera Mae, Supervising Instructor, Box 151, Fort Payne
Elder, Olivia, State Teachers College, Troy
Evans, Mrs. Zelia S., Jeanes Teacher, Shelby County, Box 29, Calera
Fain, Lillie T., Supervisor, Geneva County, Geneva
Farris, Eunora, Elementary Supervisor, Elba
Fife, Pauline, Box 245, Carrollton
Finley, John, Jr., Principal, Lexington School, Lexington
Garrison, Jessie R., Alabama Department of Education, Supervisor of Physical Education, Montgomery 4
Gilchrist, J. H., Principal, Trenholm High School, Box 418, Tuscumbia
Glisson, Ouida, Supervisor, Box 365, Prattville
Glover, May C., Supervisor of Instruction, Board of Education, Centreville
Goldthwaite, Therese, Principal, Goode Street School, Montgomery
Hadley, Laura B., Associate Professor of Home Economics Education, Alabama College, Montevallo
Hamil, Loraine, 510 S. Brundidge St., Troy
Hamilton, Mrs. E. G., Supervisor of Instruction, 515 E. Walnut St., Decatur
Henderson, Mary C., Supervisor of High Schools, Box 417, Talladega
Hitt, Nellie W., Alabama Apartment B 10, Tuscaloosa
Holmes, Ethel, Supervisor, Brewton County, Brewton
Hughes, Mary B., 1606 30th Ave., Tuscaloosa
Ingram, Foy, 1122 N. Three-Notch St., Troy
Irvine, Paul, Teacher Training Library, Alabama Polytechnic Institute, Auburn
Jackson, A. L., President, Negro Department, Stillman Institute, Southern Presbyterian Church, Tuscaloosa
Jackson, Mrs. P. S., Classroom Teacher, Peterman
Johnson, Mayme A., Primary Teacher, 711½ 15th St., W., Birmingham
Jones, Lenore, 1606 Monterey Place, Mobile 19
Kearley, Helen, Elementary Supervisor, Fayette County, Fayette
Keebler, Eloise C., Supervisor of Elementary Schools, Box 165, Talladega
Kelly, Mae, Director, Kilby Training School, 602 Morrison Ave., Florence
King, Anita, Supervisor, Lamar County Elementary Schools, Box 193, Vernon
Lea, Margaret E., Elementary Supervisor, Jefferson County Schools, Apt. 411, Claridge Manor, Birmingham 5
Leese, Joseph, Professor of Education, Alabama Polytechnic Institute
Locke, Mirian A., Supervisor of Elementary Schools, Board of Education, Jasper
Lucia, Mrs. Houston L., Supervisor, c/o Pike County Circulating Library, Pike County Schools, Troy
Mathews, Paul W., State Supervisor of Music, State Department of Education, Montgomery
McCall, W. Morrison, Director, Division of Instruction, State Department of Education, Montgomery
McClanahan, Elementary Supervisor, Cullman
McCorkle, Marietta, State Teachers College, Jacksonville
McFaddin, Geneva, Supervisor, St. Clair County, Ashville
Mixon, Lucille, Supervisor, Marion County, Hamilton
Moseley, C. C., Superintendent, Box 229, Anniston
Murphy, Esther, State Teachers College, Troy
Nichols, Luna, Elementary Supervisor, Monroeville
Obenchain, I. R., 1700 6th Ave. N., Board of Education, Birmingham 3
O'Rourke, Pauline County Supervisor, Barton Academy, Mobile 15
Owen, Dottie Pearl, Rt. 8, Box 394, Birmingham 8
Parton, Daisy, College of Education, University of Alabama, University
Penton, Mrs. J. A., County Supervisor, Clay St., Goodwater
Price, R. Holleman, 101 W. 2nd St., Montgomery 4
Samuels, J. D., Director, Division of Instruction, 907 Walnut St., Gadsden
Schurter, Elsie, Supervisor, Chilton County Elementary Schools, Box 132, Clanton
Simmons, I. F., State Teachers College, Florence
Smith, T. W., Assistant in Curriculum, State Department of Education, Montgomery 4
Sparks, Nona, Supervisor Elementary Schools, Moulton
Stone, Mrs. Ernest, Primary Supervisor, State Teachers College, Jacksonville
Tidwell, R. E., Director of Extension, University of Alabama, University
Tipton, Bess Fullerton, Supervisor, Blount County, Board of Education, Oneonta
Watson, G. M., County Superintendent of Education, Linden
Williams, Katie, Supervisor of Elementary Schools, Board of Education, Tuscaloosa
Whatley, Maude L., Principal, Central School, Tuscaloosa

ARIZONA

Meyers, George L., Principal, Keams Canyon Indian Boarding School, Keams Canyon

ARKANSAS

Baird, Lula Doyle, 605 Green St., Morrilton
Bird, C. L., Wilson

Blankenship, P. V., County Supervisor, Box 248, Huntsville
Chrisler, Verna, State Teachers College, Conway
Conrad, C. E., 2109 W. 17th St., Little Rock
Cordrey, E. E., State Teachers College, Conway
Cross, Charles H., University of Arkansas, Fayetteville
Dabney, Hazel L., Elementary Supervisor, City Schools, Pine Bluff
Hall, W. F., Elementary School Supervisor, State Department of Education, Little Rock
McKenzie, A. R., Sheridan
Nicholson, W. B., Superintendent of Schools, Blytheville
Owens, M. R., Director of Division of Instruction, State Department of Education, Little Rock
Pahotski, Minnie, Primary Supervisor, Fort Smith
Turner, Winnie Virgil, Elementary School Supervisor, Blytheville
Wright, Roy, County Supervisor, Mount Ida

CALIFORNIA

Abbey, Evelyn L., Elementary Supervisor, 115 N. Doheny, Beverly Hills
Abrams, Henry, Supervisor, Child Welfare and Attendance, Box 911, Visalia
Adams, Frances Hall, Director of Curriculum, 411 E. Wilson, Glendale
Adams, Grace Lucille, General Supervisor, 1156 Longwood Ave., Los Angeles 6
Adamson, Helena, Primary Coordinator, Box 225, Oceanside
Addicott, Irwin O., Assistant Superintendent, 2348 Mariposa St., Fresno
Albahr, A. A., 601 S. Vermont Ave., Los Angeles 5
Albert, Iris, Vocational Arts, Chamber of Commerce Bldg., Los Angeles 15
Aldridge, Ralph, Rt. 1, Box 147-A, Porterville
Alexander, Roxie E., Director, Elementary Education, 640 Virginia St., Vallejo
Alison, Lyle, Box 145, Crescent City
Allcutt, Alice P., Supervisor, Kindergarten-Primary, San Francisco State College, San Francisco 2
Alplanalp, Sarah, Elementary Supervisor, Box 772, Victorville
Anderson, Cecilia, Associate Professor of Education, San Francisco State College, San Francisco 2
Anderson, Diana, Supervisor of Instruction, 1216 N. Beverly Glenn Ave., Los Angeles
Anderson, Ida May, Art Supervisor, Chamber of Commerce Building, Los Angeles 15
Andres, Edna E., Elementary Supervisor, 429 W. 4th St., Ontario
Annear, Mrs. M. L., County Superintendent of Schools, Box 1038, Modesto
Archibald, Alice E., Principal, Mira Vista Elementary School, 635 28th St., Richmond
Argo, A. C., District Superintendent and Principal, Sequoia Union High School, Redwood
Ash, Sadie, County Superintendent of Schools, Colusa
Babcock, George T., Pacific Coast Manager, D. C. Heath, 182 Second St., San Franciso 5
Bain, Emerson, Director of Child Welfare, Madera County Schools, Madera
Barger, Anita, Elementary Supervisor, 1350 Louisiana St., Vallejo
Bartlett, Beulah D., Director of Curriculum, 640 California St., Box 723, Shafter
Baruch, Dorothy W., Professor of Education, Whittier College, 3250 Country Club Dr., Los Angeles 6
Base, Roy B., Director of Guidance, 1333 Sixth St., Santa Monica
Baxter, Bernice, Coordinator of Instruction, 1025 2nd Ave., Oakland
Bean, Minnie D., Supervisor of Rural Schools, School Office, Eureka
Beatty, Leslie S., General Supervisor, 461 S. Magnolia St., El Cajon

Bennett, Mabel, Elementary Supervisor, 601 N. Garfield, Alhambra
Bennett, Margaret E., Director of Guidance, Pasadena City Schools, 320 E. Walnut St., Pasadena
Bennett, Mildred E., Nelson Hall, Humboldt State College, Arcata
Berberick, Charlotte, Supervisor of Attendance, San Benito County, Box 660, Hollister
Bishop, F. E., District Superintendent of Schools, Corona
Bishop, H. F., Supervisor, 301 Hall of Records, Fresno
Blair, Maurice, Chamber of Commerce Building, Los Angeles 15
Bond, Jessie A., University of California at Los Angeles, Los Angeles
Borden, Hilma, Acting Vice-Principal, 1817 E. 10th St., Long Beach
Borneman, Katherine H., Assistant District Superintendent, Hayward City Schools, Hayward
Bowen, Wayne F., Treasurer California Teachers Association, 403 S. Tamarind St., Compton
Bowman, Carrie, Administration, 324 San Joaquin, Stockton 2
Boyer, Beatrice V., General Supervisor, c/o Office of Superintendent of Schools, Santa Maria
Bradford, Mrs. Leone L., Music Supervisor, Box 1007, Merced
Britton, Jasmine, 1205 W. Pico Blvd., Los Angeles
Brother, Mayme, Director of Curriculum, 534 Waverley, Palo Alto
Brown, Doris, Primary Supervisor, 8205 Locust St., Visalia
Brownlee, Robert, Director of Curriculum, 612 Vincento Ave., Berkeley
Bryant, Beatrice, Music Supervisor, San Joaquin County Schools, Stockton
Burgert, Robert, Acting Director Visual Instruction, 833 13th St., San Diego 2
Burke, Francis, General Supervisor, County Court House, Yreka
Burke, Teresa, Curriculum Director, Wasco Elementary Schools, Wasco
Burnham, Margaret, General Supervisor, County Court House, Redding
Burum, Winifred, Curriculum Consultant, Box 14, Delano
Butte, Agnes, Supervisor, 4455 Piedmont Ave., Oakland
Buttle, Agnes M., Supervisor, Elementary Education, University of California, Berkeley
Byers, Clifford E., County Court House, Bishop
Byer, Maude, Gerrior, Supervisor of Music, Santa Cruz County Schools, 23 2nd St., Santa Cruz
Byington, Barbara, Supervisor of Instruction, 526 S. Commonwealth, Los Angeles
Cameron, Christina B., Assistant Superintendent of Schools, Richmond City Schools, Administration Bldg., Richmond
Cameron, Mrs. Tene C., General Supervisor, Box 1353, Barstow
Camper, Ralph, Rural Supervisor, Glenn County, Willows
Cann, Margaret J., Health Supervisor, Office of County Superintendent of Schools, Madera
Cannon, Neva M. Cavanaugh, Rural Supervisor, 500 Harold St., Fort Bragg
Carbert, Charlotte, Supervisor of Instruction, 215 W. Hadley St., Whittier
Carpenter, Dale, Chamber of Commerce Building, Los Angeles 15
Cass, George T., Supervisor, Visual and Physical Education, Santa Clara County, Rt. 2, Box 202, Los Batos
Cassidy, Rosalind, Convener of School of Education and Community Services, Mills College, Oakland 13
Chandler, Constance, Coordinator of Research and Guidance, Education Building, Ventura
Chapman, Robert, 16 Jackson St., Woodland

LIST OF MEMBERS

Chapman, Thomas, Curriculum Director, Office of County Superintendent of Schools, Fresno
Cheathem, Wilma G., General Supervisor and Director of Reference, County Schools, Court House, Martinez
Choate, Robert, Music Supervisor, School Administration Building, Oakland 6
Christianson, Helen, Supervisor, 725 Woodruff Ave., Los Angeles
Clark, Willis, Research and Guidance Consultant, 7140 Mulholland Dr., Los Angeles 28
Cole, Stewart G., Bureau of Intercultural Education, 429 Chamber of Commerce Bldg., Los Angeles 15
Collins, Eleanor Freeman, Director of Curriculum, Office of County Superintendent of Schools, Redwood City
Combs, Julia E., Director, Tests and Measurements, Santa Rosa City Schools, Santa Rosa
Connor, Isabel, Departmental Assistant, 744 Santiago Ave., Long Beach 4
Convery, Sue, Elementary Supervisor, San Francisco Public Schools, 1761 16th Ave., San Francisco
Cook, Dorris, Music Supervisor, 421 30th St., Manhattan Beach
Cornelius, Sarah, Humboldt State College, Arcata
Covell, Eldon, Director of Elementary Education, Monterey City Schools, 1195 Franklin, Rt. 1, Box 796 A., Monterey
Cowan, Persis H., Assistant Coordinator of Instruction, Alameda County Schools, County Courthouse, Oakland
Cox, Vivian, Supervisor of Instruction, 1213 Pine St., Santa Monica
Coyner, Irean, Assistant in Instruction, Oakland Public Schools, 1025 2nd Ave., Oakland 1
Cralle Robert, City Superintendent of Schools, 8025 Maitland Ave., Inglewood
Croy, Hazel Miller, Supervising Principal, D St., Needles
Cryan, Mary M., Primary Supervisor, Box 132, Los Nietos
Curtis, Louis W., Music Section, 1205 W. Pico, Los Angeles
Dalander, Eva, Child Welfare Supervisor, San Joaquin County, Office of County Superintendent of Schools, Stockton
Dalk, David, General Supervisor, Office of County Superintendent of Schools, Hanford
Dabelich, Lillian, General Supervisor, 149 Locust, Santa Cruz
Danielson, Cora Lee, Education for Exceptional Children, Chamber of Commerce Building, Los Angeles 15
Davall, George, Chamber of Commerce Building, Los Angeles 15
Davis, Evelyn, Audio-Visual Supervisor, 270 Ravenna Dr., Long Beach
Davis, Georgia, General Supervisor, Office of County Superintendent of Schools, Modesto
Davison, Margaret, Director of Educational Measurements, 117 W. Cocoa St., Compton
Declusin, Ruth, General Supervisor, Court House, Stockton
DeJean, Marguerite, Assistant in Instruction, Oakland Public Schools, 1025 2nd Ave., Oakland
DeLappe, Maxine, Supervisor of Child Welfare, Stanislaus County Schools, Box 1, Modesto
Denlay, R. E., Superintendent, Box 710, Santa Paula
Dillon, Iva, Counselor, 725 Woodruff Ave., Los Angeles
Doak, Helen P., Supervisor of Instruction, 755 La Mirada Ave., San Marino
Dooley, Helen, Art Supervisor, Court House, Bakersfield
Downing, George M., Director, Guidance and Attendance, San Jose Public Schools, 408 Almeden St., San Jose
Drag, Francis L., Assistant Chief, Elementary Education, Civic Center, San Diego
Dubhorn, Elsie, General Supervisor, 433 W. Pueblo St., Santa Barbara

Dueker, Lois Mary, Supervisor of Instruction, 2212½ Valentine St., Los Angeles 26
Dugan, Clare K., 2140 N. Highland Ave., Hollywood 28
Dunn, Maud Wilson, Coordinator of Curriculum and Child Welfare, 715 Locust Ave., Long Beach 2
Duryee, Hazel, 432½ Palm Ave., Bellflower
Dwyr, Kathleen Ann, General Supervisor, Box 253, El Dorado
Dyke, Elmarie H., Rural Supervisor, Box 300, Pacific Grove
Eckman, O. L., Supervisor, Agriculture and Visual Education, 143 Lorimer, Salinas
Edmands, Ruth, Rural Supervisor, 820 Oak St., Colusa
Effinger, Eizabeth, Art Supervisor, 1500 E. Villa St., Pasadena
Elliott, Lila, Rural Supervisor, Court House, Hollister
Elliott, Stephen, Supervisor, 408 N. Montebello Blvd., Montebello
Erdt, Margaret, Art Supervisor, 8th and F Sts., San Bernardino
Erro, Mercedes, General Supervisor, 3535½ Park Blvd, San Diego 3
Erwin, Susie R., Supervisor of Instruction, Box 30, El Monte
Esrey, Margaret M., Supervisor, Box 336, Yreka
Esser, Birdie, Curriculum Coordinator, San Joaquin County Schools, Office of County Superintendent of Schools, Stockton
Etter, Carl, Supervisor, Chamber of Commerce Building, Los Angeles 15
Evans, Mary, County Court House, Santa Barbara
Evans, Paul, General Supervisor, Siskiyou County, Yreka
Fairman, Louise, 663 Seele, Palo Alto
Farnum, Martha T., Instructional Coordinator, 300 B. Ave., Coronado
Fathian, Maud, Supervisor, 2780 10th St., Sacramento
Favier, Florence, Supervisor, Girls Physical Education, 1526 Arch St., Berkeley 8
Fay, Arline, Special Teacher, 209 Civic Center, San Diego 1
Fields, Ralph, Assistant Superintendent, 408 Almaden Ave., San Jose
Fielstra, Clarence, Curriculum Coordinator, 209 Civic Center, San Diego 1
Findlay, Bruce, Head Supervisor, 1205 W. Pico, Los Angeles
Fitzsimons, Ethel, Primary Supervisor, Office of County Superintendent of Schools, Madera
Fleeson, Romona, County Coordinator of Arts and Crafts, Court House, Oakland
Frazier, Alexander, Secondary Curriculum Coordinator, 808 N. Spring St., Los Angeles
Fox, Dorothy Naomi, Supervisor of Health and Physical Education, 1113 13th St., Modesto
Frost, Nellie, Rural Supervisor, Riverside County Court House, Riverside
Gallagher, Dora, 6522 Orange St., Los Angeles
Gallant, Alice, Music Supervisor, County Court House, Madera
Gandy, Jannie, Art Director, 701 S. Sloan Ave., Compton
Gansberger, Dorothy, Principal, San Lorenzo Village School, 102 Lewelling Blvd, San Lorenzo
Garcia, Alys Clare, Supervisor, San Leandro City Schools, San Leandro
Geddes, Mabel, Supervisor of Health, 312 Court House, Santa Ana
Gentry, Dorothy R., Supervisor, Humboldt State College, Arcata
Gerholdt, Anna Forbes, General Supervisor, Sonona County Schools, 715 Mendocino Ave., Santa Rosa
Getsinger, J. W., Box 442, La Jolla
Gibbs, Elsie, Director of Secondary Education, 729 19th St. San Bernardino
Gibson, Carmen, Supervisor of Music, Imperial County, El Centro

Gibson, Frank, Supervisor of Physical Education, County Court House, Riverside
Gifford, Myrtie, Chairman, Art Department, 1414 Walnut St., Berkeley 7
Gilbert, Isabel, Curriculum Coordinator, Court House, Riverside
Gildea, Eva, Supervisor of Student Teaching, San Francisco State College, San Francisco 2
Glines, Dora P., Assistant Superintendent, Court House Annex, Santa Ana
Goldsworthy, Philoma, Supervisor, Art Education, San Jose State College, 1209 Glenn Ave., San Jose
Goode, Louise H., Office of County Superintendent, Nevada City
Gordon, Lola Fay, General Elementary Supervisor, Santa Clara County Schools, 466 N. 2nd St., San Jose 11
Gould, Betty, Supervisor of Child Welfare, Kern County Schools, Administration Bldg., Bakersfield
Grant, Adele L., Supervisor of Science, 6019 S. Overhill Dr., Los Angeles
Griffiths, Ciwa, Specialist in Speed and Hearing, San Diego County Schools, 209 Civic Center, San Diego 1
Grindstaff, Leonard, Curriculum Coordinator, Palo Alto City Schools, Palo Alto
Gunter, Miriam, 631 1st St., Woodland
Hall, Henry C., General Supervisor, County Court House, Redwood City
Halverson, Edna, Elementary Music Supervisor, Box 962, Oxnard
Hamm, Katherine, Supervisor of Tests, Bin 911, Visalia
Hanna, Lavone A., Supervisor of Curriculum and Educational Research, 715 Locust St., Long Beach 2
Hanna, Paul R., Professor of Education, Stanford University, Stanford University
Hansen, Botilda J., General Supervisor, Santa Clara County Schools, Hall of Records, San Jose
Hansen, Oden, General Supervisor, County Court House, Eureka
Harris, Alta, General Elementary Supervisor, San Francisco City Schools, 81 Garcia St., San Francisco 16
Hart, Anna Marie, General Supervisor, Weaverville
Hartshorn, William, Music Section, 1205 W. Pico Blvd., Los Angeles
Hartsig, Barbara, Supervisor of Instruction, Mt. View School District, El Monte, 420 Lindaraxa, Alhambra
Harville, Mae W., General Supervisor, Court House, Oakland
Haskell, Jessica, School Psychologist, 715 Locust Ave., Long Beach
Hause, Edna Mae, Primary Coordinator, Box 395, Chula Vista
Haworth, Harry H., Supervisor of Library and Visual Instruction, 1501 E. Walnut St., Pasadena
Hayes, J. D., 312 Court St. Annex, Santa Ana
Heffernan, Helen, Chief, Elementary Education and Rural Schools, State Department of Education, Sacramento 14
Helms, Walter T., City Superintendent of Schools, Richmond
Hender, Fritzi, General Supervisor, Sonora
Heryford, C. B., Rural Supervisor, Ukiah
Heurlin, Constance, Court House, Colusa
Hidden, Elizabeth, Associate Professor of Education, University of Redlands, 14 Clifton St., Redlands
Higgins, Ethel L., General Supervisor, San Louis Obispo County, Box 142, Atascadero
Hill, Ruby L., Supervisor of Junior High Elementary Education, 421 Western Dr., Richmond
Hockett, John A., Associate Director of Training, Department of Education, University of California, 405 Hilgard Ave., Los Angeles
Hodges, Rozelle G., Teacher Curriculum Worker, 806 E. Carson Blvd., Long Beach 7

Hoffman, Howardine, Elementary Education 808 N. Spring St., Los Angeles 12
Holland, Margaret, Supervisor, Guidance and Counseling, Civic Auditorium, San Francisco 2
Hord, Florence Norse, Supervisor of Art, Riverside County, Riverside
Houx, Kate, Curriculum Assistant, Los Angeles County, 808 N. Spring St., Los Angeles 12
Howe, Corinne, State Department of Education, 1515 10th St., Sacramento 14
Howell, Youldon C., Director of Art Education, 215 W. Montana, Pasadena
Hoyt, C. Russell, General Supervisor, Box 730, San Luis Obispo
Hubbard, O. S., Curriculum Coordinator of Secondary Schools, Hall of Records, San Jose
Hughes, Marie M., Curriculum Coordinator, 1660 Ramiro Rd., Pasadena
Hunt, Lucy, Superintendent of Schools, Shasta County, Redding
Hunter, Evelyn, Supervisor of Child Welfare, Box 18, Eureka
Hutcheon, Helen C., Music Supervisor, c/o County Superintendent of Schools, Hanford
Irvine, Cecilia R., Social Studies Coordinator, 11800 Texas Ave., West Los Angeles 25
Irwin, Susan B., Supervisor in Art, San Francisco State College, 555 Buena Vista Ave., San Francisco 17
Israel, Marion, Curriculum Assistant, 5010 Navarro, Los Angeles 32
James, Katrine E., Music Supervisor, 115 N St., Madera
Jans, Raymund, Supervisor of Child Welfare, Rt. 1, Durham
Jegi, Evelyn, Supervisor of Attendance, 863 Waller St., San Francisco 17
Jenkins, Marian, Coordinator, 34 S. Mentor Ave., Pasadena
Jenner, Gladys, Supervisor, South District Office, Chamber of Commerce Building, Los Angeles 15
Jensen, Harry T., Associate Professor of Education, San Jose State College, 355 S. 16th St., San Jose 12
Johnson, Loaz, Curriculum Coordinator, Office of Superintendent, Oroville
Johnson, T. D., General Supervisor, Lakeport
Kaar, Harold W., Director of Supervision, Contra Costa County Schools, 840 Lafayette St., Martinez
Kaartinen, Inez, General Supervisor, 516 1st St., Woodland
Karstetdt, Virginia W., Rural School Supervisor in Home Economics, Santa Clara County Schools, Hall of Records, San Jose 18
Kauppi, Emily Veblen, Elementary Supervisor, Office of County Superintendent of Schools, Civic Center, San Diego 1
Keagy, Mrs. William A., Supervisor, Redding
Keesler, Dean, Supervisor of Music, Box 834, Santa Cruz
Keller, Helen B., 1856 Sepulveda Blvd., Los Angeles 25
Kelley, Lorene, Director, Audio-Visual and Library Services, Alameda County Schools, 1715 High St., Oakland
Kellogg, Rhoda, 570 Union St., San Francisco
Kenneally, Finbar, Professor, San Luis Rey Seminary, The Old Mission, San Luis Rey
Kentor, Frances, Supervisor of Child Welfare, 909 14th St., Modesto
Kepley, Ruth A., Rural Supervisor, Court House, El Centro
Kindy, V. R., High School Consultant, Box 911, Visalia
King, Ben F., Supervisor of Attendance, Woodland
Kinney, Ernestine, Supervisor of Student Teaching, Occidental College, 1600 Campus Rd., Los Angeles
Kirkegaard, Lily H., Music Supervisor, Bin 911, Visalia
Knapp, W. A., Supervisor of Child Welfare, 11426th St., Merced

LIST OF MEMBERS

Koenig, Dorothy, Field Assistant, Los Angeles County, 808 N. Spring St., Los Angeles 12
Kranz, Helen, Rural Supervisor, 2451 Lexington, Ventura
Kyle, Anna, Music Supervisor, Solano County, Fairfield
Kyte, George C., Professor of Education, Haviland Hall, University of California, Berkeley
Laird, J. David, Superintendent of City Schools, Tulare
Lands, Elizabeth, Chamber of Commerce Building, Los Angeles 15
Largent, Lydia, Art Supervisor, 93 Grove St., San Francisco 2
Laws, Gertrude, Director of Education for Women, 3630 E. Mt. View Ave., Pasadena 8
Leathurby, Grace, Principal, Fredric Burk School, San Francisco State College, San Francisco 2
Lee, Mina, Rural Supervisor, Santa Cruz
Leever, Dale V., Chamber of Commerce Building, Los Angeles 15
Lewerenz, Alfred, Research and Guidance, Chamber of Commerce Building, Los Angeles 15
Leonard, F. R., Rural Supervisor, Ukiah
Leonard, J. Paul, President San Francisco State College, San Francisco
Lewis, Hazel, Director of Research, 324 N. San Joaquin St., Stockton 2
Lincoln, Cornelia A., General Supervisor, Contra Costa County Schools, Court House Martinez
Lindemann, Maud E., Rural Supervisor, Rt. 1, Box 31, Chowchilla
Lindquist, Gustave, Western District, 1740 N. New Hampshire, Los Angeles
Lindquist, Rudolph, Superintendent of Schools, Santa Barbara
Longenback, Louise, General Supervisor, County Court House, Auburn
Lonsdale, Bernard, Assistant on Course of Study, 808 N. Spring St., Los Angeles 12
Lossing, Laverna, Music Supervisor, 725 Woodruff Ave., Los Angeles
Loyd, Melba Jean, Music Supervisor, Box 1150, Porterville
Lowden, Mary, Supervisor of Elementary School, Richmond
Lund, Agnes M., Assistant Professor of Education, San Francisco State College, San Francisco 2
Lykins, Lee T., Supervisor of Music, Alameda County Schools, Court House, Oakland
MacLeod, Margaret Anne, Director of Education, 415 California St., El Monte
MacPherson, Margaret, Teacher Librarian, 1288 N. Allen, Pasadena
Madden, Richard, Director of Teacher Training, San Diego State College, San Diego 5
Malumphy, Rosanna, Art Supervisor, 1804 S. 8th St., Alhambra
Martenson, Helen, 1111 W. 60th St., Los Angeles 44
Martin, Eleanore C., General Supervisor, 1943 M St., Merced
Martin, Elsie M., Teacher, Isbell School, 615 Santa Paula St., Santa Paula
Martin, Ethel H., Supervisor of Home Economics, 11063 Massachusetts Ave., Los Angeles 25
Martin, Grace E., General Supervisor, 701 Pine St., Susanville
Martin, Vibella, Associate Director, University of California Curriculum Laboratory, 636 Hillgird Circle, Oakland
McAvoy, Eunice, Speech Department, Richmond City Schools, Administration Bldg., Richmond
McCammon, J. Harvey, Director of Audio-Visual Education, 126 N. Church St., Visalia
McCollister, Edith, Director of Elementary Music, Redlands
McElvain, Mrs. Dan
McGill, Elizabeth, Supervisor of Speech, 1492 Upham St., San Luis Obispo
McGovern, Elsie, District Supervisor, Bakersfield
McIntyre, Annie L., General Elementary Supervisor, 718 E. Harvard St., Glendale 5
McNutt, Marie, 5801 Gundry Ave., Long Beach
McQuaid, Katherine R., Rural Supervisor, Yuba County, 411 7th St., Marysville
Mead, Nelle M., Supervisor, Grades 1-4, 216 Athol Ave., Oakland
Meade, Robert J., Director, Audio-Visual Education, Contra Costa County Schools, Court House, Martinez
Melka, Katherine, 2205 Greenleaf, Santa Ana
Mellor, Bethel, Curriculum Coordinator, Office of County Superintendent of Schools, Hanford
Mendenhall, Warren O., Assistant County Superintendent, Santa Ana
Merigold, Dorothy C., Supervisor of Teacher Training, 1954 Greenfield Ave., Los Angeles 25
Merrill Anne, Supervisor, Elementary Education, School of Education, University of California, Berkeley
Messinger, Ray, Supervisor, Rm. 117, Court House, Bakersfield
Michaelis, John, Director of Teacher Training, Fresno State College, Fresno
Mickelson, Esther, 329 W. Micheltorena St., Santa Barbara
Miller, Elizabeth, Elementary Supervisor, Box 461, Placentia
Mills, Flossie E., Supervisor, 1600 K St., Bakersfield
Minch, Grace D., General Supervisor, Office of County Superintendent of Schools, Red Bluff
Mitchel, Josephine, Music Supervisor, 808 N. Spring St., Los Angeles, Calif.
Mitchell, Audry, General Supervisor, Alameda County Schools, 3050 Richmond Blvd., Oakland
Moffitt, Helen E., General Supervisor and Director of Research, Santa Clara County Schools, San Jose 12
Money, Kenneth, Curriculum Coordinator, 24 Alta Vista Way, San Rafael
Monroe, Alta, Director of Audio-Visual Education, Box 628, Eureka
Monroe, Blythe F., Principal, Primary Schools, 1001 Roberts Lane, Bakersfield
Moore, Maurine L., Supervising Coordinator, Box 851, Ventura
Moritz, Irene, Director of Research, San Mateo County Schools, 236 W. Poplar Ave., San Mateo
Morrison, Emma V., Director of Elementary Education, Santa Clara County Schools, Hall of Records, San Jose
Mortensen, Ada B., Supervisor of Health, Kings County Schools, c/o County Superintendent of Schools, Hanford
Moyes, Rhea, Principal, 2900 E. Arbot Vitae, Inglewood
Munce, Tillie C., Primary Supervisor, 14 Glenn Ave., Fresno
Murphy, Edith, Director of Home Economics, 93 Grove St., San Francisco 2
Murray, Josephine, 1235 Chapala, Santa Barbara
Murray, Katharine K., Elementary Supervisor, Court House, San Bernardino
Nance, Afton, Primary Supervisor, County Schools, Court House, Riverside
Naslund, Robert, General Supervisor, County Court House, Alturas
Neideffer, R. T., Director of Elementary Education, Administration Building, 1600 K St., Bakersfield
Nelson, Frances, Elementary Supervisor, 631 A. Virginia Terrace, Santa Paula
Newby, Ruth, Acting Curriculum Coordinator, 527 E. Washington St., Pasadena
Newton, Elda Mills, Assistant Superintendent County Court House, Oroville

Nicolls, Mary M., Attendance Coordinator, San Diego City Schools, San Diego
Noyes, E. Louise, Head, English Department, 425 Stanley Dr., Samarkand Hills, Santa Barbara
O'Neil, Agnes, Music Supervisor, 701 Paloma St., Burlingame
O'Rear, Margaret, Attendance Supervisor, 1167 E. Maple, Bellflower
O'Rourke, E. V., Curriculum Coordinator, Court House, Woodland
Ott, Eva M., Principal, 61 Agnes St., Oakland 11
Palm, Ruben R., Secondary Coordinator, 2041 Hanscom Dr., South Pasadena
Page, Amorette, Supervisor of Child Welfare, Box 730, San Luis Obispo
Paradise, Margaret, Curriculum Coordinator, 209 Civic Center, San Diego 1
Parker, J. C., Director of Curriculum, Board of Education, Civic Auditorium, San Francisco
Parrish, Maude R., Western District, 1740 N. New Hampshire, Los Angeles
Paterson, Elsie, Attendance Supervisor, Court House, Riverside
Patten, Ruth H., General Elementary Supervisor, Richmond City Schools, 2709 Dwight Way, Berkeley
Penn, Carl, Rural School Supervisor, 1119 Morgan St., Santa Rosa
Perrin, Della M., General Elementary Supervisor, Contra Costa County Schools, Court House, Martinez
Peterson, Clara F., Art Supervisor, 1235 Chapala St., Santa Barbara
Peterson, Mayme, Supervisor, Box 271, Santa Rosa
Peterson, Raymond C., Supervisor of Attendance, 715 Locust St., Long Beach 2
Pfister, Elta, Director of Individual Guidance, City Schools, Burbank
Pfleiderer, Vivian, Assistant Elementary Curriculum Coordinator, 116 N. Ave. 29, Los Angeles 31
Phelan, Arthur, General Supervisor, County Court House, Independence
Philips, Catherine, Director of Elementary Art, Box 1101, Palosverdes Estates, Redlands
Pierce, Thelma, Elementary Supervisor, 630 Main St., Santa Paula
Pinkerton, Nene, Elementary Supervisor, Eureka
Pixley, Irma, Chamber of Commerce Bldg., Los Angeles 15
Platt, Mollie S., General Supervisor, 813 13th St., Modesto
Poore, Shirley, Supervisor of Art, 715 Locust St., Long Beach 2
Poppett, Carol, Supervising Principal, County Court House, San Bernardino
Porter, Katherine Page, Supervisor of Art, 221 a S. Gale, Beverly Hills
Potter, Gladys L., Elementary School Supervisor, 715 Locust St., Long Beach 2
Prall, Lanore, Primary Supervisor, 7531 31st St., Richmond
Pratt, Meriam L., General Supervisor, 602 La Loma, Modesto
Prouty, Patricia, Music Supervisor, 4440 Lemon St., Riverside
Rademacher, Eva, Director of Elementary Education, Office of Superintendent of Schools, Redlands
Railback, Floy, General Supervisor, Court House, Oakland
Ramsdell, Carl G., Attendance and Employment of Minors, Chamber of Commerce Bldg., Los Angeles 15
Ranney, Herman, Child Welfare Coordinator, 312 Court House Annex, Santa Ana
Ransberger, Marguerite, County Court House, Santa Barbara
Rasmussen, Anne, Rt. 1, Box 476, Upland
Rea, Beatrice, General Supervisor, 309 S. L St., Madera
Rea, Josephine, General Elementary Supervisor, Contra Costa County Schools, Court House, Martinez

Redit, Edith, Supervisor, Training School, San Diego State College, San Diego 5
Reed, Helen Sue, Demonstration Teacher, 533 Mt. Holyoke Ave., Pacific Palisades
Reed, Ruth H., General Supervisor, 3239 Arrowhead, San Bernardino
Reid, Virginia, Assistant in Instruction, Oakland City Schools, 1025 2nd Ave., Oakland 6
Reinhard, Grace, Primary Supervisor, Office of County Superintendent of Schools, Hanford
Reinhard, Robert H., Assistant Superintendent, 1012 N. Main St., Santa Ana
Rhodes, Alvin E., Curriculum Director, Box 730, Office of County Superintendent of Schools, San Luis Obispo
Rice, Helen M., Elementary Supervisor, 8300 Kitty Hawk, Los Angeles 43
Rice, Mabel F., Supervisor of Student Teaching, Whittier College, Whittier
Richardson, Julia Ruth, Elementary Coordinator, 3201 30th St., San Diego 4
Richmond, Mildred, General Supervisor, 525 E. 6th St., Madera
Riecks, Eva A., Director of Guidance, 25 Parkwood Dr., Apt. 11, Redlands
Riegel, Veta R., Escondido Union Elementary School, Escondido
Risinger, Maude, Supervisor, Chamber of Commerce Building, Los Angeles 15
Robbins, Rintha, General Supervisor, 46 18th St., Apt. 10, Merced
Robinson, Jack, Director of Elementary Education, Box 140, Clearwater
Robinson, Mardelle, Elementary Supervisor, 1809 Gillette Crescent, South Pasadena
Robison, Eleanor, Assistant in Instruction, Oakland Public Schools, 1025 2nd Ave., Oakland 6
Ross, Lucile, Supervisor of Music, 3531 Park Blvd., San Diego 3
Rowley, Marion, General Supervisor, 411 E. Wilson Ave., Glendale
Russell, David H., Associate Professor, School of Education, University of California, Berkeley 4
Russell, Theresa, Supervisor of Health, Kings County Schools, Box 71, Hanford
Ryan, Lunney, Box 418, Centerville
Salisbury, Frank S., 1356 La Solona Dr., Altadena
Sampson, Mabel, General Supervisor, Alameda County Schools, 2558 E. 27th St., Oakland 1
Sanderson, Susie, Supervisor, Chamber of Commerce Building, Los Angeles 15
Sands, Elizabeth, 711 Chamber of Commerce Building, Los Angeles 15
Schoepfle, Irene, General Supervisor, Court House Annex, Santa Ana
Schwartz, Anna L., Court House Annex, Oroville
Seeds, Corinne, Principal, University of California, Demonstration School, Los Angeles
Seeling, Martha, Director of Elementary Education, Court House Annex, Oroville
Severns, Joe, General Supervisor, Visalia
Shearer, Elga M., Supervisor of Intermediate Grades, 3957 E. 3rd St., Long Beach
Sheldon, Edna R., Attendance and Employment of Minors, Chamber of Commerce Bldg., Los Angeles 15
Sherrod, Jane, General Elementary Supervisor, 320 Bonita, Piedmont
Shipp, F. T., Abraham Lincoln High School, San Jose
Short, Eleanor, 1543 Hamilton Ave., San Jose
Simpson, Vera, Rural Supervisor, 726 Arrowhead Ave., San Bernardino
Sister Mary Conciline, B. V. M., Supervisor, 2250 Franklin St., San Francisco
Sister Mary Regis, 2021 N. Western Ave., Los Angeles 27
Smallenburg, Harry, Director of Research, 804 S. Sunset Canyon Dr., Burbank
Smith, Bernice, 120 C St., Oxnard
Smitter, Faith, Coordinator of Research, Kings County Schools, 808 N. Spring St., Los Angeles

LIST OF MEMBERS

Springer, Florence, Elementary Counselor, 603 Grand Ave., South Pasadena
Stanchfield, Bessie, Curriculum Coordinator, 808 N. Spring St., Los Angeles
Standerfer, Doris, Supervisor of Art Education, 727 Bristol, Stockton
Stegeman, William H., Supervisor, Guidance and Child Welfare, Contra Costa County Schools, 1120 Shell Ave., Martinez
Steigler, Sylvia, Art Supervisor, 118 W. J St., Ontario
Stewart, Olive, Supervisor of Social Studies, Department of Education, University of California, 15 Arlington Ct., Berkeley
Straley, Ruth, Supervisor, Chico State College, Chico
Stratton, Florence M., Assistant Supervisor of Curriculum, 3983 S. Van Ness, Los Angeles
Streit, Helen E., Director, Child Care Centers, 3100 Imperial Highway, Lynwood
Stroud, Clara H., Director of Instruction, County Court House, Auburn
Sughrue, Lava, Director, Elementary Education, 2808 Stoddard Ave., San Bernardino
Sullivan, Charles Lano, 1026 Delaware St., Fairfield
Symns, Edith, Art Director, 1727 Linden, South Pasadena
Swatszel, Dorothy, Assistant, Elementary Curriculum Department, 320 E. Walnut St., Pasadena 4
Taft, Chester A., Director, Child Welfare and Attendance, 111 N. Grevillea Ave., Inglewood
Taggart, Lelia, Director of Education, Office of County Superintendent of Schools, Santa Barbara
Tantau, Louise Brier, Supervisor of Speech, Tulare County, Exeter
Terry, John Gayer, Assistant Superintendent of Schools, 816 S. Locust St., Visalia
Terwilliger, Leafy, Art Director, 523 W. School St., Porterville
Thomas, Helen S., Supervisor, San Francisco State College, San Francisco
Thomas, J. Herold, Attendance and Employment of Minors, Chamber of Commerce Bldg., Los Angeles 15
Thomas, Margaret, Director of Child Welfare, 2348 Mariposa St., Fresno 1
Thompson, Alma, General Supervisor, County Court House, Eureka
Thompson, Olive L., Elementary Coordinator, 3532 Indiana St., San Diego
Thornley, Doris M., Supervisor of Child Welfare and Attendance, Box 316, Santa Cruz
Thornton, James W., Jr., Curriculum Director, Sequoia Union High School, Redwood
Thrower, Georgeine, Supervisor, 1740 N. New Hampshire, Los Angeles
Tolle, Vernon, Director, School of Education, Redlands University, 714 11th St., Redlands
Tolman, Paulyne, Supervisor, West District Office, Chamber of Commerce Building, Los Angeles 15
Trott, Frederick, General Supervisor and Director of Curriculum, Visalia
Upholt, Liefy V., Supervisor, Court House, El Centro
Uriell, Vida, Santa Clara Union High School, Santa Clara
Van Voorhees, Margaret, Office of Superintendent of Schools, 209 Civic Center, San Diego 1
Waddell, Charles W., Director Teacher Training, University of California, 10630 Lindbrook Dr., Los Angeles 24
Walter, R. B., Chief Deputy County Superintendent, 434 N. Del Mar, San Gabriel
Walters, Paul, General Supervisor, Solano County Schools, County Court House, Fairfield
Wandling, Harry, Coordinator, 1065 E. 7th St., Chico
Ward, Ethel S., Coordinator and Director of Instruction, Alameda County Schools, Court House, Oakland
Ware, Beulah, 206 Bennett Ave., Long Beach

Weakley, G. A., Superintendent, 10th and Brighton Sts., El Centro
Wedberg, Alma, Rural Supervisor, 8215 W. 4th St., Los Angeles
White, Joseph F., Director of Visual Education, Education Bldg., Box 851, Ventura
White, Madeline, 305 Pickering Way, Montebello
White, Natalie, 533 Mt. Holyoke Ave., Pacific Palisades
Wickersham, Louise, Director of Elementary Education, 1068 Cypress Ave., Burbank
Wiese, Edna L., Supervisor, Chamber of Commerce Building, Los Angeles 15
Wiles, May B., Primary Supervisor, Rm. 301 Court House, Sacramento
Wilkinson, Dorothy Hunn, Principal, Washington School, Richmond Ave. and Wine, Richmond
Wilkinson, Hazel, Counselor East District, Chamber of Commerce Bldg., Los Angeles 15
Willey, Walter O., Principal, El Rodeo School, 605 Whittier Dr., Beverly Hills
Wilson, Douglas, Chamber of Commerce Building, Los Angeles 15
Wilson, Eleanore, Supervisor, 800 E. San Antonio Dr., Long Beach 5
Wilson, Lenore, Assistant Professor of Education, Mills College, Box 414, Oakland 13
Wisely, Edna, General Supervisor, Ventura County Schools, 453 S. Anacapa St., Ventura
Wiser, Harry D., General Supervisor, Director Child Welfare and Attendance, Box 837, Fairfield
Wolf, Beulah Paul, Director Rural Education, 2107 Mt. View, San Bernardino
Wood, El Doris, Primary General Supervisor, 424 Grand Ave., South Pasadena
Wood, Gertrude, Coordinator of Research, 808 N. Spring St., Los Angeles 12
Woods, Elizabeth L., Educational Research and Guidance, Board of Education, Los Angeles
Works, Charlotte, Office of County Superintendent of Schools, Court House, Redwood City
Wray, Ruth C., General Supervisor, Office of County Superintendent, Ventura
Wright, Francis, Music Teacher and Supervisor, 405 Hilgard Ave., Los Angeles
Wuerth, Ruth, General Supervisor, 1108 Bissell Ave., Richmond
Wulfing, Gretchen, Supervisor, Elementary Education, Oakland City Schools, 1025 2nd Ave., Oakland 6
Zinn, Mildred, Rt. 2, Box 917, El Cajon
Zumwalt, Gladys, General Supervisor, 403 McHenry, Modesto

COLORADO

Adams, Elsie W., 1640 Jackson, Denver 6
Ahrens, Maurice, Supervisor, 414 14th St., Denver 2
Alden, Ruth Viola, 1530 Grant St., Denver 5
Allphin, Helen, Supervisor, 414 14th St., Denver 2
Anderson, Ruth H., Principal, Gove Junior High School, 14th Ave. & Colorado Blvd., Denver 7
Andrews, S. M., Box 742, Walsenburg
Baerresen, Viola, 1515 Grant, Denver 5
Bellmar, Marie, Teacher, 201 S. Humboldt St., Denver
Biddle, Richard, High School Principal, Box 93, Rifle
Blixt, Lillian E., 3811 Clay St., Denver 11
Bostwick, Prudence, Supervising Teacher, 414 14th St., Denver 2
Botleman, L. J., Superintendent, High School Bldg., Trinidad
Burbrink, Teresa M., Supervisor of Physical Education, 1412 E. Pike Peak St., Colorado Springs
Burkhard, Elmer L., Superintendent, Bent County High School, Las Animas
Byrne, Helen, Teacher, 726 S. Yorke St., Denver 9

Carey, Nina, 865 S. Penn St., Denver 9
Clapp, Joy, Principal, Junior High School, 3000 Grove St., Denver 11
Coleman, Geneva E., Director, Elementary Education, 621 S. Meldrum St., Fort Collins
Daniels, Winifred J., 2155 S. Emerson St., Denver 10
Davidson, Marie, Teacher, 1337 California St., Denver 4
Doull, Frances R., Elementary Principal, 1250 Logan St., Denver 3
Dynes, John J., Chairman, Division of Education and Psychology, Western State College, Gunnison
Fox, Guy, Director, Department of Pupil Personnel, 414 14th St., Denver 2
Gebhart, Orthia, 1590 S. Ogden St., Denver 10
Gilley, C. T., Eads Public School, Eads
Glendenning, Katherine S., Teacher, 1001 Logan St., Denver 3
Goldman, Edythe, Principal, Smedley Elementary School, 1570 Fairfax St., Denver
Gore, W. R., Superintendent, 406 Penn St., Walsenburg
Gumlick, Helen R., Supervisor, 414 14th St., Denver 2
Hall, Dorothy M., Elementary Principal, 703 Polk St., Pueblo
Harper, Florence S., Social Studies Teacher, 121 E. 16th Ave., Denver 5
Hays, Catherine Downes, Principal, Boettcher School, 1000 S. Steele St., Denver 9
Henry, Edith M., Principal, Wyatt School, 700 Cherry St., Denver 7
Hill, Wilhelmina, Director, Elementary Education Workshop, University of Denver, Denver 10
Holmes, Chrystal, 1420 Logan St., Denver 3
Holmes, Ethel E., Principal, Wyman School, 2610 S. Sherman St., Denver
Jenkins, R. D., Superintendent, Englewood High School, Englewood
Kane, Anna E., Elementary Teacher, 2632 Cherry, Denver 7
Kinyon, Kate W., Director, Home Economics, Public Schools, 414 14th St., Denver 2
Lind, Nellie V., Principal, Washington Park School, S. Race and Mississippi Sts., Denver
Loomis, Arthur K., Director, School of Education, University of Denver, Denver 9
Mehl, Marie, Instructor, Elementary Education, 940 14th St., Boulder
Mills, H. H., Associate Professor of Education, University of Colorado, Boulder
Moore, Alice L., Teacher, 460 Clayton St., Denver 6
Mullins, Cecil, Superintendent of Schools, Cheraw
Neal, Bertha C., Elementary Teacher, 2081 S. Fillmore St., Denver 10
Newlon, Ruth H., Senior High Teacher, 1075 S. Fillmore St., Denver 9
Noce, Lillian, Principal, 3726 Vallejo St., Denver 11
O'Brien, Irene, Head, Department of Education and Dean of Women, Ft. Lewis College, Hesperus
O'Sullivan, Alice, 2037 Gaylord St., Denver 5
Pendleton, Claud B., Principal, Horth High School, N. Speer Blvd. and Eliot St., Denver 11
Phillips, Aleyne I., Primary Teacher, 2721 W. 25th Ave., Denver 11
Proudfit, Flora Arline, 1050 S. Ogden, Denver 9
Rawson, Kenneth A., 421 Bowen, Longmont
Rishel, J. B., Principal, Barnum School, W. 1st and Hooker Sts., Denver
Ritter, Rosamund C., Elementary Teacher, 2757 W. Denver Pl., Denver 11
Scott, Wilma, Principal Central School, Greeley
Slavens, Leon E., Principal, 1315 Grape St., Denver 7
Sparhawk, Elizabeth, 1515 E. 9th Ave., Denver 3
Staats, Pauline G., 2505 S. Bannock, Denver 10
Stewart, Dorothea H., Elementary Principal, Rt. 1, Durango
Stone, Clark H., Principal, Grant Junior High School, S. Pearl and Colorado Ave., Denver 9
Swan, Carla, Parent Education, Pre-school, 461 Humboldt St., Denver 3
Taylor, Esther F., 325 Birch St., Denver 7
Wagnild, Lillian, Primary Teacher, 2818 Gaylord St., Denver 5
Waldhauser, D. W., Superintendent, Craig
Warren, Hugh M., Principal, Washington and Lowell Schools, 3500 S. Sherman St., Englewood
Wasson, Roy J., Superintendent, 406 N. Weber St., Colorado Springs
Willey, Gilbert S., Director of Instruction, Public Schools, 2275 S. Columbine, Denver
Worley, Vivienne S., 1019 Logan, Apt. 8, Denver 3
Yardley, Hattie, Director of Instruction, New Junior High School, Greeley

CONNECTICUT

Alexander, William M., USNR, Yale University, New Haven
Bourgeois, William L., Griswold High School, Jewett City
Condon, Anna A., Elementary School Principal, 74 Garden St., Stamford
Daniels, Katharine, Director, Elementary Instruction, School Administration Bldg., Hartford
Fuller, Harvey, Superintendent, 200 Main St., Wethersfield 9
Gustin, Margaret, Assistant Field Supervisor, State Board of Education, Unionville
King, Lois J., Supervisor of Student Teaching, New Haven State Teachers College, 2 Howe St., New Haven 11
Lawerence, L. Gertrude, Elementary Supervisor, Mitchell School, Wethersfield 9
Leister, LeRoy L., Superintendent Towns of Montville and Waterford, Box 1027, New London
Lewis, Gertrude M., Teaching Assistant, Yale University, 715 York St., New Haven
Lyons, John H., Director of Guidance and Visual Aids, Box 142, Thompsonville
Lyons, Margaret A., Curriculum Consultant, Public Schools, New Haven
Nybakken, Ernest O., Field Superintendent, State Department of Education Canaan
Rein, Dorothy E., Principal, 32 Girard Ave., Hartford
Schwartz, Pauline P., 84 Howe St., New Haven 11
Seidel, Ida E., Assistant Supervisor, State Department of Education, 1 Essex Sq., Essex
Sister Mary Laura, 1335 Enfield St., Enfield
Tompkins, Harriett, Primary Supervisor, 528 Wood Ave., Bridgeport 4
Walker, Eleanor, President, Educational Publishing Corp., Darien
Wathley, Rose J., Elementary Supervisor, 51 Memorial Rd., West Hartford

DELAWARE

Armstrong, W. E., University of Delaware, Newark
Bonine, Beatrice L., Acting Supervisor, Delaware Trust Bldg., Wilmington 28
Burnett, Marguerite H., Director of Curriculum, Public Schools, Wilmington
Dennison, Mary C., Principal, George Gray School, 22nd and Locust Sts., Wilmington
Devine, Bessie C., Assistant Superintendent of Schools, 11th and Washington Sts., Wilmington 9
Ehlers, Emma C., Assistant Professor of Education, Box 162, W. C. D., Newark
Heck, Phyllis Mason, Supervisor of Rural Schools, Delaware Trust Bldg., Wilmington
Holley, Ella J., Rural Supervisor, State Department of Public Instruction, Delaware Trust Bldg., Wilmington

LIST OF MEMBERS

Hoyle, Dorothy, Vice-Principal, Friends School, Wilmington 284
Johnson, Catherine S., Vice-Principal, 1718 N. Broom St., Wilmington 35
Laker, Sara M., 1st Grade Teacher, 125 W. 35th St., Wilmington 204
Lynam, Lela A., Supervisor of Mathematics, High School, Wilmington
Milligan, May L., Supervisor of War Nursery Schools, c/o Board of Education, 11th and Washington Sts., Wilmington
Pell, Walden, II, Headmaster, St. Andrews School, Middletown
Raffle, Mary E., Supervisor, Art Education, Sussex County Court House, Georgetown
Shields, R. A., Superintendent Lewes Special School District, Lewes
Stradley, Elsie W., Teacher, Kirkwood School, Elliott Heights, Rt. 2, Newark
Vansant, J. A., Superintendent, Rehoboth Special School District, Rehoboth

DISTRICT OF COLUMBIA

Amidon, Edna P., Chief, Home Economics Educational Services, U. S. Office of Education, Washington 25
Annan, Elizabeth, Director of Middle School, National Cathedral School, Washington 16
Armes, Ella D., Administrative Principal, Benning Schools, Washington 19
Arndt, C. O., U. S. Office of Education, New Interior Bldg., Washington 25
Beust, Nora, Senior Specialist in Library Materials, 3133 Connecticut Ave., Washington
Bowes, Fern A., 5812 Nevada Ave., N. W., Washington 15
Brown, William B., USNR, 1638 16th St., N. W., Washington
Bull, Evelyn L., Blow School, 3905 Davis Pl., N. W., Washington 7
Burson, Susan M., Home Economics Agent, U. S. Office of Education, Washington 25
Christie, Mary E., Administrative Principal, Elementary Schools, 7931 Orchid St., N. W., Washington 12
Clark, Eugene A., President, Miner Teachers College, Georgia Ave. and Euclid St., N. W., Washington
Clark, Lois M., Assistant Director, Division of Rural Service, NEA, 1201 16th St., N. W., Washington
Coon, Beulah I., U. S. Office of Education, Washington 25
Cornell, Florence N., J. Q. Adams School, 19th and California Sts., N. W., Washington 9
Cramer, Bessie W., 4220 45th St., N. W., Washington 16
Daiches, Dan S., Attache, British Embassy, 3100 Massachusetts Ave., N. W., Washington 8
Davis, Mary Dabney, Specialist, Lower Elementary Education, U. S. Office of Education, Washington 25
Dore, Bernadette L., Principal, 2725 31st St., N. W., Washington 8
Fox, James Harold, Dean, School of Education, George Washington University, Washington 6
Frutchey, Fred P., Senior Education Analyst, Extension Service, U. S. Department of Agriculture, Washington 25
Fryer, Thelma E., Principal, J. R. Keene School, 3051 Idaho Ave., N. W., Washington 16
Gabbard, Hazel F., Specialist, Parent Education, U. S. Office of Education, Washington 25
Goodykoontz, Bess, U. S. Office of Education, Washington 25
Green, Elsie, Administrative Principal, Whittier School, 3151 Tennyson St., N. W., Washington
Hager, Walter E., President, Wilson Teachers College, 11th and Harvard Sts., N. W., Washington 9
Halberg, Anna D., Head, Division of Education and Psychology, Wilson Teachers College, Washington

Harper, Helen V., Supervisor of Student Teaching, 3846 Cathedral Ave., N. W., Washington
Haworth, Ellis, Professor of Science, Wilson Teachers College, Washington 9
Henderson, Mary A., Elementary Principal, 2412 Observatory Pl., N. W., Washington 7
Hickman, Clara, Principal, Rose Lees Hardy School, Foxhall Road and Q St., N. W., Washington 7
Hilder, Janie Frost, 3809 Ingomar St., Washington 15
Hiscox, Nell F., Administrative Principal, George Truesdall School, 1820 Upshur St., N. E., Washington 18
Hodgkins, George W., Teacher, 1821 Kalorama Rd., N. W., Washington 9
Israel, Raymond, Elementary Teacher, 4044 7th St., N. E., Washington 17
Jenkyns, Ernest S., Assistant Principal, Randall Junior High School, First and I Sts., S. W., Washington
Kefauver, Grayson N., Science Education, Department of State, Washington 25
Kirkland, Mineola, Supervising Principal, 1106 B St., N. E., Washington 2
Kyle, May T., Administrative Principal, 2129 32nd St., S. E., Washington 20
Lewis, Dorothy M., Administrative Principal, Kimball School, Minnesota Ave. and Ely Pl., S. E., Washington 20
Lind, Ida Mary, Director Elementary Instruction, Park View School, Warder and Newton Sts., N. W., Washington
Lockwood, Margaret M., Principal, Horace Mann School, 45th and Newark Sts., N. W., Washington
Mackintosh, Helen K., Elementary Education, U. S. Office of Education, Washington 25
Mallory, Berenice, Federal Agent, Home Economics Education, U. S. Office of Education, Washington 25
Reta McDonald, Girl Scout Leader, 1704 Rhode Island Ave., N. W., Washington 6
Melroy, Ruth M., Elementary Science Teacher, 1651 Primrose Rd., N. W., Washington 12
Noll, Frances F., Teacher, 3437 14th St., N. W., Washington 10
Patterson, W. B., Elementary School, South Capitol St., S. W., Washington 22
Perry, Leon L., Supervising Principal, 913 P St., N. W., Washington 1
Peterson, Gladys T., Principal, Randall Junior High School, First and I Sts., S. W., Washington
Pitts, Clara, Administrative Principal, 1705 Kenyon St., N. W., Washington 10
Proffitt, Maris M., Chief General Instructional Services, U. S. Office of Education, Washington 25
Rawlins, G. M., Jr., Head, Department of Science, Woodrow Wilson High School, Washington 16
Roby, Maud F., Teaching Principal, Shepherd School, 14th & Calmea Rd., N. W., Washington 12
Ruediger, Imogene I., Principal, H. D. Cooke School, 2836 28th St., N. W., Washington 8
Savoy, A. Kiger, Assistant Superintendent in charge of Elementary Schools, 217 T St., N. W., Washington
Savoy, Ruth Gordon, 1834 Vernon St., N. W., Washington 9
Schult, Veryl, Head, Mathematics Department, Wardman Park Hotel, Washington 8
Scrivener, Katherine, Raymond School, 10th and Spring Rd., N. W., Washington 11
Sister M. Agneze, Supervisor, 1726 N St., N. W., Washington 6
Sister Margaret Marie, Dean of Studies, Dunbarton College of Holy Cross, 2935 Upton St., N. W., Washington 8
Smith, Hugh S., Principal, Jefferson Junior High School, 8th and H Sts., S. W., Washington
Smith, Josephine C., Administrative Principal, 1948 2nd St., N. W., Washington 1

Taliaferro, Julia, Blow School, 19th and Bennings Rd., N. E., Washington 19
Taylor, Bertha E., Director of Special Classes for Exceptional Children, Franklin Administration Bldg., 13th and K Sts., N. W., Washington 5
Tripp, Dorothy, Principal, 217 9th St., S. E., Washington 3
Van Horn, Rua, Federal Agent, Home Economics Education, U. S. Office of Education, Washington 25
Wakeman, L. J., Principal, Emory-Eckington School, 4817 46th St., N. W., Washington 16
Ward, Douglas S., Director of Inter-American Education Relations, U. S. Office of Education, Washington 25
Warde, Ethel May, Horace Mann School, 44th and Newark Sts., N. W., Washington 16
Webb, Ruth K., Supervisor, Washington 9
White, Emilie M., Board of Education, 13th and K Sts., N. W., Washington
White, Marie, Federal Agent, Home Economics Education, U. S. Office of Education, Washington 25
Wiler, Jessie, Administrative Principal, Eckington-Seaton, 113 7th St., S. E., Washington 3
Williams, Edith M., Administrative Principal, 5703 14th St., N. W., Washington 11

FLORIDA

Alexander, Martha King, Director of Elementary Education, Box 1424, Tampa
Allen, Donald R., Field Supervisor, State Department of Education, 1608 High St., Leesburg
Allen, L. Claudia, Box 1124, Orlando
Bailey, Thomas D., Supervising Principal, Box 1424, Tampa
Bainum, Mary I., Supervisor, 125 24th Ave., S. E., St. Petersburg 5
Banning, F. J., County Superintendent, Court House, Tavares
Barnes, Lillian O., General Supervisor, Naples
Bates, Evelyn, Visiting Teacher, Board of Public Instruction, Madison County, Florida
Beal, Beulah, Principal, Elementary School, 1940 Silver Street, Jacksonville
Black, Marian W., Blountstown
Blackburn, J. Hartley, Bradenton
Boutelle, Margaret, Assistant Professor, English Education, 309 N. Oak, Gainesville
Burhans, Edna K., Supervisor, Box 1221, Ft. Myers
Burns, J. W., County Superintendent, Lake City
Butts, Mrs. John L., Supervisor, 6100 N. W. 2nd Ct., Miami 38
Campbell, D. S., President, Florida State College for Women, Tallahassee
Christen, Irene S., General Supervisor, Box 264, Macclenny
Cox, Carl S., Supervising Principal, Lakeland
Culver, Lola M., Elementary Principal, 1835 Silver St., Jacksonville 6
Davies, J. M., Supervisor, Secondary Schools, Cross City
Drayer, Erma, Principal, Spring Park School No. 72, Jacksonville 7
Edwards, W. T., Acting Director, Division of Instruction, State Department of Education, Tallahassee
Elkins, Annice Davis, Supervisor, Office of Public Instruction, Kissimmee
Erwin, Edna B., Principal, Broward School, 812 S. Oregon St., Tampa 6
Ferguson, Sara, Principal, Memorial Junior High, 632 E. Amelia St., Orlando
Frojen, Boletha, Supervisor of Home Economics Education, State Department of Education, Tallahassee
Geiger, A. J., Principal, St. Petersburg High School, St. Petersburg
Geiger, Winnifred R., General County Supervisor, Lake Butler
Goulding, R. L., Professor of Education and Superintendent of Demonstration School, Florida State College for Women, Tallahassee
Grant, Arabelle, Supervisor, Box 820, Panama City
Graves, Theresa, Supervisor Secondary Schools, Box 409, Gainesville
Hall, John E., Principal, Hungerford School, Winter Park
Hand, Ruth, 1301 Park Ave., Sanford
Hart, M. Lucile, General Supervisor, Box 68, Mayo
Henderson, E. B., Senior High School, Fort Meyers
Hindman, B. M., 275 N. W., 2nd St., Miami
Holland, Frank L., Supervisor, Board of Public Instruction, Box 820, Panama City
Hosic, James F., 1521 Highland Rd., Winter Park, Fla.
Kelley, J. T., Principal Bay County High School, Box 109, Panama City
Kent, Mary, Principal, Seminole Heights School, 2802 Sitios St., Tampa
Krentzman, Sara Malcolm, Consultant, Libraries, State Department of Education, Tallahassee
Leonard, John I., Box 2469, West Palm Beach
Leps, Joseph M., University of Florida, Gainesville
Martin, Minnie Mae, Board of Public Instruction, Vero Beach
Mead, A. R., Director of Research, P. K. Yonge Bldg., University of Florida, Gainesville
Meade, Buena Lee, General Elementary Supervisor, Ft. Pierce
Miller, Mozelle, General Supervisor, Westville
Milton, W. H., Macclenny
Moore, Jean, General Supervisor, LaBelle
Moorer, Sam H., Field Supervisor, State Department of Education, 1913 Harding St., Hollywood
Morse, C. Marguerite, Board of Public Instruction, Clearwater
Mosher, Frank, USNR, 1822 Lilly Rd., Jacksonville 71
Nutter, H. E., Director, Curriculum Laboratory, 317 P. K. Yonge Bldg., University of Florida, Gainesville
Osborne, Grace W., General Supervisor, Bradford County Schools, Starke
Owen, Ray A., 1153 Miramar Ave., Jacksonville 7
Pearson, I. T., Director of Instruction, 275 N. W. 2nd St., Miami
Pickens, E. Verdelle, Spencer Bibbs School, 1422 N. Davis St., Pensacola
Plumb, Kathleen G., Director Elementary Education, 718 Lakeview St., Clearwater
Preston, Carleton E., 1716 N. Ft. Harrison Ave., Clearwater
Ruediger, Mrs. J. J., 1009 Gadsden St., Tallahassee
Shaffner, Gertrude, Assistant Director of Instruction, 1636 S. W. 19th Ave., Miami
Sister M. Dorothy, O. P., Barry College, Miami
Skipper, Dora, Box 1103, Florida State College, Tallahassee
Snyder, D. R., Superintendent, Health and Physical Education, County School Administration Bldg., 275 N. W. 2nd St., Miami
Southerland, Ruth V., Elementary Supervisor, 306E. Bay St., Wauchula
Stimmel, Barbara, 30 Central Ave., St. Augustine
Stone, Nobie H., Supervisor, Box 245, Port St. Joe
Swain, Jewell, Elementary School Supervisor, Sarasota
Swearingen, Mildred E., Supervisor of Instruction, State Department of Education, Tallahassee
Trottman, Warren E., Dixie County School Supervisor, Zephyrhills
Vergason, A. L., Field Supervisor, 232 Ave. B, N. E., Winter Haven
Vinal, Emma K., Principal, Shorecrest Outdoor School, St. Petersburg

LIST OF MEMBERS

Vories, Marian, 119 S. 7th St., Fernandina
Walker, Mrs. Herman, Principal, Box 9, Bradenton
Wells, Ophelia, General Supervisor, 825 Waukeenan St., Monticello
Wilkerson, Emma D., General Supervisor, Sumter County Schools, Box 62, Coleman
Williams, Colly V., Supervisor of Instruction, Washington County, Department of Public Instruction, Chipley
Wimberly, Beatrice R., Elementary Supervisor, Hernando County, Brooksville
Withers, Mrs. Rex Todd, State Department of Education, Tallahassee
Wolverton, Ethel G., c/o Superintendent of Public Instruction, County Court House, Pensacola
Yawn, Maude, Supervisor of Elementary Schools, Highlands County, De Soto City

GEORGIA

Arden, Alice, Principal, Massie School, Savannah
Bailey, Elizabeth Moss, Supervisor, Department of Education, Canton
Barnes, Editha, Perry
Benson, Frances, Tift County Public Schools, Tifton
Bivins, Mrs. C. W., Supervisor, Jones County Schools, Haddock
Bowman, C. W., Rt. 4, Rossville
Burnham Reba, Supervisor of Schools, Oglethorpe County, Lexington
Burroughs, Cecil B., Principal, Massie School, Savannah
Carnell, Sara, J. C. Winston School, 441 W. Peachtree St., N. E., Atlanta 3
Champion, Frances, Assistant State Superintendent of Home Economics, West Georgia College, Genola
Coleman, M. E. Assistant Superintendent, 10th Floor, City Hall, Atlanta 3
Cox, Johnnye, Supervisor, Pulaski County Schools, Wadley
Cox, Mrs. L. G., Supervising Principal, Elementary Schools, Moultrie
Deariso, Elizabeth J., Supervisor, Worth County Schools, Box 98, Sylvester
Dickerson, James L., Box 302, Americus
Divine, Sara, Supervisor, General Delivery, Griffin
Donovan, Elizabeth, Instructional Consultant, State Department of Education, State Department Office Bldg., Atlanta
Downs, Katie, Director of Teacher Training, West Georgia College, Carrollton
Elder, Mrs. C. G., Supervisor, Baxley
English, Mildred, Superintendent, Peabody Training School, Georgia State College for Women, Milledgeville
Folger, D. W., Dean of Instruction, West Georgia College, Genola
Folger, Ruth M., Principal, Oglethorpe Avenue School, Savannah
Franseth, Jane, University of Georgia, College of Education, Athens
Gammage, Ruby O., Office of County School Superintendent, Thomasville
Golden, Frankie N., Supervisor, Chatham County Elementary Schools, 611 E. Henry St., Savannah
Goodman, Mrs. Fielder B., Primary Supervisor, 8-D Massee Apts., Macon
Hall, Myra L., Supervisor of Instruction, Blackshear
Heard, Virginia Lord, Assistant Superintendent, 208 Bull St., Savannah
Jeter, Lamar, Supervisor of Girls, High School, Rosalie St., Atlanta
Jimmerfield, Verda, Box 865, Rome
Jones, Lucille D., Principal, John B. Gordon School, 1205 Metropolitan Ave., S. E., Atlanta
Jones, Wanda, Instructional Supervisor, Dahlonega

Jordan, Floyd, Schools Services Consultant, 20 Collier Rd., N. W., Atlanta
Kendall, Mrs. C. M., Supervisor of Rural Schools, Funston
Kent, Vada, Box 295, Gainesville
King, J. B., Elementary Principal, Brinson Vocational School, Brinson
Lester, L. M., Director Teacher Education and Certification, State Department of Education, 229 New State Office Bldg., Atlanta 3
Lipscomb, Grace, Supervisor, Box 413, Madison
Lumsden, Isabel, Box 346, Elementary Supervisor, Toccoa
Lyon, Ralph M., Collegeboro
Mayes, Elizabeth, 446 Evans St., Bainbridge
McCall, Martha, Box 32, Jasper
McCord, George M., Principal, Murphy Junior High School, 1425 Memorial Dr., S. E., Atlanta
McCune, W. W., Assistant Superintendent of Schools, Board of Education, Bull and Hull Sts., Savannah
McJenkin, Virginia, 345 Washington St., S. W., Atlanta
Mitchell, Mary Edward, Supervisor, Box 143, Rockmart
Mitchell, Pendleton, 618 Love Ave., Tifton
Moore, Katherine, Supervisor, County Schools, Douglas
Munro, Paul M., Superintendent of Schools, Box 176, Columbus
Neighbors, Jean, Elementary Supervisor, 302 Hines Ter., Macon
Norvell, Mrs. Crane, Principal, Pape School, 906 Drayton St., Savannah
Nussbaum, Lillian B., Principal, Moore Avenue School, 511 Forsyth Apt., Savannah
Pafford, W. E., 204 State Office Bldg., Atlanta 3
Parker, Laura M., 211 E. Gwennett St., Savannah
Perkins, Mary Ellen, Supervisor, Jefferson County, Wadley
Pool, Jewel, Elementary School Supervisor, Summerville
Renfroe, Olive, Office of County Superintendent, Dublin
Riley, Romana, Principal, Waters Avenue School, Savannah
Seawright, Margie, Supervisor of Elementary Schools, 603 E. 55th St., Savannah
Shannon, Mary Neal, Elementary Supervisor, 521 Court House, Atlanta
Shearouse, H. S., Supervisor, 514 2nd Ave., Albany
Singleton, Sara, County Supervisor, Box 262, Clayton
Slocumb, Josie, Supervisor, Grades 4-6, 165 E. 14th St., Atlanta
Snipes, Sue, Supervisor, Bullock County Schools, Department of Education, Statesboro
Strickland, Jessie, County Supervisor, Hiawassee
Sutton, Rachel S., Professor of Education, University of Georgia, Athens
Walker, Knox, Supervisor, Fulton County Schools, 979 Los Angeles Ave., N. E., Atlanta 3
Wallace, Inez, Supervisor of Home Economics, 219 State Office Bldg., Atlanta 3
Watson, Martha, Supervisor, County Schools, Box 71, Pearson
West, Mabel, Instructional Supervisor, Box 275, Catoosa County, Ringgold
Wills, Mary Lizzie, State Department of Education, Abac
Wimberly, Kathleen, Supervisor, Floyd County Schools, Rome
Winn, Nell, Supervisor, Floyd County Schools, Box 409, Rome
Woodward, Lamar, Principal, Tubman High School, Augusta

IDAHO

Bjorkman, S. R., Superintendent of Schools, Cassin and Twin Falls Counties, Burley

Carlson, L. L., Superintendent of Schools, Lewiston
Click, Leo E., 916 11th Ave., Lewiston
Hendricks, Lorene, Director of Practice Teaching, Southern Branch University of Idaho, Pocatello
Hughes, La Verne, Principal, Lewiston Senior High School, Lewiston
Lame, C. C., Registrar and Instructor, Lewiston State Normal School, Lewiston
Pratt, R. W., Superintendent of Schools, Grangeville
Rankin, Vera E., County Superintendent of Schools, Orofino
Snyder, R. H., Albion State Normal School, Albion

ILLINOIS

Adams, Agnes L., National College of Education, Evanston
Ahlenius, Ruth E., Supervising Principal, Irving School, 701 W. Mill St., Bloomington
Ashbaucher, Daisy B., Elementary Principal, 618 E. 9th St., Moline
Ball, Lester B., Superintendent, District # 108, Lincoln School, Highland Park
Banson, Hilda J., Principal and 5th Grade Teacher, 430 Park Blvd., Glen Ellyn
Batchelder, Mildred, Chief, School and Children's Library Division, American Library Association, 520 N. Michigan Ave., Chicago, 11
Bell, Millard D., Superintendent of Schools, 900 Central Ave., Wilmette
Bellis, Bertha, Teacher Training, Northern Illinois State Teachers College, DeKalb
Blaha, M. Jay, Psychologist and Coordinator, Cicero Public Schools, 5110 W. 24th St., Cicero 50
Blair, Clarence D., Superintendent, Office of County Superintendent of Schools, Belleville
Boyd, Grace, Primary Supervisor, 2337 S. 53rd Ave., Cicero 50
Breed, Blanche, Elementary Supervisor, 117 Thrush, Apt. 4, Peoria
Brewington, Ann, Associate Professor of Business Education, University of Chicago, School of Business, Chicago 37
Burrell, Marjorie, Primary Supervisor, 601 S. Douglas Ave., Springfield
Burt, C. Vinton, Office of Superintendent, Board of Education, River Forest
Butts, L. A., Principal, Junior High School, Belleville
Buzzell, Leonard A., Principal, Kingshighway and Forest Blvd., East St. Louis
Campbell, Minnie, National College of Education, Evanston
Carpenter, Robert H., Teacher, New Trier High School, Winnetka
Cooper, Margaret, Director, Elementary Education, Illinois State Normal University, Normal
Corey, Stephen M., Professor of Education, University of Chicago, Chicago 37
Crackel, Verne E., Superintendent of Schools, 65 E. Cass St., Crete
Crodian, J. P., 810 Hyde Park Blvd., Chicago 15
Curtis, Ina L., Principal, Glen Flora School, 1110 Chestnut St., Waukegan
Davis, Melvin G., Superintendent of Schools, 300 N. Monroe St., Peoria
DeYoung, C. A., Head, Department of Education, Illinois State Normal University, Normal
Dierzen, Verda, 636 N. Madison St., Woodstock
Douglas, Faye, Teacher, 295 W. Barnes St., Bushnell
Dummer, Mrs. W. F., 679 N. Michigan Ave., Chicago 11
Endres, Mary P., County Superintendent of Schools, McHenry County, Woodstock
Entsminger, Mary, Elementary Supervisor, 302 N. Springer St., Carbondale
Ferguson, J. C., Ginn and Co., Box 277, Wheaton
Flynn, Ella M., Principal, Le Moyne School, 851 Waveland Ave., Chicago
Fosse, Frances, 1721 N. Church St., Rockford
Gaffney, Matthew P., Superintendent, New Trier Township High School, Winnetka
Gray, William S., Department of Education, University of Chicago, Chicago 37
Halkyard, Marcita, Elementary Supervisor, Public Schools, 153 S. Ottawa St., Joliet
Hamilton, William J., 122 Forest Ave., Oak Park
Hanna, Grace, Avery Coonley School, Downers Grove
Hauser, L. J., Superintendent of Schools, Board of Education, District No. 96, Riverside
Heise, Bryan, Director of Extension, Eastern Illinois State Teachers College, Charleston
Honor, Leo L., Executive Director, Board of Jewish Education, 72 E. 11th St., Chicago 5
Hough, Arleigh R., Managing Editor, Rand-McNally Co., 536 South Clark St., Chicago 5
Howard, Harriet, Director, Supervision Department, National College of Education, Evanston
Johnson, Maude E., Supervisor of Instruction, Board of Education, Rockford
Jordon, Marion, 700 N. Mayfield Ave., Chicago
Kaar, Galeta M., 2143 Hudson Ave., Chicago 14
Keener, E. E., Principal, 250 Forest Ave., Oak Park
Keith, Linton J., Editor, Follett Publishing Co., 1257 S. Wabash Ave., Chicago
Kilburn, George W., Superintendent, Chicago Junior School for Boys, Elgin
Koos, L. V., College of Education, University of Chicago, Chicago 37
Larson, Irene, 719 Buckbee St., Rockford
Lauing, Walter, 128 11th Ave., Melrose Park
Lindsey, Richard V., Superintendent of Schools, Galesburg
Lundeen, Alma, Field Visitor School Libraries, Illinois State Library, Springfield
McIntire, Alto, 7125 Stanley Av., Berwyn
McNamara, Loretta M., Elementary Supervisor and Principal, 15 W. 1st St., Hinsdale
McSwain, E. T., Professor of Education, Northwestern University, School of Education, Evanston
Messenger, Helen R., Professor of Education, Northern Illinois State Teachers College, DeKalb
Misner, Paul J., Superintendent of Schools, Glencoe
Monroe, Walter S., Professor of Education, 300 Gregory Hall, University of Illinois, Urbana
Morgan, Lewis V., County Superintendent, County Bldg., Wheaton
Muffley, E. J., Principal, 701 W. Grand Ave., Decatur 20
Newell, Eva H., Rural Teacher, Rt. 2, Smithfield
Oftedal, Laura, Laboratory Schools, University of Chicago, Chicago 37
Ott, Hazel H., Director, Curriculum Research Department, F. E. Compton and Co., 1000 N. Dearborn St., Chicago 10
Pease, Marion O., 2256 Lincoln Pk., West, Chicago
Pence, Helen M., Training Teacher, 827 W. Adams St., Macomb
Perkins, E. L., Vice-President, A. J. Nystrom and Co., 3333 Elston Ave., Chicago 18
Pinkstaff, H. E., Superintendent, Public Schools, Anna
Pratt, Marjorie, Educational Consultant, John C. Winston Co., 623 S. Wabash Ave., Chicago 5
Pygman, C. H., Superintendent, Washington School, Maywood
Reichert, Edwin C., School District 107, 233 N. Sheridan Rd., Highland Park
Reiffel, Sophie M., Principal, Hibbard School, 3244 Ainslie St., Chicago 25
Reinhardt, Emma, Head, Department of Education, 859 11th St., Charleston

LIST OF MEMBERS

Rice, Agnes, Associate Professor of Education, Illinois State Normal University, Normal
Richards, Mrs. H. L., Superintendent, Community High School, 12915 S. Maple Ave., Blue Island
Russell, Lillian, Supervisor, Language Arts, 1911 Ridge Ave., Evanston
Sanders, Agnes L., Elementary Supervisor, District 76, 2428 Greenleaf, Chicago 45
Seyfert, Warren C., Laboratory School, 1362 E. 59th St., Chicago 15
Shaw, Mary Dwyer, 638 Elmwood Ave., Evanston
Sheldon, Vera G., Supervisor, 901 Maple Ave., Evanston
Sifert, F. R., Superintendent, Proviso Township High School, Maywood
Sister Eileen Marie, 3000 N. Mango St., Chicago 34
Sister M. Agathene, Instructor in Education, College of St. Francis, Joliet
Sister Mary Laetitia, R. S. M., Principal, St. Mary School, Lake Forest
Sister M. Fidelia, Superintendent, Lourdes High School, 4038 W. 56th St., Chicago 29
Sister M. Sanctoslaus, Supervisor, 3800 Peterson Ave., Chicago 45
Smith, Bertrand L., Assistant Superintendent of Schools, 6th and Langdon Sts., Alton
Smith, B. Othanel, Associate Professor of Education, College of Education, University of Illinois, Urbana
Stateler, C. B., Sales Manager, A. J. Nystrom and Co., 3333 Ellston Ave., Chicago 18
Sugden, W. E., Curriculum Department, Board of Education, River Forest
Swanson, Nellie, Elementary Supervisor, Board of Education, Galesburg
Sweat, C. H., Assistant Superintendent, Lincoln High School, Wheaton Ave. and Park Ridge, Wheaton
Taba, Hilda, Professor of Education, University of Chicago, Chicago 37
Theman, Viola, School of Education, Northwestern University, Evanston
Tipton, Gladys, Illinois State Normal University, Normal
Traenkenschuh, Amelia, Director of Curriculum and Instruction, Office of Superintendent of Schools, Rock Island
Trimmer, Carmen A., Supervisor of Art, 555 N. 14th St., East St. Louis
Troyer, Raymond E., High School, Lake Forest
Weedon, Vivian, Curriculum, Consultant, 204 5th St., Wilmette
Winslow, Harry D., Superintendent, Lincoln School, Park Ridge
Williams, O. S., 1035 Greenwood Ave., Wilmette
Witty, Paul A., Professor of Educational Psychology, Northwestern University, Evanston
Wood, Dinsmore, Principal, High School, Edwardsville
Yale, John R., Executive Editor, Science Research Associates, 228 S. Wabash Ave., Chicago 8

INDIANA

Andrews, L. O., Director of Supervised Teaching, Indiana University, Bloomington
Armstrong, Leila, Supervisor of Elementary Education, 905 Tyler St., LaPorte
Bagwell, Olive B., Supervisor, 317 Maple W., Wabash
Baldwin, Susan M., Elementary Supervisor, 1534 W. Armstrong St., Kokomo
Bell, Eva H., 856 Woodrow St., Indianapolis 8
Bicking, Ada, Director, Arthur Jordon Conservatory of Music, 1204 N. Delaware St., Indianapolis 2
Bookwalter, Karl W., Assistant Professor, Indiana University, 527 S. Highland St., Bloomington
Boston, Paul F., Superintendent, La Porte Public Schools, La Porte
Breed, F. S., Dune Acres, Chesterton
Champion, Grace, Elementary Supervisor, 810 E. Market St., New Albany
Christian, Thomas L., Superintendent, Lebanon Public Schools, Lebanon
Church, Harold H., Superintendent, Board of School Trustees, Elkhart
Clark, Marie, Washington School, Vincennes
Coleman, C. T., Hammond High School, Hammond
Cooper, Helen, Primary Supervisor, 4819 Magoun Avenue, East Chicago
Craig, M. Dorothy, Director of Elementary Education Roosevelt Bldg., 7th and Broadway, Logansport
Delbridge, Maude, Supervisor of Music, 3325 Ruckle St., Indianapolis
Dunn, Pearl, Elementary School Supervisor, New Castle City Schools, New Castle
Ellerbrook, L. W., Supervising Principal, University School, Bloomington
Foltz, Elsie, Elementary School Principal, 2427 Garfield Ave., Terre Haute
Fuqua, Blanche E., Director of Instruction, 667 Walnut St., Terre Haute
Gorman, Frank H., Director, Department of Elementary Education, Butler University, Indianapolis
Gray, Merle, Director, Elementary Grades, 217 Webb Street, Hammond
Hamilton, Otto T., Assistant Professor of Education, Oklandon
Holmes, Doris F., Director of Instruction and Curriculum Studies, 150 N. Meridian St., Indianapolis
Hunt, Margaret, Supervising Principal, 11 Martin Pl., Franklin
Johnson, Harold S., High School Principal, Huntington
Jones, Daisy Marvel, 316 N. Mulberry St., # 313, Muncie
Kauffman, Geraldine, Supervisor, 4819 Magoun St., East Chicago
Kimber, Grace W., Principal, School No. 47, 1240 W. Ray St., Indianapolis
Knapp, M. L., Superintendent, Isaac C. Elston Junior High School Bldg., Michigan City
Lacey, Florence R., Senior High School, Richmond
Lange, P. W., Board of Education, 524 Garfield St., Gary
Lindahl, Hannah, Supervisor of Elementary Education, Mishawaka Public Schools, Mishawaka
Miller, Inez G., Elementary Supervisor, 1312 N. Jefferson St., Huntington
Morrison, Nellie C., Supervisor of Elementary Education, 148 Central High School Bldg., Muncie
Mossman, Isabelle, Assistant Supervisor of Music, 3358 Ruckle St., Indianapolis 5
Patterson, Ruth, Associate Professor of Kindergarten Education, Butler University, 717 N. Alabama St., Indianapolis 2
Peed, Emma Grayce, 5784 Central Ave., Indianapolis 5
Rausch, Oscar P., Research Assistant, School of Education, Indiana University, Bloomington
Redman, Ruth N., State Manager, Encyclopedia Britannica, 1672 N. Seventh, Terre Haute
Reed, Mary D., Assistant Director, Division of Training, Indiana State Teachers College, Terre Haute
Simpson, Dorothy, 815 N. Ninth St., Lafayette
Sister M. Agness Cecile, Instructor in Education, St. Mary's College, Notre Dame, Holy Cross
Smith, L. Frances, Elementary Supervisor, 734 7th St., Columbus
Spangler, Mamie, Kindergarten and Primary Supervisor, Lake County, Box 290, 307 N. Court St., Crown Point
Staninger, Ruth E., Elementary Supervisor, 607 Upper 11th St., Vincennes
Strickland, Ruth, Assistant Professor in Education, Indiana University, Bloomington
Tabbert, Mildred E., Supervising Principal, 813 Georgiana St., Hobart

Trefz, Lettie P., Assistant Supervisor of Handwriting, 953 N. Audubon Road, Indianapolis
Wadsworth, Elsie, Griffith, Lake County
Witmer, Mildred, 1608 S. 8th St., Goshen
Wright, Wendell W., School of Education, Indiana University, Bloomington
Zehner, Effie T., Director of Elementary Instruction, 1517 Bayou St., Vincennes

IOWA

Ahlborn, Irene L., Elementary Supervisor, Public Schools, Fort Dodge
Bennett, H. K., Superintendent, Tipton
Berg, B. C., Superintendent, Newton
Bloedel, Elfred P., 1603 Maple Dr., N. W., Cedar Rapids
Bly, Gordon M., Principal, Junior and Senior High Schools, Independence
Brown, Nina H., Elementary Supervisor, Simpson College, 311 N. D St., Indianola
Davis, Floyd, Superintendent, Public Schools, Knoxville
Docken, F. L., 407½ E. Jefferson St., Bloomfield
Ehrhorn, Principal, East High School, Sioux City
Fallgatter, Florence, Head, Home Economics Education, Iowa State College, Ames
Frank, Emily, Director of Student Teaching, College Hill, Decorah
Friant, Regina J., Iowa State College, Ames
Hagie, L. L., Osceola
Hall, Mary E., 1600 Wilson Ave., Webster City
Hamm, Bess, 1077 27th St., Des Moines
Harken, Urban, Principal, Horace Mann Junior High, 625 S. Garfield St., Burlington
Hartnett, Ellen, County Superintendent, Box 746, Newton
Hawk, R. A., Superintendent, Grinnell
Helff, Bernice, Campus School Iowa State Teachers College, 2304 Olive, Cedar Falls
Horn, Ernest, Professor of Education and Director of University Elementary School, W107 East Hall, Iowa City
Howland, Adelene E., Assistant Director of Elementary Education, 629 3rd St., Des Moines 9
Hudson, Eva L., 218 N. 1st St., Keokuk
Jacobson, P. B., Superintendent of Schools, Davenport
Kirn, Gerald W., Principal, Abraham Lincoln High School, Council Bluffs
Koehring, Dorothy, Kindergarten Supervisor, Iowa State Teachers College, Cedar Falls
Kraft, Edna, State Supervisor, State House, Des Moines
Kratzer, Ferne, 232 E. Bloomington St., Iowa City
Logan, Jack, Superintendent of Schools, Waterloo
Marquis, Norwood, Principal, 1310 Orleans, Keokuk
McBurney, J. H., Superintendent, Webster City
McCleery, Helen E., 629 3rd St., Des Moines 9
McLaughlin, Samuel J., Cornell College, Mount Vernon
McNee, Irene Faye, Assistant Principal, Senior High School, Keokuk
McPhail, H. R., Superintendent of Schools, 813 Blondean, Keokuk
Miller, B. R., Principal, Senior High School, Marshalltown
Miller, Jennie H., Principal, 503 W. 12th St., S., Newton
Morgan, Doris M., Elementary School Principal, 2404 Forest Dr., Des Moines
Nodland, Marvin T., Superintendent of Schools, 1240 Orchard Dr., Ames
Parker, Jessie M., Superintendent of Public Instruction, Department of Public Instruction, Des Moines 4
Pattison, Mattie, Home Economics Hall, Iowa State College, Ames
Peterson, Evelyn, Director of Elementary Education, East High School Bldg., Waterloo
Plotts, Sylvia F., Superintendent, Marion County Schools, Knoxville

Prehm, Ernest, Superintendent of Schools, Northwood
Pritchard, Ruth B., Elementary School Principal, 2901 Grand, Des Moines 12
Rhea, W. L., Principal, Junior High School, 1501 Gnahn St., Burlington
Sorum, Marie, Court House, Estherville
Spitzer, Herbert F., Professor of Education, and Elementary Principal, 901 Melrose Ave., Iowa City
Thomas, Hazel V., County Superintendent, Court House, Mason City
Vanderlinden, J. S., Superintendent of Schools, Perry
Van Dyke, L. A., Associate Professor Education and Director of University High School, State University of Iowa, Iowa City

KANSAS

Bergman, F. V., Superintendent of Schools, Public Schools, Manhattan
Carroll, Jane M., Professor of Elementary Education, Kansas State Teachers College, Pittsburg
Cooke, Dorothy E., Administration Bldg., 415 W. 8th St., Topeka
Evans, Mildred I., Elementary Supervisor, Board of Education, Emporia
Gammon, Delore, Elementary Supervisor, 4288 Broadway, Wichita 2
Guthridge, Wallace H., Superintendent of Schools, Box 526, Parsons
Harnly, Paul W., 428 S. Broadway, Wichita 2
Higgins, Harold H., Principal, Waco Elementary School, Wichita 4
Hobson, Cloy S., Director, Guidance and Curriculum, 3633 Leahy Ct., Planeview, Wichita 10
Kier, Hazel, Supervisor, Intermediate Grades, Library Bldg., Kansas City
Leasure, Ernestine, General Supervisor, Box 164, Arkansas City
Lind, I. R., Hesston College, Hesston
Martin, Mabel F., Wichita Guidance Center, 3422 E. Douglas Ave., Wichita 8
McPherson, Dorothy, Elementary School Supervisor, Board of Education, Coffeyville
O'Brien, Professor of Education, University of Kansas, Lawrence
Perrill, Ariel Smith, Coordinator of Language Arts, 117 W. 13th St., Hutchinson
Soderstrom, Lavern W., Superintendent of Schools, Lindsborg
Stewart, Grace E., Elementary School Supervisor, Supervisor's Office, Bartlett Bldg., Salina
Streeter, Helen, Kindergarten-Primary Supervisor, Board of Education, Kansas City
Thorpe, B. R., Superintendent of Schools, Tonganoxie
Tissue, Kathryn, Assistant Professor, Home Economics, 118 Fraser Hall, Lawrence
Wiens, Esther, Teacher, 901 N. Grove, Wichita 6
Wolfe, W. D., Superintendent of Schools, Atchison
Woodard, R. C., Elementary Supervisor, Junior College, Hutchinson
Zeller, Dale, Professor of Education, Kansas State Teachers College, Emporia

KENTUCKY

Abrams, Burnace, Helping Teacher, Clover Bottom
Adams, Elizabeth, Supervisor, Magoffin County, Leatha
Allen, Ida Nice, Elementary Supervisor, Allen County, Settle
Angel, Flossie, Savoy
Ashby, Mrs. Clemon C., Rt. 4, Madisonville
Barker, Elmer, Winchester
Barton, Eva, Summershade
Belcher, E. W., Principal, Elementary School, 671 Madlon Ct., Louisville 11

LIST OF MEMBERS 141

Bernstorf, Lydia S., Elementary Supervisor, High School, Winfield
Berkeley, Ina M., Helping Teacher, Greenup
Boyd, Lillian, 417 E. Madison St., Franklin
Britton, Elizabeth, 2628 Virginia Ave., Louisville 11
Brown, Myrel C., Helping Teacher, Whitsburg
Brown, Stevie, Teacher, 114 Boggs Lane, Richmond
Browning, Mary, Supervisor, Primary Grades Administration Bldg., 5th and Hill, Louisville 8
Burress, Nona, Box 126, Greensburg
Butler, Suda E., Elementary Supervisor, 224 Stilz Ave., Louisville 6
Callaghan, Mary, County Supervisor, Owenton
Carneal, Mrs. W. M., Nebo Consolidated School, Nebo
Carter, Mozelle, Teacher, Rt. 4, Franklin
Caudill, Margie, Helping Teacher, Swamp Branch
Cave, Mary Laurine, Munfordville
Chambers, Marjorie, Helping Teacher, Pineville
Chidester, Albert J., Head, Education Department, Berea College, Box 433, Berea
Cochran, Estelle, Helping Teacher, Chilton
Coe, Mrs. B. P., Elementary Supervisor, Box 203, Jamestown
Cohron, Marie, Elementary Teacher, Richardsville
Cole, Mary I., Associate Professor of Education, Western Kentucky Teachers College, Bowling Green
Coleman, Mabel, Stone
Combs, Louise, Assistant Director of Certification, State Department of Education, Frankfort
Compton, Christine, Helping Teacher, Middleburg
Cooper, J. Bryant, Supervising Principal, 3212 Dumesnil St., Louisville 11
Currier, Mrs. A. H., Principal, Box 420, Hopkinsville
Dame, Waurika, Hanson School, Hanson
Davis, Frances L., 1158 Laurel, Bowling Green
Day, Mary Vance, Elementary Supervisor, City Schools, 502 W. Columbia St., Somerset
Diseker, Mildred, Helping Teacher, Williamsburg
Dotson, John A., Director of Curriculum and Research, Louisville 8
Duncan, May K., Head, Department of Elementary Education, University of Kentucky, Lexington
Dunn, Ruth, Primary Supervisor, Jefferson County Schools, 618 W. Jefferson St., Louisville
Durham, Mrs. O. A., Professor, Lindsey Wilson Junior College, Columbia
Edwards, Lucy Byrd, Barren County Superintendent's Office, Glasgow
Esch, Bianca, Elementary Principal, 1857 Princeton Dr., Louisville 5
Evans, Laura Katherine, Supervisor, 517 S. 2nd St., Richmond
Evans, Thelma, Critic Teacher, Morehead Teachers College, Morehead
Ewan, Mrs. J. V., Elementary Principal, Kenwick School, Henry Clay Blvd., Lexington
Gardner, Elsie, Helping Teacher, Somerset
Gatlin, Kathleen, Rt. 4, Morganfield
Good, Mrs. Lewis, Rt. 1, Dawson Springs
Graham, Charles C., Coordinator, 54 Estill, Berea
Graham, Rozelle, Box 35, Earlington
Griggs, Rozellen, Teacher, 201 Erlanger Rd., Erlanger
Hamm, Mary E., Teacher, 200 Jarvis Ave., Somerset
Hansen, May C., Associate Professor of Education, 532 Main St., Richmond
Harris, Reba T., Associate Director, Bureau of Public Health Education, State Department of Health, Louisville 2
Hart, Ruby Evans, Supervisor, 116 Goodrich Ave., Lexington
Hatfield, Esthel, Helping Teacher, Monticello
Hinton, Evelyn, Elementary Supervisor, Allen County, Adolphus
Holloway, Lucy, Woodstock Farm, Lexington
Hood, Lucile, Attendance Supervisor, Morgantown
Hopkins, P. H., Superintendent, Public Schools, Somerset
Horton, Emery S., Helping Teacher, Faye
Horton, Jewel, Helping Teacher, Carter County, Grayson
Howard, Bonnie C., Supervisor of Intermediate Grades, 409 Kensington Ct., Louisville
Hunt, Erma Daniel, 330 15th St., Bowling Green
Hunt, Roxie, Supervisor, Whitley City
Jackson, Mrs. H. A., Teacher, Anton School, Rt. 3, Madisonville
Jaggers, R. E., Chief, Bureau of Instruction, State Department of Education, Frankfort
Jasper, Susan E., Hogue
Jenkins, Gertrude, Box 437, Somerset
Kimbler, Mara D., Elementary Teacher, Buechel
King, Lera, Helping Teacher, Knob Lick
Lacy, Nan, Elementary School Supervisor, 120 Walton Ave., Lexington
Lawson, H. Bentley, Assistant Superintendent, Harlan County, Loyall
Lingenfelser, Margaret, Critic Teacher, Training School, Richmond
Lyon, Cecil H., Supervisor, Monroe County Schools, Tompkinsville
Lytle, Mrs. William, Helping Teacher, Bourbon County, 242 Parrish Ave., Paris
Martin, Ruth, California School, 1638 W. Kentucky St., Louisville 10
Maupin, Audrey, Supervisor, Clinton County, Albany
Mays, Allie, Helping Teacher, Barbourville
Mercer, Fannie May, White Plains School, White Plains
Molloy, Jeanette, 326 Grosvenor Ave., Lexington 8
Moore, Bess, Elementary Supervisor, 518 Allen, Owensboro
Moore, Kathleen, Associate Professor of Education, Union College, Barbourville
Morris, Marell, Teacher, Rt. 2, Paducah
Neal, Edna, Supervising Teacher, State Teachers College, 440 Main St., Morehead
Noel, Mrs. Michael, Fourth Grade Teacher, Rt. 2, Madisonville
Northcutt, Ruby Castle, Elementary Supervisor, 3001 Carter Ave., Ashland
Oates, W. Newton, Elementary Principal, White Plains
Oppenheimer, J. J., Dean of College of Liberal Arts, 2818 Saratoga Drive, Louisville 5
Parker, Ethel L., University of Kentucky, Lexington
Parker, Evadine, Teacher Training in Home Economics, College Station, Murray State Teachers College, Murray
Patterson, Mary M., Hodgeville
Patterson, Wilma, Teacher, Rt. 2, Slaughters
Peyton, Cressa, Teacher, Dalton
Peyton, Lillie K., Teacher, 12th St., Sturgis
Prater, Olga Marie, Supervisor, Salyersville
Preece, Forrest L., Helping Teacher, Inez
Ragland, Anna Lou, Helping Teacher, Morgantown
Ramsey, Imogene, West Main St., Lebanon
Ray, Annie, Supervisor, Training School, Murray State Teachers College, Murray
Reimer, Sibbia, Burlington
Rice, Mrs. W. H., Morehead High School, Morehead
Richards, Edith, Elementary Teacher, Dalton
Rives, Sara, Supervisor, Intermediate Grades, 25 E. 7th St., Covington
Roome, Elizabeth, Critic, Morehead State Teachers College, Elizabeth St., Morehead
Ross, C. C., Professor of Educational Psychology, College of Education, University of Kentucky, Lexington 29
Ross, Uel W., Principal, Central Park School, McHenry

Rudisill, Mabel, Department of Education, Western Kentucky State Teachers College, Bowling Green
Rupard, Nancy, RT. 1, Winchester
Scaggs, Maxine Kiser, Elementary Teacher, Greenup
Sexton, Agnes, Whitesburg
Shirley, Curtis E., Rt. 9, Frankfort
Short, Goldia, Helping Teacher, Allen
Smith, Bert L., Western Kentucky State Teachers College, Box 187, Bowling Green
Sneed, Ruth, Itinerant Teacher Training, Home Economics, College of Education, University of Kentucky, Lexington 29
Spikard, Ronella, College of Education, University of Kentucky, Lexington 29
Stamper, Mary Edwin, Elementary Supervisor, Hopkinsville
Stewart, Ruth Burton, 1509 State St., Bowling Green
Sutton, Elizabeth W., Supervisor, Breathitt County Schools, Jackson
Swain, Mary, Reading Consultant, Scott-Foresman Company, 230 N. 3rd St., Danville
Taylor, Willam S., College of Education, University of Kentucky, Lexington 29
Tarter, Lela, Helping Teacher, Mintonville
Travelstead, Mary Lee, Teacher, Junior High School, 312 West Cedar St., Franklin
Vanderpool, Thelma S., Royalton 7
Virgin, Vera, Director of Census and Attendance, Greenup
Walden, Gladys M., Helping Teacher, 311 Duffield St., Harlan
Walters, Ovelia, Elementary Supervisor, Fonthill
Ward, Emma B., Helping Teacher, Lawrenceburg
Warren, Pansy, College Heights, Box 54, Bowling Green
Whalin, E. B., Superintendent, Raceland Independent Schools, Raceland
Wilhoite, Naomi, Supervisor, State Department of Education, New Capitol Bldg., Frankfort
Williams, Thersa Hacker, Box 62, Whitley City
Williamson, Mary L., State Department of Education, Frankfort
Wilson, Mattie Mae, Suebennett College, London
Wolfe, Mary Elizabeth, Elementary Teacher, 1241 Indianola St., Bowling Green
Woodard, Sallie, Secretary-Treasurer, Hopkins County Board of Education, Court House, Madisonville
Woods, Charles, Helping Teacher, Hyden
Young, Arline, Primary Supervisor, 25 E. 7th St., Covington
Young, Lula B., 135 Winn Ave., Winchester
Zurfluh, John, 1531 Southgate Ave., Louisville

LOUISIANA

Aiken, E. S., Supervisor, Rapides Parish School Board, Alexandria
Babin, Larry J., Superintendent, Donaldsonville
Bassich, Joseph B., Professor of Education, 6363 St. Charles Ave., New Orleans
Bauduit, A. Leonie, Principal, 4849 Chestnut St., New Orleans
Bergeron, H. J., Supervisor of Instruction, St. Landry Parish, Opelousa
Best, Camilla, Division of Audio-Visual Aids, 1835 Erato St., New Orleans 13
Burnham, Joy, Assistant Supervisor, 205 Cypress St., Natchitoches
Causey, J. P., Principal, Oak Ridge High School, Oak Ridge
Collette, Mabel, Supervisor of Primary Grades, Calcasie Parish School Board, Lake Charles
Craton, Ruby, Supervisor, Webster Parish Schools, Minden
Davis, Beatrice, Parish Supervisor of Instruction, Braithwaite
Ducote, S. C., Supervisor, Avoyelles Parish School Board, Marksville
Eisely, A. M., Mrs., Elementary Supervisor, Box 949, Tallulah
Ferran, Rose, Primary Supervisor, 3515 Napoleon Ave., New Orleans
Goldenberg, Principal, 142 N. Herndon, Shreveport 70
Green, Thomas, Supervisor, 407 Hillary St., New Orleans 18
Guilbeau, Lolita, Supervisor, Marksville
Harris, Margaret, Dean of Lower School, Metarie Park County Day School, Metarie Park, New Orleans 20
Haws, Maggie, Supervisor of Schools, Bastrop
Hay, Dorothy A., Specialist in Guidance, Orleans Parish School Board, 703 Carondelet St., New Orleans 13
Hefley, Sue, Supervisor of School Libraries, State Department of Education, Baton Rouge 4
Hinrichs, Amy H., Principal, Robert M. Lushes School, 315 Willow St., New Orleans 18
Jackson, Kara V., Instructor in Education, Louisiana Negro Normal, Grambling
Janvier, Carmelite, Director, Division of Special Services, New Orleans Public Schools, 703 Carondelet St., New Orleans 13
Kolb, May L., Elementary Principal, 1828 Franklin Ave., New Orleans 17
Landry, Thomas, Plaquemine
Lane, Caro, State Supervisor of Health, State Department of Education, Baton Rouge 4
Marionneaux, P. E., Principal, Shady Grove School, Box 58, Maringouin
Markey, Ruth, Supervisor, 6038 Canal Blvd., New Orleans
Mayfield, Henry L., Supervisor, 1700 Jefferson Ave., Covington
McBride, A. A., Lafayette Parish Supervisor, Lafayette
McClendon, W. C., Supervisor, Acadia Parish Schools, Hotel Monteleone, New Orleans
Miller, Blanche, Supervisor of Instruction, Richland Parish Schools, Box 396, Rayville
Molony, Miss A. J., Principal, B. M. Palmer School, 1339 Clouet St., New Orleans
Montegut, M. O., Superintendent of Schools, Reserve
Morrison, Irene Clark, Supervision of Instruction, Union Parish School Board, Farmerville
Nelson, Bertha G., Supervisor of Schools, Box 231, Winsboro
Oliver, Marjorie, 210 Louisville Ave., Monroe
Pearce, H. L., Jr., Supervisor, Denham Springs
Perkins, Mrs. J. L., Elementary Supervisor, East Baton Rouge School Board, Baton Rouge
Pitre, Ruth, Supervisor of Elementary Schools, 476 Sala Ave., Westwego
Poncet, Aimee J., High School Supervisor, School Administration Bldg., 703 Carondelet St., New Orleans 13
Richards, Georgette, Materials and Library Supervisor, Ascension Parish, Donaldsonville
Rousseve, Charles B., Principal, Johnson Lockett School, 3240 Law St., New Orleans 17
Roy, Jeanne, Specialist in Homemaking, 703 Carondelet St., New Orleans 13
Roy, P. A., Loyola University, New Orleans 15
Sawyer, Rita, Junior High School Head Teacher, 189 Oakley Drive, Shreveport 67
Schmalzrid, Alma, Supervisor of Primary Grades, State Department of Education, Baton Rouge 4
Schwartz, H. O., Supervisor of Instruction, Winnfield
Short, Alice, Elementary Principal, Box 403, Cedar Grove Station, Shreveport
Sister Cornelia, Principal, St. Vincent's College and Academy, Shreveport
Slocum, J. S., Parish Supervisor, School Board Office, Alexandria
Statum, Mrs. Leslye M., 324 Haynes Ave., West Monroe
Taylor, Elizabeth, Assistant Superintendent, School Board Office, 501 Court House, Shreveport
Terrebonne, L. P., Superintendent, Iberville Parish School Board, Railroad Ave., Plaquemine

LIST OF MEMBERS

Terrell, Catherine, Elementary Supervisor, 64 Chestnut St., New Iberia
Tharp, Fanny Rives, Parish Supervisor, Box 45, Mansfield
Thomas, Josephine, John McDonought High School, Esplanade Ave. & Dorgenois St., New Orleans
Trezevant, Blanche, Supervisor of English and Language Arts, State Department of Education, Baton Rouge 4
Tubre, R., Principal, Rosenthal Grammar School, 1712 Monroe St., Alexandria
Walsworth, M. M., Supervisor, E. Carroll Parish Schools, Lake Providence
Whelan, James F., Chairman, Department of Education, Loyola University, 6363 St. Charles Ave., New Orleans
Williams, Chrissie H., Supervisor, 1419 S. Grand St., Monroe
Williams, Fannie C., Principal, Valena C. Jones Elementary School, 2121 Annette St., New Orleans
Woodard, C. T., Supervisor of Schools, Jackson Parish School Board, Jonesboro
Woodard, Helen, Teacher Personnel Advisor, Division of Extension, LaPolytechnic Institute, Ruston
Yeiser, Idabelle, Director, Department of Education, Dillard University, New Orleans

MAINE

Bagley, L. P., Superintendent of Schools, Island Falls
Beverage, Wentworth, Principal, Jay High School, Chisholm
Brown, Zeta I., Elementary Supervisor, State Department of Education, Augusta
Buker, Lou M., Elementary Supervisor, Cony High School Bldg., Augusta
Bull, Lucy W., Supervisor, State Department of Education, Augusta
Carpenter, R. J., Superintendent of Schools, 183 Harlow St., Bangor
Cobb, Beatrice, Teacher, Gray
Cox, Julia B., 34 High St., Farmington
Doring, Jessie, Perry
Dresser, Irene L., 12 High St., Kennebunk
Edminister, W. H., Superintendent of Schools, Norway
Estey, Mildred F., Teacher, R. R. # 1, Ellsworth
Foster, Frank C., Associate Director, "Save the Children Federation," Friendship
Hayden, Villa E., Field Supervisor of Rural Education, State Department of Education, Augusta
Kendall, Glenn, Dean, School of Education, University of Maine, Orono
Ladd, Harland A., State Department of Education, Augusta
Storer, Clayton A., Superintendent, Union No. 110, Box 66, Lee
Wieden, Clifford O. T., Principal, Washington State Normal, Machias
Woodman, Orlando C., Superintendent, 145 Dresden Avenue, Gardiner

MARYLAND

Adams, Ruby M., Director of Elementary Education, 108 Wash. St., Cumberland
Alder, Grace, Supervisor of Elementary Schools, Lexington & Liberty Sts., Baltimore
Bannatyne, Kate, Supervising Teacher, Garrett Co., Grantsville
Bard, Harry, Curriculum Specialist, 3 E. 25th St., Baltimore 18
Billows, Marjorie J., Art Supervisor, Bd. of Education, Rockville
Blackford, F. Pauline, General Supervisor, Washington County, Board of Education, Hagerstown
Botsford, Jane E., Supervising Teacher, 307 Bedford, Cumberland
Bowie, B. Lucile, Supervisor of Elementary Education, La Plata
Brechbill, Henry, Professor of Education & Director of Student Teaching, University of Maryland, College Park
Broome, Edwin W., Superintendent, Public Schools of Montgomery County, Rockville
Brown, Edward W., Headmaster, Calvert School, 105 Tuscany Rd., Baltimore
Brown, Stella E., Director of Student Teaching, State Teachers College, Towson 4
Chadwick, Gail, Supervisor of Elementary Schools, Ellicott City
Chrissinger, Mary Helen, Director of Art Education, 38 Wayside Ave., Hagerstown
Compton, Lillian C., President, State Teachers College, Frostburg
Coulburn, Alice Mae, Supervisor of Elementary Schools, Board of Education, Princess Anne
Daniel, Etheline, Supervisor, Bd. of Education, Rockville
Dawson, Leah W., McDonogh School, McDonogh
Dean, Myrtle E., Principal, John Hunbird School, 233 Elder St., Cumberland
Devilbiss, Wilbur, Principal, 4619 College Ave., College Park
Dowling, Nellie F., Principal Hammond St. School, Western Port
Eckhardt, Myrtle S., Supervising Teacher, Baltimore County, Glyndon
Fisher, Hazel L., Supervisor of Elementary Schools, Board of Education, Bel Air
Gaskin, Emma F., 1224 Druid Hill Ave., Baltimore 17
Grau, Mary L., Supervisor of Elementary Schools, Board of Education, Bel Air
Greene, Winifred, Supervising Teacher of Primary Grades, 86 Mt. Pleasant, Frostburg
Hawkins, Earle T., Supervisor of Secondary Schools, 1111 Lexington Bldg., Baltimore 1
Hoffman, Miriam Lee, Supervisor of Music, Board of Education, Hagerstown
Hoyle, Mildred, Supervisory Teacher, Chestertown
Hull, G. R., Supervisors Office, Hyattsville Elementary School, Hyattsville
Hyson, S., Superintendent, Carroll County, Westminster
Johnson, Lucille E., Supervisor of Music, Board of Education, Rockville
Laws, Margaret, Board of Education, Snowhill
Matthews, Anna H., Supervisor of Student Teaching, 107 E. College Ave., Salisbury
Meany, Elizabeth, Elementary Supervisor, Rockville
Mendenhall, James E., 5 W. Saul Rd., Kensington
Parker, Harry R., 2304 Druid Hill Ave., Baltimore
Pierson, Mildred B., 329 No. Calhoun St., Baltimore
Pogue, Nell Jones, 4506 Elm St., Chevy Chase 15
Richardson, Anne H., Supervisor of Elementary Education, Board of Education, Hagerstown
Sammis, Ethel E., Department of Education, Lexington Bldg., Lexington & Liberty Sts., Baltimore 1
Schindler, Alvin W., Associate Professor of Education, College of Education, University of Maryland, College Park
Shugrue, Alma M., Administrative Principal, 8509 Hazelwood Drive, Bethesda 14
Smith, Josie G., Acting Supervisor of English, 2326 Madison Ave., Baltimore
Stack, Margaret S., Supervisor of Elementary Schools, Centreville
Steele, Irene M., State Teachers College, Towson
Thompson, A. May, Supervisor of Elementary Schools, 402 South Second St., Denton
Thompson, Louise Freeman, Supervisor of Elementary Education, 115 E. Church St., Frederick
Ward, Lula D., Principal and Supervisor, Ridgely
Whitelaw, John B., USNR, 4626 Western Ave., Chevy Chase 16

Williams, Maud L., Supervisor of Kindergarten and Primary Grades, 629 George St., Baltimore
Willis, Benjamin C., Superintendent of Schools, Board of Education, Hagerstown
Wilson, Caroline, Elementary School Supervisor, Kitzmiller
Young, E. Violette, Leonardtown

MASSACHUSETTS

Abbott, S. L., Jr., Principal, School Street School, Middleboro
Bain, Winifred E., President, Wheelock College, Riverway and Pilgrim Rd., Boston 15
Bartell, Madeline E., Elementary Supervisor, 87 Winter St., Haverhill
Boyer, Laurenda A., 415 Hamilton St., Southbridge
Bradbury, Hazel, Elementary Supervisor, Barnstable Schools, Training School, Hyannis
Burton, W. H., Director of Apprenticeship, Harvard University, Lawrence Hall, Kirkland St., Cambridge 38
Bussell, Esther S., Shays St., Amherst
Butler, Elizabeth F., Supervisor, Primary Grades, 12 Fresh Pond Lane, Cambridge
Carson, Olive G., Supervisor of Elementary Grades, School Department, Hall Ave., Medford 55
Chase, W. Linwood, Boston University School of Education, 84 Exeter St., Boston 16
Cole, Eleanor F., The Pilgrim Press, 14 Beacon St., Boston 8
Cockrell, Dura Louise, Assistant Regional Supervisor, 99 Chauncey St., Boston
Colvin, Wilson, J. W. Weeks Junior High School, Newton Centre 59
Cox, Philip W. L., Professor of Education, Box 663, Oak Bluffs
Daniels, Laura A., Principal, The Tapley School, Sherman and Bay Sts., Springfield 9
Dingley, Vivian A., Principal, Winthrop L. Cheney School, 75 Washington St., Belmont 78
Draper, Mabel S., Old Sudbury Rd., Wayland
Driscoll, Martina McDonald, Supervisor in State Department of Education, 93 Moraine St., Jamaica Plain
Fernow, Alice, Supervisor of Elementary Education, 166 Hancock St., Stoneham 80
Flagg, Sadie E., Principal White St. School, 300 White St., Springfield
Gregory, Katherine T., Supervisor of Elementary Education, 23 Maple St., Arlington 74
Grover, Eldridge C., Superintendent of Schools, School Department, Reading
Ireland, Everett W., Superintendent of Schools, School Committee Rooms, Somerville
Lincoln, Elizabeth M., Elementary Supervisor, 226 Union St., Leominster
Marble, Sarah A., Supervisor of Primary Grades, Room 14, City Hall, Worcester 8
Marsh, Harry B., Superintendent, 32 Spring St., Springfield
Mitchell, Mary Alice, Director of Elementary Education, 32 Eden Ave., West Newton 65
Nelson, Edwin A., Superintendent, School Department, Brockton 8
Nichols, Marjorie H., Elementary Supervisor, School Department, Southbridge
O'Connor, Mary E., Teacher, 158 Highland St., Taunton
O'Leary, Joseph M., 15 Chesbrough Rd., West Roxbury
Page, John C., Superintendent, West Newbury
Piper, Helen J., Supervisor, Grades 4-6, 55 Eastern Ave., East Lynn
Pottenger, Mary O., General Supervisor of Elementary Education, 32 Spring St., Springfield 5
Pottle, Annie C., Principal, Underwood District, 570 Centre St., Newton 58
Prouty, Etta F., Head, Geography Department, 38 Spring St., Shrewsbury
Quinnam, Bertha C., Elementary Supervisor, 113 Thacher St., Milton 87
Remon, Marion E., Director of Elementary Education, Office, Superintendent of Schools, Main St., Melrose
Sauer, Edith, Principal, Lincoln and Jefferson Avenue Schools, 732 Chestnut St., Springfield
Shaver, Erwin L., Congregational-Christian Churches, 14 Beacon, Boston 8
Simmons, Charles G., Teacher, 12 Commonwealth Ave., Boston 16
Sister Mary Christina, U. S. C., Dean and Director of Teacher Training, 466 Prospect St., Fall River
Somers, Ruth V., Aberdeen Apts., Andover
Sullivan, Helen Blair, Associate Professor of Eduation, Boston University, 84 Exeter St., Boston 16
Sweeney, Ellen C., Elementary Supervisor, 48 Morgan St., New Bedford
Varney, Charles E., Superintendent of Schools, Stoneham 80
Wadleigh, Verna L., Editorial Department, Ginn and Company, Statler Bldg., Boston 17
Wallace, Jennie, Williams Junior High School, Chelsea 50
Wesley, Marian J., Supervisor Elementary Education, Rm. 14, City Hall, Worcester
Wilmarth, Madelin A., 535 Chandler St., Worcester 2
Wilson, Guy M., Professor of Education, 30 Pine St., Wellesley Hills

MICHIGAN

Alexander, Effie, Supervisor of Elementary Schools, 153 E. Church St., Adrian
Althouse, A. D., Supervisor of Vocational Education, 467 W. Hancock, Detroit 1
Anderson, Superintendent of Schools, 2340 Third St., Trenton
Ayres, F. M., Superintendent, Dundee
Bader, Edith M., 1305 Baldwin, Ann Arbor
Barnes, C. C., Director of Social Studies, Division of Instruction, 467 W. Hancock, Detroit 1
Beck, Elsie M., Supervisor of Instruction, Department of Social Studies, 467 W. Hancock, Detroit 1
Boyne, Edwin M., Superintendent, Mason
Brennan, Lenora, Supervising Teacher, Western Michigan College of Education, 204 Woodward Ave., Kalamazoo
Champion, Clara E., Assistant Professor of Education, Wayne University, 467 W. Hancock, Detroit 1
Clark, Bertha, County Normal Principal, 909 Dakota Ave., Gladstone
Collins, Laurentine B., Assistant Director, School-Community Relations, 1354 Broadway, Detroit
Courtis, S. A., Professor of Education, University of Michigan and Wayne University, 9110 Dwight Ave., Detroit
Crofoot, Bess L., Warren
Crull, Howard D., Superintendent, Port Huron
Dewey, Joseph C., Director of Training, State Teachers College, 123 E. Magnetic, Marquette
Dimond, Stanley E., Director, Citizenship Education Study, Detroit Public Schools and Wayne University, 436 Merrick St., Detroit
Downer, Effie M., Assistant Professor, College of Education, Wayne University, Detroit 1
Ellingson, Evelyn A., Regional Consultant, Public Health Nursing, Michigan Department of Health, Lansing
Everill, Winifred, Elementary Supervisor, 197 Cass Ave., Mt. Clemens
Faunce, Roland C., Department of Public Instruction, Lansing 2
Frederick O. I., Western State Teachers College, 311 Woodward Ave., Kalamazoo 47

LIST OF MEMBERS   145

Garrison, Noble Lee, Head of Department of Education, Michigan State Normal College, Ypsilanti
Graybill, Clara, Director of Elementary Education, 428 W. South St., Kalamazoo
Gregory, Kathleen, Teacher, 707 W. Ludington Ave., Ludington
Gutzler, Grace. 114 Charles St., East Lansing
Haley, Nelle, Director of Elementary Education, 620 S. Jefferson St., Saginaw
Hanlon, Helen J., Division of Instruction, 467 W. Hancock, Detroit
Hazel, F. M., Superintendent, Lakeview School, Battle Creek
Heilbronn, Edna M., Supervisor of Practice Teaching, 810 S. College Ave., Mt. Pleasant
Howard, Ervin, Assistant Superintendent of Schools, Fordson Board of Education, Dearborn
Irwin, Manley E., Division of Instruction, 467 W. Hancock Ave., Detroit 1
Jameson, Mary S., Supervisory Teacher, 2615 Barlum Tower, Detroit
Johnson, Eleanor L., Elementary Supervisor, 545 Maffett St., Muskegon Heights
Johnson, Erwin M., 501 W. Columbia Ave., Belleville
Johnston, Edgar, School of Education, University of Michigan, Ann Arbor
Kane, Ruth F., Principal, 650 Philip, Detroit 15
Kaufman, Jennie M., County Helping Teacher, Court House, Grand Haven
Kelley, Earl C., Associate Professor of Education, Wayne University, 467 W. Hancock, Detroit 1
King, Ira F., Superintendent, Coldwater
Laurence, Helen M., 1352 College Ave., N. E., Grand Rapids 5
Lewton, Opal S., 806 W. Michigan, Lansing 14
Martin, Frances K., Consultant in Elementary Education, Central State Teachers College, Mt. Pleasant
Mason, Katherine A., Counselor & Instructor, Western Michigan College of Education, Kalamazoo
Massey, Emil L., Supervisor of High School Science. 467 W. Hancock, Detroit
McClusky, Howard Y., Professor of Educational Psychology, School of Education, University of Michigan, Ann Arbor
McGee, D. Reed, Superintendent, North Branch
McNeil, Ella E., School of Public Health, University of Michigan, Ann Arbor
Meighen, Mary, Grade Supervisor, Escanaba
Mosier, Earl E., State Consultant in Secondary Education, 1814 William St., Lansing
Mulder, Fred J., Head of Mathematics Department, Edwin Denby High School, 12800 Kelly Rd., Detroit
Neumann, Frederic T., 1141 N. Pine St., Lansing
Northey, Thomas J., 219 Healy Ave., Negaunee
Olson, Willard C., Director of Research in Child Development, University of Michigan Elementary School, Ann Arbor
Park, Charles B., Superintendent, Mt. Pleasant
Randall, Don, Wayne High School, Wayne
Rankin, Paul T., 16823 Plainview Rd., Detroit
Riddering, A., Board of Education, Melvindale
Robinson, Roy E., Elementary Principal, 143 Farrand Park, Highland Park
Robinson, William McKinley, Director of Department of Rural Education, Western Michigan College of Education, 1414 Low Rd., Kalamazoo
Rogers, Virgil M., Superintendent, Battle Creek
Rojas, Pauline M., Assistant Professor, University of Puerto Rico (on Leave) 1020 S. University, Ann Arbor
Rudduck, Lillian W., Principal, 4920 Grandville Ave., Detroit 2
Rugen, Mabel E., Associate Professor of Physical Education and Health, 4014 University High School, Ann Arbor
Seibert, Alvena, Secondary School Supervisor, 1111 Beers St., Port Huron

Shattuck, Marquis E., Assistant Superintendent, 1354 Broadway, Detroit 26
Shaw, Lena A., Assistant Director of Language Education, 467 Hancock W., Detroit 1
Shibler, H. L., Superintendent, 12541 Second Ave., Highland Park
Shimel, Vesta M., Supervisor of Elementary Grades, 143 Bostwick Ave., N. E., Grand Rapids
Shimmel, Ethel, 118 Buckley St., Kalamazoo
Sister Mary Nolasco R. S. M., Supervisor, 8200 W. Outer Dr., Detroit
Sister Mary Richard, Dean, Marygrove College, 8425 W. McNichols Rd., Detroit 21
Sommers, Mildred E., Director of Elementary Education, City Public Schools, Jackson
Stauffer, Gladys, Lakeview School, Battle Creek
Stenson, Helen Elaine, Central Michigan College of Education, Mt. Pleasant
Stephens, Pearl, Critic Teacher, 215 Austin Ave., Albion
Stone, R. H., Manufacturer of Educational Equipment, P. O. Box 414, Detroit
Swan, Agnes E., Assistant Supervisor, 2281 W. Grand Blvd., Detroit
Thayer, Howard C., Rural Supervisor, County Bldg., Ann Arbor
Varson, Nina F., Supervisor of Social Studies, 291 Elmhurst, Highland Park 3
Waltmire, Helen H., 16 Lafayette S. E., Grand Rapids
Warner, Mary M., Kalamazoo College, Kalamazoo
Wellever, Edith L., Rural Supervisor, 22517 Law, Dearborn
Whipple, Gertrude, Supervisor of Reading, 467 W. Hancock Ave., Detroit
Wilson, Zeal Z., Elementary Principal, Pearl School, Jackson
Woody, Clifford, School of Education, University of Michigan, Ann Arbor

MINNESOTA

Anderson, Walter A., Assistant Superintendent, 305 City Hall, Minneapolis, 15
Andrews, Walter A., Director of Elementary and Secondary Schools, State Department of Education, 301 State Office Bldg., St. Paul 1
Archer, Clifford P., 1381 N. Cleveland Ave., St. Paul 8
Boardman, Charles W., Director of Student Teaching and Professor of Education, 4500 Upton Ave., S., Minneapolis
Bossing, Nelson L., Professor, College of Education, University of Minnesota, Minneapolis 14
Brother J. Leo, St, Mary's College, Winona
Brueckner, Leo J., Professor of Elementary Education, University of Minnesota, Minneapolis 14
Bryne, May E., Director of Special Education, Jackson School, 15th Ave., S. at 4th St., Minneapolis
Cahlander, Loren L., Corcoran School, 19th Ave. S. and 34th St., Minneapolis 7
Carleton, Mary E., Principal, Hiawatha School, 42nd Ave. S. and E. 42nd St., Minneapolis 6
Cook, Walter W., Associate Professor of Education, 305 Eddy Hall, University of Minnesota, Minneapolis 14
Cross, C. W., Superintendent, Faribault Public Schools, Faribault
Cutright, Prudence, Assistant Superintendent, 305 City Hall, Minneapolis 15
Davis, Vera, Director of Elementary Education, 226 1st St., N. W., Chisholm
Fisher, Marie, Supervisor of Tests and Measurements, 727 City Hall, St. Paul 2
Gallagher, Agnes, 220 N. 1st Ave., W., Duluth
Giere, Cora A., Grade Supervisor, Mankato
Goslin, Willard E., Superintendent of Schools, Board of Education, Minneapolis
Hood, Edith G., Principal, 2328 Seabury, Minneapolis

Ivey, Mae J., Supervisor of Elementary Grades, 316 Vinehurst, Albert Lea
Jasperson, Lillian, Principal, Bancroft School, 38th St. and 13th Ave., Minneapolis 7
Jensen, Myrtle E., Supervisor, 167½ Center St., Winona
Johnston, Ruth V., Counselor, University of Minnesota, Minneapolis 14
Knox, Bess J., Supervising Principal, 515 5th Ave., S. E., Minneapolis 14
Lichtenberger, J. F., Principal, Seward School, 24th St. and 28th Ave. S., Minneapolis
Maass, Harry H., Principal, North High School, Minneapolis
Murphy, Edna I., Supervisor, School District #1, Box 354, Grand Rapids
Narveson, Carl R., Superintendent, Lake Park
Nelson, Ethel V., Supervisor, Elementary Grades, Box 107, Mountain Iron
Newell, Bernice, Supervisor of Instruction, Board of Education, 305 City Hall, Minneapolis 15
Nolte, Karl F., Director of Elementary Education, Hibbing High School, Hibbing
Nystrom, Ellen C., Board of Education, Boys Vocational High School, Minneapolis 8
O'Neill, M. Lucille, Elementary Grade Supervisor, c/o Hotel Arcana, Coleraine
Parker, Mrs. H. J., President, PTA, 5128 Thomas Ave., S., Minneapolis 10
Paull, Mabel A., 112 7th St., S., St. Cloud
Perry, Dora C., Junior High School Supervisor, State Teachers College, St. Cloud
Petersen, Edith, Principal Keewaydin School, 30th Ave. and 52nd St., Minneapolis
Raymond, Ruth, Professor of Art Education, 1000 University S. E., Minneapolis 14
Refsland, Martha B., Associate Supervisor of Elementary Education, Houston
Rose, Ella J., Assistant Professor of Home Economics Education, University of Minnesota, University Farm, St. Paul 8
Roverud, Ella M., Principal, Gordon and Baker Schools, 622 Grand Ave., St. Paul 5
Sister Mary Ellen de Lourdes, Supervisor, St. Agatha's Conservatory, 26 E. Exchange St., St. Paul 2
Sorensen, R. R., Superintendent of Schools, Tracy
Van Brussell, Martha, Grade Supervisor, Central Junior High School, St. Cloud
Voigt, Alfreda H., Principal, Hay School, 10th Ave. N. & Penn., Minneapolis 11
Waller, Beulah, Principal, Cooper School, 44th Ave., S. & 33rd St., Minneapolis
Weidner, Rose B., Principal, Bremer School, Lowry and Emerson N. Sts., Minneapolis
Wiecking, Anna M., Principal, College Elementary School, State Teachers College, Mankato

MISSISSIPPI

Andrews, Annie, Supervisor of Elementary Schools, Amite County, Liberty
Bourland, Mrs. Harry, Elementary Supervisor, Monroe County, Aberdeen
Brazeale, J. L., Superintendent, Lambert Consolidated School, Lambert
Coffee, Olive, 549 Main St., Jupelo
Collins, Mary E., Supervisor, Elementary Schools, New Albany
Fishburn, Ynez, Box 582, Brookhaven
Ford, Minnie, Mississippi South College, Station A., Harriesburg
Hunter, Mrs. Earle, Elementary Supervisor, Newton County, Decatur
Jobe, E. R., High School Supervisor, Old State House, Jackson
Lewis, T. L., Superintendent High School, Hickory
McKee, Clyde V., State Rural and Elementary Supervisor, Jackson
Newman, Sallie B., Office of Director of Elementary Instruction, Central High School Bldg., Jackson 19

Patterson, D. R., Director of Instruction, State Department of Education, Jackson 113
Ratliff, T. J., Elementary Supervisor, Ripley
Richey, Elizabeth, Elementary Supervisor, Oxford
Stevens, Nora, Principal, Elementary School, 209 S. 31st Ave., Hattiesburg
Thompson, Louise G., Box 225, Vicksburg
Weathersby, Mary E., Associate Professor, Home Economics Education, Mississippi State College, State College
Zeigel, William H., Dean, Delta State Teachers College, Cleveland

MISSOURI

Amen, C. E., 513 N. Williams, Columbia
Blackburn, Helen I., Principal, 3401 S. Benton St., Kansas City 3
Blackwell, G. L., Superintendent of Schools, 10th and Felix Sts., St. Joseph 54
Bottrell, Harold R., Director, Burrall Service Projects, 1207 University St., Columbia
Brown, Elmer B., Associate Professor of Education, State Teachers College, Warrensburg
Bush, Mildred B., Primary Supervisor, 6807 Waterman Ave., St. Louis
Casey, Martha S., Principal, Carondelet School, 8221 Minnesota Ave., St. Louis
Charters, W. W., Stephens College, Columbia
Clarke, Katherine, Principal, Meramec School, 400 S. Meramec, Clayton
Collins, Anne J., Principal, Howard School, 4948 Labadie Ave., St. Louis 15
Cone, David A., Superintendent, Lathrop
Croy, Wallace, Superintendent of Schools, Tarkio
Cusack, Alice M., Director of Kindergarten-Primary, 210 Library Bldg., 9th and Locust Sts., Kansas City
Elliott, Lucy C., Supervisor of Special Schools, 911 Locust St., St. Louis 8
Evans, W. L., 1 W. 10th St., Fulton
Fleischaker, Ruth R., Sight-Saving Class Teacher, S. B. Ladd School, 3640 Benton St., Kansas City 3
Gilbert, A. W., Director of Research and Curriculum, Office of the Superintendent, Kansas City
Haldaman, D. H., Superintendent, Rt. #4, Farmington
Hamrick, Clyde S., County Superintendent of Schools, Hillsboro
Henderson, Barbara, Director of Intermediate Grades, Rockhill Manor, 43rd and Locust Sts., Kansas City
Hollister, Mary L., Principal, 520 W. 40th St., Kansas City 2
Hooss, Ida M., Elementary Principal, 5330 Pershing Ave., St. Louis
Hopkins, Mary Sue, Department of Education, 202 Broad St., Warrensburg
Hunt, Herold C., Superintendent, 9th & Locust St., Kansas City 6
Jackson, Euris J., 1055 Tuxedo Blvd., Webster Groves 19
Johnson, B. Lamar, Dean of Instruction and Librarian, Stephens College, Columbia
Keith, L. G., Superintendent of Schools, Cardwell
Knight, Riley F., Superintendent of Schools, Bloomfield
Kretzmann, P. E., Director, Library, Concordia Seminary, Pritzlaff Memorial Library, 801 De Mun, St. Louis 5
Ledbetter, Enola, Elementary Teacher, 6062 Cates Ave., Apt. C-1, St. Louis 12
Lee, Charles A., Professor of Education and Director of Educational Service, Washington University, St. Louis 5
Lewallen, Fred, Superintendent of Schools, Chaffee
Lloyd, Elizabeth C., 7270 Stanford, St. Louis 5
MacKay, J. L., 573 S. Clay Ave., Kirkwood 22
Manley, Helen, Director of Health and Physical Education, Public Schools, University City 5

LIST OF MEMBERS

Manuel, Dessa Jane, State Supervisor of Public Schools, 817 E. Belmont, Springfield
Martinez, D. F., State Supervisor of Negro Schools, Capitol, Jefferson City
McClure, Worth, Superintendent, Board of Education, 6701 Delmar Blvd., University City 5
Meyering, H. R., 231 E. 72nd St., Kansas City 5
Myers, Anna G., Assistant Director of Research, 217 Library Bldg., Kansas City 6
Oliver, Stanley C., Professor of Education, State Teachers College, Springfield
Phillips, C. A., Rm. 209, Education Bldg., University of Missouri, Columbia
Prevey, Esther, Director, Family Life Education Department, 3845 McGee St., Kansas City 2
Rennison, A. M., 2103 Mulberry, St. Joseph
Schmidt, Julia B., Principal, Shenandoah School, 3828 Wilmington, St. Louis 16
Schultze, L. J., Superintendent of Schools, Cape Girardeau
Seidlitz, Mabel, Primary Supervisor, 5084 Maple Ave., St. Louis
Sparling, E. A., Superintendent of Schools, Crystal City
Sperry, Lochie E., Supervisor of Language Arts, 940 N. Jefferson St., Springfield
Taylor, J. F., Superintendent of Schools, Deering
Tucker, Leona, Training School Director, 219 Lillian St., Bolivar
Wahlert, Jennie, Elementary Principal, 2918 Harper St., St. Louis 7

MONTANA

Aikins, Lincoln J., Superintendent, Glendive
Ames, W. R., Professor of Education, Montana State University, Missoula
Baldwin, Boyd F., 2300 Hilda, Missoula
Bergan, K. W., Superintendent, School District Number 9, Browning
Brockman, L. O., Assistant Professor of Education and Psychology, Montana State College, Bozeman
Brown, Maude, A., State Board of Health, Helena
Carleton, Linus J., Superintendent, Helena
Crump, P. C., Superintendent, St. Ignatius
Flores, Zella N., Elementary Supervisor, 514 8th Ave. S., Lewistown
Forster, Thelma Allen, State Music Supervisor, 924 11th Ave., Helena
Gullidge, A. O., Department of Public Instruction, Helena
Jones, Kyle, 1620 Toole Ave., Missoula
Lausted, Alice, Elementary Principal, 205 N. 26th St., Billings
Manning, C. J., Superintendent, Junior High School Bldg., Lewistown
Peterson, Lillian L., State Department of Public Instruction, Helena
Ragsdale, 501 Avenue F, Billings
Ryan, Estelle B., Consultant in Elementary Education, 45 Maryland Hotel, Great Falls
Sands, R. F., Superintendent, Poplar
Solvie, A. J., Superintendent, Saco Public Schools, Saco
Stegner, Warren E., Superintendent of City Schools, Miles City
Williams, D. S., Superintendent, Box 547, Bozeman

NEBRASKA

Aller, Blanche C., Assistant Professor of Education, Hastings College, Hastings
Beattie, Merle M., Director of Elementary Education, Board of Education Office, Lincoln 8
Bimson, O. H., Assistant Superintendent of Schools, 720 S. 22nd St., Lincoln 8
Black, Leo P., State Capitol, Lincoln
Burnham, Archer L., Executive Secretary, Nebraska State Teachers Association, 605 S. 14th St., Lincoln 8
Ellwood, Robert S., Nebraska State Teachers College, Chadron
Harding, Dorothy L., Supervisor of Elementary Instruction, Grand Island

Marrs, R. M., South High School, Omaha
McNickle, T. R., Superintendent, Public Schools, York
Mielenz, Mary M., 3241 Holdrege, Lincoln
Morton, W. H., University of Nebraska Teachers College, Lincoln 8
Newell, Ethel K., 2555 Ellison Ave., Omaha 11
Rainey, Elizabeth, Supervisor of Primary Grades, 1425 S. 8th St., Omaha
Rice, John D., Superintendent, Kearney
Roys, Cassie F., Principal, Harrison and Walnut Schools, 2609 Bristol St., Omaha 10
Saylor, Galen, Associate Professor of Secondary Education, Teachers College, University of Nebraska
Taylor, L. O., 4842 Farnam St., University of Omaha, Omaha
Traster, Stella, Supervisor, 909 Lincoln St., Wayne
Wetzel, Marie E., 192 Drake Ct., Omaha 2
Williams, Ruth M., Station A, Box 55, Wayne
Wilson, Clara O., Chairman, Department of Elementary Education, Teachers College, University of Nebraska, Lincoln 8

NEVADA

Bray, Mildred, State Superintendent of Public Instruction, Carson City
Chapman, Joanna, Teacher Trainer, 942 Sierra, Reno
Morrison, Ida E., Reservation Principal, Carson Indian Agency, Stewart

NEW HAMPSHIRE

Hoctor, Cathryn R., Elementary Supervisor, Parker School, Concord

NEW JERSEY

Baldwin, Ruth L., Primary Supervisor, Franklin School, Prospect St. and Newton Pl., Westfield
Ballou, John L., Assistant Principal, High School, 305 New Jersey Ave., Point Pleasant
Batey, Eva, Teacher, 23 N. Ohio Ave., Atlantic City
Bergen, Dorothy, Teacher, Garfield School, Long Branch
Bigelow, Merrill A., Elementary Principal, Franklin School, Curtis St., Bloomfield
Bosshart, John H., 617 Trenton Trust Bldg., Trenton
Boutillier, Jessie W., Chairman, Department of English, Central C. and T. High School, Newark
Burd, Philip C., Assistant Principal, High School, Scotch Plains
Burns, Loretta L., School #8, 6th St., Elizabeth
Carr, Louis D., Principal, School #23, Romaine Ave., Jersey City 6
Cassel, Lloyd S., Superintendent of Schools, 6 Berkeley Pl., Freehold
Caswell, Hollis L., Professor of Education, Teachers College, Columbia University, 209 Hillcrest Ave., Leonia
Conway, Wm. F., Supervising Principal, Edgewater
Crowley, Luella J., Lindy Lake, Butler
Davis, C. V., Principal, Evergreen School, Plainfield
Delaney, Eleanor, Principal, Woodrow Wilson School, Edgar Rd., Elizabeth 2
Diamond, I. Victoria, Elementary Supervisor, School #6, 62nd St. and Broadway, West New York
Durrell, T. J., Department of Public Instruction, Trenton Trust Bldg., Trenton
Everett, Marcia A., Helping Teacher, Warren County, 319 Market St., Belvidere
Finger, Mary H., Principal, Gregory School, Trenton
Fisher, Gilmore J., Supervising Principal of Schools, Ewing Township, Parkway School, Trenton 8

Forrester, Gertrude, Director of Guidance, 71 Overpack Ave., Ridgefield Park
Geisser, Lillie J., Director of Instruction, 583 Mt. Prospect Ave., Newark 4
Hargrove, William B., Principal, Elliott St. School, Newark 4
Harrison, Eunice, Principal, Girls Vocational School, 108 Green St., Woodbridge
Hawkes, Evelyn J., Associate Professor of Education, New Jersey College for Women, New Brunswick
Haynes, Grace B., Elementary Supervisor, 449 Main St., Orange
Hayward, W. George, Principal, Elmwood School, 6 Emerson St., East Orange
Hendrickson, Mary, 27 Sheffield St., Jersey City 5
Hoppock, Anne, Assistant in Elementary Education, State Department of Public Instruction, Trenton
Hudgins, Charles F., 10 Chestnut St., East Orange
Hummer, H. Myrtle, Parker School, Union St., Trenton
Husk, Miriam, Newton School, Newark 3
Johnson, Eliza, 7 Joane Ter., Trenton
Johnston, Ruth S., Principal, George Washington Elementary School, Ridgewood
Keller, Ethel M., Elementary Principal, 711 Glen Ave., Westfield
Libby, Herschel S., Superintendent of Schools, 1253 Clinton Ave., Irvington 11
Lomax, Paul S., Professor of Education, New York University, 21 Beach Pl., Maplewood
Matthews, W. B., City Superintendent of Schools, High School, Cape May
McConnell, R., 801 Verona Ave., Pleasantville
McKendree, E. Wallis, Supervisor of Elementary Schools, Camden
McLean, William, Mt. Hebron Junior High School, Bellevue Ave., Upper Montclair
Miller, Fannie E., Helping Teacher—Rural School Supervisor, 413 N. Main St., Elmer
Morrison, Howard D., Supervising Principal, S. Clinton and Park Aves., Trenton 10
Myers, Lanning, Superintendent, High School Bldg., Wildwood
Petersen, Anna J., Supervisor of Elementary Education, 10 Suydam St., Apt. 12, New Brunswick
Potter, Floyd A., County Superintendent of Schools, Court House, Mays Landing
Pratt, Doris E., Camden County Helping Teacher, Black Horse Pike, Blackwood
Roach, Marian J., Intermediate Grade Supervisor, 610 15th St., Union City
Salsbury, Jerome C., Secondary Supervisor, Administration Bldg., Broad St. and Belleville Ave., Bloomfield
Saul, Anna E., Supervisor of Upper Elementary Grades, 259 Woodlawn Ave., Jersey City
Shaver, John J., Supervisor, 2 Harrison Ave., Jersey City
Shotwell, Fred C., Supervising Principal, Franklin
Shotwell, Harry W., Director of Secondary Guidance, 40 74th St., North Bergen
Sickler, Edna F., Gloucester County Helping Teacher, 61 Pitman Ave., Pitman
Sister M. Wenceslaus, St. James High School, Penns Grove
Smith, Ethel L., Director of Elementary Education, 9 S. Stockton St., Trenton
Smith, Florence M., Supervisor, 74 S. Munn Ave., East Orange
Storen, Helen, Tenafly High School, Tenafly
Taplin, Ida, Supervisor of Speech, Board of Education, Newark
Todd, Mrs. H. H., 1138 Boulevard, Bayonne
Truesdell, Marguerite, Helping Teacher, 389 Bath Ave., Long Branch
Van Syckle, Edith L., Helping Teacher, Salem County, 258 Giles, Bridgeton
Weber, Julia, 303 3rd St., Belvidere
Weidberg, Joseph M., Headmaster, Oxford Academy, Pleasantville

NEW MEXICO

Bradley, William T., Catholic Teachers College of New Mexico, Albuquerque
Diefendorf, J. W., University of New Mexico, Albuquerque
Drummond, Esther, Manzano Day School, Albuquerque
Gray, Howell, Box 111, Farmington
Leason, Marjorie, Principal, 421 N. 4th St., Raton
Low, Frank, 3013 N. Arno, Albuquerque
Lusk, Georgia L., Superintendent of Public Instruction, State Department of Education, Santa Fe
Mazurvek, Eleanor G., Coordinator-Junior and Senior High School, 3rd and Lead Ave., Albuquerque
Mills, Charles L., Hobbs Municipal School, Box Y, Hobbs
Pierson, Maude, Rural Supervisor, Curry County Board of Education, Clovis
Sanchez, Victoria D. de, Director of Remedial Work, Box 708, Las Vegas
Sands, Lester B., Assistant Professor of Education, Box 563, Las Vegas
Schroeder, Erna, Elementary Supervisor, 816 E. Silver Ave., Albuquerque
Schupp, Ona E., Principal, 223 N. High St., Albuquerque
Tireman, L. S., Professor of Education, University of New Mexico, 453 N. Sycamore, Albuquerque
Watson, Mary, State Department of Education, Santa Fe
Westerfield, Elizabeth, Headmistress, Manzano Day School, 1801 W. Central, Albuquerque
Woodruff, Fannie, Primary Supervisor, 107 N. Eighth St., Artesia
Zohn, Roberta H., Supervisor of Public School Music, Las Vegas

NEW YORK

Aldworth, Eleanore, County Health Teaching Supervisor, 704 Loew Bldg., Syracuse
Alterman, Harry, Chairman Women's Clothing Manufacturing Department, 2435 Ocean Ave., Brooklyn 29
Anderson, Howard R., Stone Hall, Cornell University, Ithaca
Arnold, Mary S., Whittier Hall, 1230 Amsterdam Ave., New York
Arnspiger, V. C., Encyclopedia Britannica Films, Inc., 1841 Broadway, New York 23
Babcock, Essie E., District Superintendent of Schools, 136 S. Main St., Cattaraugus
Babcock, Ruth F., School Library Supervisor, New York State Department of Education, Albany
Bacon, Clara S., Assistant Superintendent of Schools, 41 Division St., Amsterdam
Baker, Adelaide Woodall, 108 E. Garden St., Rome
Baker, Harold V., Principal, Daniel Webster School, Glenmore Dr., New Rochelle
Barnes, Georgia L., 314 Rowland St., Syracuse
Barry, Winifred A., Elementary Supervisor, Oceanside School No. 5, Oceanside
Bartholomew, Mrs. Bennett, District Superintendent, Whitehall
Beaumont, Florence S., Principal, 3323-85th St., Jackson Heights
Beecher, Dwight E., Supervising Principal, 201 Church St., Adams Center
Betzner, Jean, Associate Professor of Education, Teachers College, Columbia University, 262 Pondfield Rd. West, Bronxville
Binzel, Cora E., Cornell University, Ithaca
Blake, Ailene M., 101 Woodbine Ave., Syracuse
Blom, E. C., Principal, State Normal Training School, 75 Forest Place, Fredonia
Boardman, Walter S., Superintendent, Oceanside Schools, Oceanside
Bock, Doris L., Instructor, New York University, 1 Christopher St., New York

LIST OF MEMBERS 149

Boros, Arnold L., Mathematics Teacher, 396 E. 170th St., New York
Boughner, Lillian M., 1629 Eighth St., Niagara Falls
Bowen, Mary E., Head of Department of Health Teaching, Board of Education, 401 W. Genessee St., Syracuse
Brickman, Benjamin, Department of Education, Brooklyn College, Bedford Ave. and Ave. H., Brooklyn
Bristow, William H., Assistant Director of Reference, Research and Statistics, Board of Education, 110 Livingston St., Brooklyn
Brown, Clayton H., District Superintendent, Box 237, Hadley
Brumbaugh, Florence, Principal, 695 Park Ave., New York
Burk, Cassie, Supervisor and Instructor in English, 147 Temple St., Fredonia
Burns, Suzette, Principal, 949 West End Ave., Apt. 9, New York 25
Carey, Elizabeth B., Division of Elementary Education, New York State Education Department, Albany
Carlson, Clara H., Principal, Belmont Boulevard School, 9042 206th St., Queens Village, L. I.
Coolidge, Anne, Director of Reading Service and Institute of Personality Development, 17 E. 96th St., New York
Cottrell, Donald P., Professor of Education, Teachers College, Columbia University and Executive Director Horace Mann-Lincoln High School, 425 W. 123rd St., New York
Courson, Grace S., Critic Teacher, State Teachers College, Fredonia
Craig, Gerald S., Professor of Natural Sciences, Teachers College, Columbia University, New York
Crist, Ammy Bull, District Superintendent, Orange County, Montgomery
Cunningham, Ruth, Curriculum Consultant, Institute for School Experimentation, Teachers College, Columbia University, New York
Daly, Robert J., Director of Curriculum Guidance and Research, 163 Bishop St., Watertown
Davis, Vesta F., Chairman of Department of English, 81 Columbia Heights, Brooklyn
Dawson, Mildred A., F. A. Owen Publishing Company, Dansville
Donohue, John J., Principal, Public School 16, Bronx, 2219 Lyon Ave., New York
Ebeling, Elsa, Principal, Public School 208, Avenue D. and E. 49th St., Brooklyn
Ellis, Scott M., Principal, Greenville Central Rural School, Greenville
Ernst, Christine, Supervisor of Elementary Education, 366 Quail St., Albany
Faddis, Gabrielle Joan, Director of After School Center, Greenwich House, 27 Barrow St., New York
Feldman, Mina, 119-95th St., Brooklyn 9
Ferriss, Emery N., Professor of Education, Stone Hall, Cornell University, Ithaca
Fitzgerald, James A., Professor of Education, Fordham University, 5 Croydon Dr., Baldwin
French, Harold P., District Superintendent of Schools, Town Hall, Newtonville
Frey, Martha R., Principal, 12 Burton Rd., Larchmont
Gastwirth, Paul, 192-21 80th St., Jackson Heights, Long Island
Gates, Arthur I., Teachers College, Columbia University, 525 W. 120th St., New York
Giles, H. H., Bureau for Intercultural Education, 1697 Broadway 14th Floor, New York 19
Goodman, Katherine M., Director of Intermediate Grades, 134 Lakeview, Jamestown
Gould, Clifford M., Supervisor of Elementary Education, 98 Washington Ave., Kenmore
Gould, Lyttleton B. P., Educational Relations Consultant, 141 E. 53rd St., New York
Gray, Dorothy, Instructor in Education, Queens College, 405 W. 118th St., New York

Gunther, Theresa, Instructor, Brooklyn College, 385 E. 18th St., Flat Bush Station Brooklyn
Hageman, Genevieve A., Homemaking Supervisor, 108 Union St., Schenectady
Haines, Millicent, Curriculum Coordinator, Secondary Schools, 216 Pine St., Lockport
Hakes, Elton J., District Superintendent, District #1, Rennsalear County, Rt. 3, Troy
Haskew, L. D., Coordinator of Teacher Education, 525 W. 120th St., New York
Healy, Helen, 22 Parkwold Drive East, Valley Stream, L. I.
Hoffman, Augusta M., Art Supervisor, Public Schools, 329 E. Walnut St., Oswego
Hopkins, Johanna M., Principal, Public School 92, Bronx, 179th St. and Clinton Ave., New York 57
Hopkins, L. Thomas, Teachers College, Columbia University, New York
Hoppe, Arthur A., 509 W. 121st St., New York 27
Horton, Lena Mary, Director of Research, Silver Burdette Company, 45 E. 17th St., New York
Hughson, Arthur, Principal, 1412 Caton Ave., Brooklyn 26
Hulse, M. L., Associate Professor, Cornell University, 251 Goldwin Smith Hall, Ithaca
Hutchins, Margaret, Associate Professor of Rural Education, 208 Stone Hall, Cornell University, Ithaca
Jammer, George F., Superintendent, 60 Chestnut St., Lockport
Johnston, Ruth M., District Superintendent of Schools, Port Leyden
Kayfetz, Isidore, 81-19 Grand Central Parkway, Jamaica
Kearney, Leo I., Assistant Director of Reference, Research and Statistics, Board of Education, 311 Bedford Park Blvd., New York
Kengla, Elsie R., Associate Professor of Education, Hunter College, 3007 143rd St., Flushing, L. I.
Kennedy, Anna Clark, School Library Supervisor, New York State Education Department, 257 State St., Albany
Kennedy, Mabel, 204 W. 94th St., New York
Kennedy, Mary A., Assistant Superintendent, 1339 Park Place, Brooklyn
Ketcham, M. Kathleen, Elementary Supervisor, 80 Clinton St., Tonawanda
Kneerim, Margaret, New York University Film Library, 71 Washington Square South, New York
Knowlton P. A., Editor, The Macmillan Co., 60 Fifth Ave., New York 11
LaGrasse, Benjamin A., Science Teacher, 214 Marlborough Rd., Brooklyn
Lawson, Dorothy A., Supervisor, University of the State of New York, State Department of Education, Albany
Leavens, Edith B., c/o Alexander Hamilton School, 16th St. and John Ave., Binghamton
LeBaron, Walter A., Associate Supervisor, University of the State of New York, State Department of Education, Albany
Lefkowitz, Abraham, Principal, Samuel J. Tilden High School, Tilden Ave., and E. 57th St., Brooklyn 3
Leiman, Harold I, Superintendent, 350 Stone Ave., Brooklyn
Lodato, August, Principal, Public School 167, 1025 Eastern Parkway, Brooklyn
Lucke, Elmina R., Lincoln School, Teachers College, Columbia University, 425 W. 123rd St., New York 27
MacArthur, Edith H., Director of Department of Home Economics, Skidmore College, Saratoga Springs, New York
MacKenzie, Gordon N., Director, Institute for School Experimentation Teachers College, Columbia University, New York 27
Mantell, Herman P., 52 Clark St., Brooklyn
Mayfarth, Frances, Editor, "Childhood Education", 52 Clark St., Brooklyn

McAtavie, Margaret M., Teacher, 102-35 129th St., Richmond Hill
McCartha, Carl W., Principal, Gastonia, North Carolina, Junior High School, Hotel Albert, University Place at 10th St., New York
McLean, Francis H., Family Welfare Association of America, 122 E. 22nd St., New York
Meisel, Carl L., Teacher of Applied Physics, 161 W. 75th St., New York 23
Melchior, William T., Professor of Educational Supervision, Syracuse University, 140 Westminster Ave., Syracuse
Merry, Liona, Principal, Hamilton School, Schenectady
Meyer, Charles E., 725 W. 184th St., New York 33
Miel, Alice, Assistant Professor in Curriculum and Teaching, Teachers College, Columbia University, New York 27
Miller, Ward I., Superintendent, Eastchester High School, Tuckahoe
Molendyk, Clara A., Chairman of English Department, Lafayette High School, Benson Ave. and Bay 43rd St., Brooklyn
Moore, Clyde B., Stone Hall, Cornell University, Ithaca
Moore, E. Carleton, Administrative Assistant, Hempstead High School, Hempstead
Morrison, J. Cayce, Assistant Commissioner for Research, State Education Department, Albany
Mosher, Frank K., 53 N. Main St., Marion
Munro, Mary, Grade Supervisor, 8 Mill St., Cazenovia
Martagh, Anna L., Principal, Intermediate School, Solvay 9
Myers, Alonzo, School of Education, New York University, New York
Myers, Clyde deB., District Superintendent of Schools, Scipio Center
Nestrick, W. Virgil, Department of Education, Queens College, Flushing
Neuner, Elsie Flint, Director of Instruction, Department of Education, New Rochelle
Nifenecker, Eugene A., 800 Riverside Drive, New York 32
Norton, Louise M., Director of Training, St. Normal School, Plattsburg
Norvell, Annabel, Supervisor and Teacher, 108 Union, Schenectady
Olsen, Edward G., Director of School of Education, Russell Sage College, Troy
Osborne, Kathaleen I., District Superintendent of Schools, North Creek
Painter, Fred B., Superintendent, Gloversville
Park, Martha A., Professor of Home Economics Education, Rt. #1, Plattsburg
Pease, Ethel G., Principal, 287 Elmdorf Ave., Rochester
Peterson, A. G., Director of the Training School, State Teachers College, Plattsburg
Phelps, Margaret, Director of Instruction in the Intermediate Grades, 409 W. Genesee St., Syracuse
Platt, Clara Skiles, Instructor in Education, New York University, 19 W. 10th St., New York 11
Pollock, Kathryn M., 466 South Avenue, Elmira
Power, Leonard, Independent Educational Consultant, 2 West 45th St., New York
Powers, S. Ralph, Teachers College, Columbia University, New York
Praeger, Rosamond, Supervisor of Early Childhood and Parent Education, Board of Education, 409 W. Genesee St., Syracuse 4
Pratt, Martha S., Head Teacher of Home Economics, 355 Linwood Ave., Buffalo
Prehm, Hazel, Supervisor of Later Elementary Education, Board of Education, Rochester 4
Pugsley, Chester A., Professor of Elementary School Administration, 666 Auburn, Buffalo
Rappaport, Mary B., Supervisor of Health Teaching, New York State Education Department, Albany 1
Reagan, G. Agnes, Head of Primary Department, 1340 W. Colvin St., Syracuse

Reed, Paul, U. S. Office of Education, 116 Crosman Terrace, Rochester 7
Reiser, Charles W., Principal Public School 122, Queens, 21-21 Ditmars Blvd., Long Island City
Richman, J. Maurice, Social Studies Teacher, 1001 E. Ninth St., Brooklyn 30
Rommei, Herman L., Supervising Principal, Valhalla Junior High School, Valhalla
Ross, Jacob, Principal, Midwood High School, Bedford Ave. and Glenwood Rd., Brooklyn 10
Ryan, Francis A., Associate Professor of Education, Fordham University, 340 W. 57th St., New York 19
Scherer, Doris C., Elementary School Supervisor, 31 Seneca St., Geneva
Schneider, Perry L., Assistant to the Director of Evening School, Board of Education, 110 Livingston St., Brooklyn 2
Scott, Dorothy D., Teachers College, Columbia University, New York
Segner, Esther F., Assistant Professor of Home Economics Education, Buffalo State Teachers College, Buffalo
Seidlin, Joseph, Director, Graduate Division, Alfred University, Alfred
Siegel, Benjamin, Chairman, Curriculum Committee, Drum Hill Junior High School, Peekskill
Sipp, Mildred L., State Teachers College, Buffalo
Sofejko, Jennie, Supervisor, 66 Maple Avenue, Cortland
Spence, Ralph B., State Education Department, Albany
Stevenson, Elizabeth, Itinerant Teacher Trainer, 400 W. 119th St., New York
Stratemeyer, Florence B., Teachers College, Columbia University, 525 W. 120th St., New York
Taylor, Bent, Director of Public Relations, Community Chests and Councils, 155 E. 44th St., New York 17
Thayer, V. T., Fieldston School, Fieldston Road, New York
Thurston, Flora M., Professor of Education, Stone Hall, Cornell University, Ithaca
Tompkins, Charlotte C., National Staff of Department of Christian Education, Episcopal Church, 281 Fourth Avenue, New York
Travis, Zena R., District Superintendent of Schools, Roxbury, New York
Troyer, Maurice E., Professor of Education, School of Education, Syracuse University, Syracuse
Van Ness, Carl, Editor, D. Appleton-Century Co., 35 W. 32nd St., New York
Van Til, William, Bureau for Intercultural Education, 1697 Broadway, New York 19
Vitarelli, William, Consultant, Horace Mann-Lincoln Institute of School Experimentation, Teachers College, Columbia University, New York
Voss, Edna R., Secretary, Unit of Education and Medical Work, Board of National Missions of the Presbyterian Church in the U. S. A., 156 Fifth Ave., New York 10
Wallstein, D. Daniel, Principal, Edgar D. Shiner Junior High School, Linden Blvd. and 142nd St., Jamaica
Walther, Herbert K., American Council on Education, 437 W. 59th St., New York
Watkin, Earl P., Board of Education Office, Ilion
Weber, E. M., Principal, Menands School, Menands, Albany
Welch, Cornelius, 504 Dryden Rd., Ithaca
Welch, Earl E., Administrative Editor, Silver Burdett Co., 45 E. 17th St., New York
Whalen, Frank D., Assistant Superintendent, 330 E. 152nd St., New York 51
Wiles, Marion E., Supervisor Primary Grades, School Department, Great Neck
Williams, Byron B., Charles E. Merrill Co., Inc., 373 Fourth Ave., New York

LIST OF MEMBERS 151

Williams, Lt. Maurice C., Regimental Headquarters, 121 Staff Infantry, APO 8, c/o Postmaster, New York
Winch, Ruth B., District Superintendent, Sherman Rd., Westfield
Winterble, Margaret, Research Assistant, Bureau of Reference, Research and Statistics, 110 Livingston St., Brooklyn
Wofford, Kate V., State Teachers College, Buffalo
Wrightstone, J. Wayne, Assistant Superintendent, Board of Education, 110 Livingston St., Brooklyn
Wylie, Anna, Supervisor of Kindergarten and Primary, 2223 Whitney Ave., Niagara Falls
Young, William E., Director, Division of Elementary Education, State Department of Education, Albany
Zamory, Stanley S., 304 East Ave., East Syracuse
Zeitler, Mrs. Blodwen Williams, 178 Manning Blvd. S., Albany

NORTH CAROLINA

Beck, Mae, Teacher, Central High School, 308 Green St., Fayetteville
Bostian, Annie, Principal, A. T. Allen School, Salisbury
Brownell, W. A., Professor of Educational Psychology, Box B., College Station, Durham
Bullock, W. L., Superintendent, City Schools, Kannapolis
Edwards, Charles T., Principal, 312 E. Highland Ave., Rocky Mount
Fitzgerald, Ruth, Professor of Education, 308 S. Aycock St., Greensboro
Garinger, Elmer H., Principal, Central High School, Charlotte 4
Gwynn, J. Minor, Associate Professor of Education, University of North Carolina, Chapel Hill
Hearne, Clara, Elementary Principal, Box 68, Roanoke Rapids
Hicks, Clara B., Supervisor, 1919 Oaklawn Ave., Charlotte
Horwich, Frances R., Visiting Professor, University of North Carolina, Box 810, Chapel Hill
House, Ralph W., Professor of Education and Psychology, State Teachers College, Boone
Jenkins, Sarah Burton, 2203 Ridgecrest, Raleigh
Lacy, Frances, Elementary Supervisor, Board of Education, Raleigh
Mann, Clara D., Supervisor of County Schools, Box 6, New Bern
O'Briant, Mary Vann, Supervisor, Northampton County, Box 232, Jackson
Peedin, Minnie Lee, Elementary Supervisor, 403 S. Chester St., Gastonia
Phillips, G. K., Superintendent, City Schools, Gastonia
Pitts, Maurie Simpson, Supervisor, Davidson County Elementary Schools, Box 6, Lexington
Pope, O. R., Supervising Principal, Booker T. Washington High School, 606 Atlantic Ave., Rocky Mount
Tripp, Madeline, Elementary Supervisor, Scotland Neck
Underwood, Myrtle, Principal, Hayes-Barton School, 1200 Glenwood Ave., Raleigh
Washington, B. T., Principal, Williston Primary School, Wilmington
Wells, Mrs. A. H., Elementary Principal, F. A. Woodard School, Wilson
Wetherington, Julia, Division of Instructional Service, State Department of Public Instruction, Raleigh
Yount, M. E., Superintendent of Schools, Alamance County, Box 591, Graham

NORTH DAKOTA

Barnes, James A., Director of Elementary Training, State Teachers College, Mayville
Eininger, H. J., Emerson H. Smith School Bldg., Fargo
Estensen, E. V., Superintendent of Schools, Cooperstown
Fortsch, L. E., 917 N. Main, Williston
Grindstuen, Iver I., Supervisor, Secondary Teaching, State Teachers College, Dickinson
Hulbert, Helga, 424 12th St. N., Fargo
Martinson, Esther C., Supervisor, State Teachers College, Valley City
Selke, Erich, Professor of Education, University of North Dakota, Grand Forks

OHIO

Adell, James C., Director, Division of Educational Research, Board of Education, 1380 E. 6th St., Cleveland
Alberty, Harold, Professor of Education, Ohio State University, 1982 Berkshire Rd., Columbus 8
Appel, Marguerite, 312 E. State St., Athens
Augspurger, R. E., Superintendent, Franklin Public Schools, Franklin
Baker, Emily V., Elementary Supervisor, Miami University, Oxford
Bancroft, Clara M., Assistant Professor, Home Economics Education, Ohio State University, Columbus 10
Beery, Althea, Supervisor of Language Arts, 315 Terrace Ave., Cincinnati
Bertermann, Helen A., Assistant Principal, 1339 Cryer Ave., Cincinnati 8
Bixler, Lorin E., Professor of Education, Muckingum College, New Concord
Bloser, R. E., President, Zoner-Bloser Company, Box 4006, Station 11, Columbus 8
Boda, H. L., Assistant Superintendent in charge of Curriculum, 232 N. Main St., Dayton 2
Bradley, Helen, Principal, Guilford School, 2401 Salutario Ave., Cincinnati
Brown, Francis W., Superintendent Ottawa Hills Schools, Toledo 6
Burwick, Charlotte D., DeVilbis High School, Upton Ave., Toledo 6
Callow, Harriet T., 48 S. Valley St., Akron 3
Chandler, Elizabeth W., 69 14th Ave., Columbus
Dale, Edgar, Ohio State University, 13 Page Hall, Columbus 10
Dunsmore, Philo C., Supervisor, Social Studies and Curriculum, Board of Education Bldg., 121 Southard, Toledo
Edmiston, R. W., Professor of Education, 117 W. Walnut St., Oxford
Elliott, Irene, Supervisor, 77 W. State St., Athens
Fishel, Dorothy L., Elementary Principal, 802 Park Ave., S. W., Canton 6
Fordyce, W. G., Principal, Euclid Central High School, 1520 Chardon Rd., Euclid
Fowler, Lena, 1332 Logan N. W., Canton
Frahm, Olive M., Principal, 362 Piedmont Rd., Columbus
Fraser, Jean, Director of Elementary Education, Otterbein College, Westerville
Gilchrist, Robert S., Director, University School, Ohio State University, Columbus 10
Gilmore, M. E., Supervising Principal, Wells School, 1422 25th St., N. W., Canton 3
Gleason, Emma M., Assistant Superintendent, Lorain County Schools, Rt. 2, Lorain
Graham, E. B., Principal, 325 Crestview Rd., Columbus 2
Griffith, Ruth Margaret, Director, Extra-Mural Teacher Training, Miami University, Oxford
Haddow, Mary A., Director, Elementary Curriculum, Board of Education, Youngstown 3
Hargitt, Ruth A., Director, Kindergarten and Primary Grades, 11 Glenmary Ave., Cincinnati 20
Harry, David P. Jr., Graduate School, Western Reserve University, Cleveland 6
Heer, A. L., Director of Teacher Training, 312 S. Willow St., Box 366, Kent
Hickok, Jessie L., Elementary Supervisor, High School Bldg., 208 S. Arch Ave., Alliance

Holmes, Jay William, Principal, 1415 Lexington Ave., Dayton 6
Holt, E. E., Superintendent of Schools, 445 S. Prospect St., Marion
Horrocks, John E., College of Education, Department of Psychology, Ohio State University, Columbus
Howard, Ethel K., 1470 Warren Rd., Lakewood 7
Humphreys, Phila, Director of Curriculum, Mt. Union College, Alliance
Kemler, Clara M., Associate Professor of Elementary Education, 1100 Copley Rd., Akron 2
Kirby, Theresa K., 532 County Court House, Cincinnati 2
Leum, Clara L., Professor of Education, Capital University, 886 S. Roosevelt, Columbus 9
Lyons, Olive, Department of Elementary Education, Otterbein College, Westerville
Masson, J. S., Assistant Superintendent, 1102 10th St., Lorain
Mathews, C. O., Professor of Education, Department of Education, Ohio Wesleyan University, Delaware
McClintock, Anna E., 2026 3rd St., Cuyahoga Falls
McConnell, Mrs. Russell A., Primary Teacher, 887 Greenwood Ave., Akron 2
McDill, Blanche L., Assistant Professor of Education, 300 N. College Ave., Oxford
McFarland, Mildred, 754 Hamilton Ave., Lorain
McKim, Margaret, Teachers College University of Cincinnati, Cincinnati 21
McKnight, John A., Superintendent of Schools, Glendale
Metts, D. E., Director of Research, Euclid Public Schools, 310 E. 216th St., Cleveland
Miller, C. L., Principal, Garfield School, Elmore and Beekman Sts., Cincinnati
Nystrom, W. C., Director of Teacher Training, Wittenberg College, Springfield
Oechsler, Hazel, Principal, Nathan-Hale School, Shenandoah and Foster Ave., Toledo
Parker, Constance, Teacher, 5901 Franklin Blvd., Cleveland 2
Pasch, Dorothy F., Supervisor, Special Education, Board of Education, 121 Southard Ave., Toledo 2
Pennekamp, Dorothy, 517 Nashoba Ave., Columbus 4
Pressey, Alice D., School of Home Economics, Ohio State University, Columbus 10
Purdy, Ralph D., 819 Main St., Conneaut
Ragland, Fannie J., Director Upper Elementary Grades, 216 E. Ninth St., Cincinnati 12
Ricketts, Gladys E., 5th Grade Teacher, 1301 N. Oakland Ave., Columbus 8
Roemer, Kathryn, Elementary Principal, 830 Western Ave., Zanesville
Schroeder, Esther L., Principal, Elementary School, 590 Ludlow, Cincinnati 20
Sister M. Adelbert, 1111 W. Bancroft St., Toledo 6
Sister M. Benigna, O. S. U., Supervisor of Elementary School, Ursuline Convent, 2413 Collingwood Blvd., Toledo 10
Sister Marie Emilie, S. N. D. De N., Mt. Notre Dame, Reading, Cincinnati 15
Sister M. Euphrasia, O. S. F., Elementary Supervisor, 436 W. Delaware, Toledo 10
Sister Mary St. Agatha, Diocesan Supervisor, Mt. Notre Dame Academy, Reading
Sister M. Teresa, 2013 Cherry St., Toledo 8
Spafford, Ivol, Curriculum Consultant, Rock Creek
Stine, J. Ray, Principal, Central High School, Akron
Tanruther, E. M., Division of Elementary Education, Miami University, Oxford
Teeters, Ruth C., Teacher, 531 Columbus Ave., Washington C. H.
Toepfer, Carl W., Principal, Glenwood School, Detroit and Glenwood Ave., Toledo 10
Waldron, J. Harley, Supervisor of General Education, S. Detroit St., Rt. 1, Xenia

Walters, Verna Fogg, State Supervisor, Elementary Curriculum, State Department of Education, Columbus 15
Warnking, May, Principal, 4792 Rapid Run Rd., Cincinnati
Willcockson, Mary, Associate Professor of Education, Miami University, 2 N. Bishop St., Oxford
Wilcox, George M., Dean, Youngstown College, Youngstown 2
Yates, Leah, Elementary Supervisor, Shelby County Schools, Sidney

OKLAHOMA

Adair, Mrs. D. W., Primary Director, 528 N. Second St., Seminole
Bender, John F., University of Oklahoma, Norman
Black, M. M., Principal, Central High School, Tulsa 3
Bruner, H. B., 400 N. Walnut Ave., Oklahoma City
Chambers, W. Max, Superintendent, City Schools, Okmulgee
Drewry, Agnes M., Director, Elementary Education, Sepulpa City Schools, Sepulpa
Elder, Ruth E., Faculty Exchange, University of Oklahoma, Norman
Frederick, C. G., Superintendent, Box K, Heavener
Gaither, F. F., Director, Teacher Education, University of Oklahoma, Norman
Greer, Lola B., Primary Teacher, 1201 N. E. 8th St., Oklahoma City 4
Harrell, Gordon M., Supervisor, 831 E. 15th, Ada
Hooper, George J., Principal, Bryant School, Board of Education Bldg., Tulsa
Llewelyn, Ardelle, Coordinator of Instruction, Inman Page School, 317 N. Geary St., Oklahoma City
Manahan, Ethel H., Professor of Education, Box 2275, University Station, Enid
McGoodwin, Irene Pate, Supervisor of Elementary Education, Ardmore City Schools, Ardmore
McIntosh, D. C., Dean, Graduate School, Oklahoma A. & M. College, Stillwater
Melton, Cleo, Elementary Supervisor, 201 S. 5th St., Ponca City
Nichols, Helen, District Supervisor, Home Economics Education, Box 3007, State Capitol, Oklahoma City 5
Pauly, Frank R., Director of Research, Tulsa Public Schools, Tulsa
Quinn, Lila, 817 S. W. 36th St., Oklahoma City 9
Ragan, W. B., Teacher Training, College of Education, University of Oklahoma, Norman
Rice, Ted, Coordinator of Instruction, 400 N. Walnut, Oklahoma City
Russell, Mary, Box 263, Oklahoma College for Women, Chickasha
Scales, Pearl, Director of Elementary Schools, 1401 N. Walnut St., Oklahoma City
Simms, W. E., Langston University, Langston
Stayton, Winifred, Supervisor of Teacher Training, Central State Teachers College, 224 E. 4th St., Edmond
Stover, John H., Director, Character Research, 5808 Military, Oklahoma City 6
Templeton, Flossie B., Supervisor, 3308 N. Pennsylvania, Oklahoma City 6
Terrill, Pearl W., Teacher, Box 612, Weleetka
Tippie, Mrs. James R., 1205 Ash, Muskogee
Watts, Winifred, Coordinator of Elementary Grades, Junior College Bldg., Okmulgee
Welch, Lila M., Professor of Home Economics Education, Faculty Exchange, University of Oklahoma, Norman

OREGON

Anderson, Robert E., Supervisor, Curriculum and Publications, State Department of Education, 950 N. 15th St., Salem

LIST OF MEMBERS 153

Anderson, Vernon E., Director of Curriculum, 631 N. E. Clackamas, Portland 8
Aschenbrenner, Carl E., Principal, Parrish Junior High School, Salem
Bond, Ruth E., Curriculum Librarian, 1729 N. E. 17th St., Portland 12
Crumm, Winona, 5847 N. E. 27th Ave., Portland 11
Dallas, Neva, County Supervisor, Rt. 3, Box 888, Grants Pass
De Bernardis, Amo, 4519 N. E., 36th Ave., Portland 11
Donaldson, Mary A., Supervising Teacher, 1055 Monmouth St., Independence
DuBois, May, Oregon State College, Corvallis
Emerson, D. A., Director of School Administration and Secondary Education, State Library Bldg., Salem
Ernst, Karl D., Assistant Professor of Education, 631 N. E. Clackamas St., Portland
Fenn, Lucile E., Director, Elementary Education, Administration Bldg., 631 N. E. Clackamas, Portland 8
Ferrin, H. B., Superintendent, High School Bldg., Cottage Grove
Forest, Ruth M., Supervisor of Family Life Education, 631 N. E. Clackamas St., Portland 8
Gilstrap, Carlie, Supervisor of Social Studies, 405 N. Russet St., Portland 11
Hedrick, E. H., Superintendent, School District 49, Medford
Henkle, Emma, Department of Education, Oregon Normal School, Monmouth
Hills, Joy, Principal, Leslie Junior High School, Salem
Hines, Clarence, Assistant Superintendent, City Hall, Eugene
Hoel, Lesta, 631 N. E. Clackamas St., Portland 8
Hoenig, Vivian S., 1475 S. Commercial, Salem
Katterlee, Zeno B., Assistant Superintendent, 631 N. E. Clackamas St., Portland 8
Knighten, Wily W., County School Superintendent, Moro
Logan, Greba, Supervisor, Health Education, 631 N. E. Clackamas, Portland 8
Long, Watt A., Director of Intermediate Education, 631 N. E. Clackamas St., Portland 8
Longfellow, J. J., Superintendent, City Schools, Oregon City
Mattley, Maud, Supervisor, Physical Science, 631 N. E. Clackamas St., Portland 8
McCormack, R. E., City School Superintendent, 420 E. 3rd St., Albany
Milhous, Ivan C., Professor, Oregon College of Education, 560 W. Main St., Monmouth
Patton, Mrs. Fred, Superintendent, 4th and M Sts., La Grande
Pinckney, Paul W., Director, Secondary Education, 631 N. E., Clackamas, Portland 8
Posey, C. W., 2207 N. E. Going St., Portland 11
Read, Earnest A., Principal, Training School, 131 Powell St., Monmouth
Skeen, Bearnice, Principal, 4228 N. Overlook Dr., Portland 17
Snyder, Walter E., Curriculum Director, Salem Public Schools, Salem
Stephers, Eleanor, Librarian, Oregon State Library, Salem
Trenholme, Kingsley, Supervisor, Visual Education, 546 N. Stafford, Portland 3
Turnbull, J. L., Superintendent of Schools, Ontario
Weddle, Carmalite I., Supervisor, 1365 Broadway St., Salem
Williams, Mildred, Vice Principal, Roosevelt Junior High School, Eugene

PENNSYLVANIA

Amberson, Jean D., Professor Home Economics Education, Pennsylvania State College, State College
Bailey, Helen C., Principal, Stetson Junior High School, 300 Winona Ave., Philadelphia 44
Beatty, Evelyn, Principal, Crescent School, Bennett & Tokay Sts. Pittsburgh 21
Betts, Emmett A., Director, Reading Clinic, Temple University, Philadelphia
Boehm, Charles, Superintendent, Bucks County, 75 N. Main St., Doylestown
Booth, Miriam B., Supervisor of Secondary English, 640 West Ninth St., Erie
Bowers, Frances L., Elementary School Principal, 65th Ave. & Limekiln Pike, Philadelphia 38
Brewer, Karl M., Superintendent of Schools, 133 E. Washington Ave., Dubois
Carback, Clarence H., Principal, Theodore Roosevelt Junior High School, E. Washington Lane & Musgrave St., Philadelphia
Carson, J. O., Director of Curriculum, School District of Abington Township, Abington
Champlin, Carroll D., Professor of Education, Burrowes Bldg., Pennsylvania State College, State College
Christian, Grace, J. B. Stetson Junior High School, 2725 East Lehigh Ave., Philadelphia 25
Cockerille, Clara E., Supervisor of Elementary Schools, Lincoln Bldg., Altoona
Cressman, Paul L., Director, Bureau of Instruction, Department of Public Instruction, Harrisburg
Cushman, C. L., Associate Superintendent of Schools, Board of Education, 21st at Parkway, Philadelphia 3
Dawes, Dorothy D., 4840 Pine St., Philadelphia
Deck, Clara M., Head, Dept. of Social Studies, 1409 North 13th St., Reading
Diem, Marie L., Supervisor, Grades 4-7, 944 Taylor Ave., Scranton
Dimmick, E. A., Associate Superintendent, Elementary Schools, 341 S. Bellefield Ave., Pittsburgh 13
Doyle, Florence A., Director, Teacher Education, Muhr School, 12th & Alleghany Ave., Philadelphia 33
Dungan, A. D., Assistant Superintendent, Aliquippa Public Schools, Aliquippa
Esterline, Irene, Principal, McClure School, 6th & Hunting Park Ave., Philadelphia 40
Evans, Walter P., Principal, Hopkinson Schools, L and Luzerne Sts., Philadelphia 24
Everett, Samuel, Director, Junior Red Cross, S. E. Pennsylvania, 41 Shady Hill Rd., Moylan
Floyd, Oliver R., Supervising Principal, Ben Avon Schools, 200 Dickson Ave., Pittsburgh
Foreman, Anna B., Director of Curriculum, 31 S., Penn St., Allentown
Frankenfield, Ira M., Elementary Principal, 637 Center St., Bethlehem
Garver, F. M., Professor of Elementary Education, 112 Bennett Hall, University of Pennsylvania, Philadelphia 4
Geary, Catherine E., Director of Elementary Education and Curriculum, 9th and Crosby Sts., Chester
Gilland, Thomas M., Director of Student Teaching, State Teachers College, California
Greenberg, Simon, Professor of Education, 2253 N. 53rd St., Philadelphia 31
Grimes, Helen K., Mathematics Supervisor, 1114 Haywood St., Farrell
Grizzell, E. D., Professor of Secondary Education, Eisenhohr Hall, University of Pennsylvania, Philadelphia 4
Hanna, Edith B., Principal, Vare Junior High School, 24th and Snyder Ave., Philadelphia
Haven, Jessie G., 121 W. Fairmount Ave., State College
Hay, Charles K., John M. Patterson School, 70th St. and Buist Ave., Philadelphia
Hedge, John W., Superintendent, Broughal Bldg., Bethlehem
Hinkle, Thomas L., Superintendent, Green St. Administration Office, Hazleton
Hoffman, Jane, Supervisor of Elementary Grades, Phoenixville School District, Phoenixville
Hoffman, M. David, Head of English Department, Simon Cratz High School, 17th and Luzerne Sts., Philadelphia

Jones, Arthur J., Professor of Secondary Education, School of Education, University of Pennsylvania, Philadelphia 4
Jones, Mary F., Principal, Highland Park School, Upper Darby
Kerstetter, Newton, Principal, Box 242, Danville
Kirk, Mabel E., Associate Professor of Education, Pennsylvania State College, State College
Kirk, S. Elisabeth, Elementary Principal, Garrettford School, Drexel Hill
Krall, Helen, Director of Elementary Education, 3121 Columbia Ave., Camp Hill
Krause, Mildred C., Centre Valley
Kurtz, Virginia, 4211 Tyson St., Philadelphia, 35
Lafferty, Genevieve E., Supervisor of Music Education in the Elementary Schools, 3339 Vista St., Philadelphia 36
Landis, Robert C., Superintendent, Conshohocken
Lantz, W. W., County Superintendent, 345 County Office Bldg., Pittsburgh
Laws, Catherine B., Elementary Supervisor, 19 W. 4th St., Media
Lembke, Glenn L., Editor-in-Chief, John C. Winston Co., 1010 Arch St., Philadelphia 7
Lilly, Mabel H., Livingston School, 730 Union St., Allentown
Liveright, Alice K., Elementary School Principal, 1512 Spruce St., Philadelphia
Lukens, Mary L., Senior High School, Lansdowne Ave. and School Lane, Upper Darby
Lumley, John M., County Superintendent of Schools, Dushore
McConnel, Clarence H., Assistant Superintendent Lycoming County Schools, Court House, Williamsport
McCormick, Ethel, Lincoln School, Altoona
McDermott, Irene E., Senior Supervisor of Home Economics, Board of Public Education, 341 Bellefield Ave., Pittsburgh
McElroy, Howard C., 1116 Craig St., McKeesport
McKee, Margaret, Assistant County Superintendent, 345 County Office Bldg., Pittsburgh
Miller, C. S., Professor of Education, Allegheny College, Meadville
Milliette, Earl B., Director of the Division of Fine and Industrial Arts, Board of Education, 21st at Parkway, Philadelphia
Moll, Richard M., Assistant County Superintendent, 313 West Penn, Robesonia
Moyer, James H., Assistant Professor, Pennsylvania State College, State College
Newman, Raymond S., 629 E. Mt. Airy Ave., Philadelphia
Nitrauer, W. E., Supervising Principal, Manheim Township High School, Neffsville
Noar, Gertrude, Principal, 935 N. 65th St., Philadelphia
Olander, Herbert T., Assistant Professor, School of Education, University of Pittsburgh, Pittsburgh
Pollock, Lucile V., George School, Bucks Co.
Pooler, Mary Hardy, Supervisor of Special Education, 518 Holland St., Erie
Powers, Leversia L., Education Bldg., Harrisburg
Puff, Clinton M., Scottdale Public Schools, Scottdale
Quigley, Thomas J., Superintendent of Catholic Schools, 11 Tunnel St., Pittsburgh
Raker, William W., Director of Laboratory School, State Teachers College, Kutztown
Ralston, Alene, Psychology Consultant, 709 Church Lane, Philadelphia
Rannells, Emilie, Bureau of Pupil Personnel and Counseling, Administration Bldg., Parkway at 21st St., Philadelphia
Roffe, Pauline E., Senior High School, Lansdowne Ave. and School Lane, Upper Darby
Rowland, Sydney V., Superintendent, Wayne
Sauvain, Walter H., Associate Professor of Education, Bucknell University, 1413 West Market St., Lewisburg
Scanlon, Kathryn I., Director of Teacher Training, Education Department, Rosemont College, Rosemont

Scorer, Sadie M., Teacher of Mental Deviates, Box 404, Homestead
Seegers, J. Conrad, Teachers College, Broad and Montgomery Ave., Philadelphia
Sharlip, Lou N., Elementary School Principal, 5058 N. 8th St., Philadelphia
Sinsenig, E. Susan, Principal, Nathan C. Schaeffer School, 875 Pleasure Rd., Lancaster
Sister Mary Borromeo, 161 S. Washington St., Wilkes-Barre
Smith Gall, Elizabeth, 126 N. Lime St., Lancaster
Snyder, Warren P., Superintendent, Bristol High School, Wilson Ave. and Garfield St., Bristol
Sones, W. W. D., School of Education, University of Pittsburgh, Pittsburgh 13
Sprague, Stella H., Director of Secondary Education, 53 Elm St., Bradford
Stack, Katherine I., Principal Junior High School, 4733 Cedar Ave., Philadelphia
Stevens, A. M., Elementary Principal, 222 Riley St., Harrisburg
Stock, L. V., Board of Education, Biglerville
Strickland, Helen L., Principal, Apt. G-1, Windermere Ct. Apts., Wayne
Sussman, Samuel, Principal, 2258 Georges Lane, Philadelphia 31
Taylor, Florence E., Director of Elementary Education, Pennsylvania State College, 205 E. Beaver Ave., State College
Trabue, M. R., Dean, School of Education, Pennsylvania State College, State College
Webb, Ella, Principal, A. Wilson School, 46th St. and Woodland Ave., Philadelphia
Wolf, R. Olive, Principal, 581 Moorhead Place, Pittsburgh
Wright, Anne, Elementary School Principal, Ridge Ave. and Kales St., Philadelphia
Young, May I., Supervisor of Special Education, 2206 Wallace Street, Philadelphia
Yundt, John H., Newtown, Bucks County

RHODE ISLAND

Hoye, Monica M., Elementary Supervisor, 262 Gano St., Providence
Quirk, Mary V., Principal and State Critic, 15 Wheaton St., Warren
Watrous, Mildred L., Supervisor of Elementary Grades, 109 Turner Ave., Oak Lawn

SOUTH CAROLINA

Brooks, J. F., County Superintendent of Education, Court House, Spartanburg
Brunson, Mrs. De Witt, State Department of Education, Wade Hampton Office Bldg., Columbia
Clayton, Mrs. M. F., Supervisor of Intermediate Grades, 129 Carlyle St., Spartanburg
Connor, Lila, Box 138, Chester
Flora, A. C., Superintendent of Schools, 1311 Marian St., Columbia
Grayson, W. H., Supervisor of Negro Schools, 89 Columbus St., Charleston
Johnson, C. A., Supervisor of Negro Schools, Carver Junior High School, Columbia
Loggins, W. F., Superintendent, 17 Westfield St., Greenville
Martin, Zona M., Mayo High School, Darlington
McCormick, L. B., Superintendent, Mullins Public Schools, Mullins
Moore, Lena, State Department of Education, 307 Wade Hampton Bldg., Columbia
Payne, J. M., Assistant Superintendent, City Public Schools, Columbia
Southerline, W. B., Superintendent, Drawer 60, Winnsboro
Thomas, Martha E., Director of the Division of Elementary Education, State Department of Education, Columbia
West, Dean, Principal, Belton Public Schools, Belton

LIST OF MEMBERS

SOUTH DAKOTA

Arntz, Genevieve, County Superintendent of Schools, Aberdeen
Cummings, Mable E., Elementary Grade Supervisor, Rise Bldg., Rapid City
Gilbert, Alice, Elementary Supervisor, Huron City Schools, Huron
Ketelhut, La Vis E., Chamberlain
Lindsey, John, Superintendent, Mitchell
Notehoom, Charlotte M., Associate Professor of Education, University of South Dakota, Vermillion
Risk, Thomas M., Professor of Education and Director of Teacher Training. University of South Dakota, 319 Elm St., Vermillion

TENNESSEE

Arrants, Frances, Elementary School Supervisor, Green County, Greenville
Bales, J. D., Principal, Soddy Elementary and Junior High Schools, Soddy
Barker, Viva, Supervisor, Dunlap
Bell, Hazell, Supervisor, Box 116, Lewis County, Hohenwald
Betts, Mary Florence, Elementary Supervisor, Dover
Birdwell, Elza Price, Supervisor, Sumner County Elementary Schools, Gallatin
Bizzell, Winnie Lee, Box 266, Ripley
Brandon, Eleanor S., Supervisor of Elementary Grades, Ashland City
Brumit, Pauline, Supervisor, Carter County Schools, Elizabethton
Cannon, Mary E., Elementary Supervisor, Box 466, Paris
Carpenter, Anne Leah, Assistant Supervisor of Elementary Education, Court House, Chattanooga
Carter, Nelle, Supervisory Teacher, Crockett County, Alamo 4
Cawthon, Hilda Robbs, Elementary Supervisor Court House, Jackson
Chilton, Mrs. W. B., Springfield
Christenbury, E. S., 719 James Blvd., Chattanooga
Cook, May R., Supervisor, Loudon
Dye, Neelie, Supervisor, Bedford County, Belle Buckle
Elam, Mary, Elementary Supervisor, Howell School, Clarksville
Erwin, Clara Hudgens, Elementary Supervisor, Sparta
Essery, Florence V., Associate Professor of Education, University of Tennessee, Knoxville 16
Evans, Blanche Rousseau, Professor of Elementary Education, 4513 Division Ave., Jackson
Evers, Lorraine Long, County Supervisor, Madisonville
Farrell, Emma E. Tennesse State College, Box 97, Johnson City
Flowers, Dorothy, Covington
Frost, Norman, Peabody College for Teachers, Nashville
Garcia, Hector G., Peabody College for Teachers, Box 683, Nashville
Garrison, Leatha M., Box 55, Pikesville
Goforth, Lillian, County Supervisor, Elementary Schools, 451 Love St., Erwin
Graff, Orin B., Superintendent, 35 Dogwood Road, Norris
Greene, Zella Mae, 911 W. Hill Crest Drive, Johnson City
Hall, Mary, Regional Elementary Supervisor, State Teachers College, Murfreesboro
Harap, Henry, George Peabody College, Nashville 4
Hardy, A. D., Science Teacher, 310 Stonewall St., Jackson
Harper, Mrs. J. S., Principal East Ridge Elementary School, Hotel Patten, Chattanooga
Hayes, Elsie, Elementary Supervisor, Box 738, Clarksville
Highsmith, Ruth, RFD 4, Springfield

Hill, Evelyn, Jeanes Supervisor, Henderson County Board of Education, Lexington
Hill, Lucille, Supervisor of Elementary Schools, Anderson County, Clinton
Hilliard, C. D., County Superintendent, Obion
Hobgood, Baxter E., Middle Tennessee State College, Murfreesboro
Hoover, Souci, County Elementary Supervisor, Beech Grove
Hunter, Vallie, Elementary Supervisor, Department of Education, Cookeville
Hyder, Gretchen, Regional Elementary Supervisor, E. Tennessee State Teachers College, Johnson City
James, Virginia White, Principal, 311 W. Glenwood Ave., Knoxville
Johnston, Eula, Supervisor of Elementary Schools Court House, Department of Education, Chattanooga
Jones, Mary Sneed, Intermediate Supervisor, RFD 1, Brentwood
Kaiser, D. H., Elementary Supervisor, Giles County, Pulaski
Kelley, Audley, Supervisor of Elementary Schools, Jasper
Kennedy, L. Blanche, General Supervisor of Elementary Schools, 1412 Valley St., Kingsport
Kirksey, Howard G., High School Visitor, Middle Tennessee State College, Murfreesboro
Knudsen, Charles W., Professor of Secondary Education, George Peabody College, Nashville 4
Kriger, Margaret, Cedar Hill
Ladd, Margaret, Supervisor, Jefferson County, Department of Education, Dandridge
Leavell, Ullin W., Professor of Education, George Peabody College, Nashville 4
Lockhart, Mrs. Wyly C., Elementary Supervisor, Box 218, Camden
Mackinlay, Mary, Primary Supervisor, 530 Baldwin St., Chattanooga
Mason, Bessie Lee, Rt. 5, McMinnville
McAfee, Marian, Supervisory Teacher, Lincoln County Elementary School, Fayetteville
McCafferty, Ruth R., 4208 Anderson Ave., Chattanooga
McCray, Ann, Elementary School Supervisor, Rt. 1, Limestone
McMillan, Mayme J., 707 W. Washington, Athens
McNulty, Susie, 611½ Houston St., Chattanooga
Minton, Marjorie, Columbia, Tennessee
Mitchell, Ruth Lee, Overton County Supervisor, 216 East Main St., Livingston
Mooney, Ruby, Elementary Supervisor, Box 162, Rogersville
Moore, C. H., Superintendent, Clarksville
Moore, Donald, Supervisor, Granville
Mueller, Walter, Principal, Pleasant Hill Academy, Pleasant Hill
Oakley, Bertha C., County Elementary Supervisor, White Bluff
Oakley, Louise, Elementary Supervisor, Henderson County Schools, 204 Broad St., Lexington
Parker, Dixie, Elementary Supervisor, Humphreys County, Waverly
Penney, Sara Mae, Elementary Supervisor, Piney Flats
Petty, Eva, Supervisor, Van Buren County, Spencer
Pitt, Catherine H., Elementary Supervisor, 403 Locust, Springfield
Pope, Margaret, Visiting Teacher, Dyer County Schools, Dyersburg
Ramer, Earl, College of Education, University of Tennessee, Knoxville
Rauscher, Arthur C., Elementary Supervisor, Department of Education, Memphis
Rawls, Flora H., Principal of Training School, 3586 Watauga, Memphis
Rigsby, J. F., Lawrenceburg
Rose, Mary Ruth, Kingston
Rudsill, Zelia I., Principal, Rozelle School, Roland and Walker Sts., Memphis
Schulze, Bertha, Elementary Supervisor, Box 84, Tracy City

Smithson, Henrietta, Elementary Supervisor, Cannon County Schools, Woodbury
Southall, Maycie, George Peabody College, Nashville
Stevens, Allie Mae, Decaturville
Steverson, C. M., 1508 Leola St., Springfield
Stinson, Ruth, District Supervisor of Vocational Home Economics, 103½ South Market, Jackson
Tarpley, Louise, Nursery School Technician, State Department of Education, Nashville
Thomas, Beulah, County Supervisor of Elementary Schools, Box 275, Lexington
Thomas, R. Lee, Supervisor, Division of Elementary Schools, State Department of Education, Nashville
Walker, Margaret, Sharon School, RFD 2, Greenbrier
Waters, E. A., Associate Professor, University of Tennessee, Knoxville
Waters, G. H., Professor of Education, 2003 Greenwood Ave., Nashville
Webster, Mrs. George, Mt. Pleasant School, RFD 1, Greenbrier
Wehrle, Helen, Board of Education, Crossville
Williams, Margaret, Board of Education, 317 Poplar Ave., Memphis
Witcher, Lucile, Supervisor of Macon County Schools, Red Boiling Springs, Tennessee

TEXAS

Allen, Corrie W., Associate Professor of Curriculum and Instruction, University Station, University of Texas, Austin 12
Ayer, Fred C., Professor of Education and Administration, University of Texas, Austin 12
Baccus, Nettie, Elementary Principal, Granbury
Bollman, Thelma Anderson, Assistant Professor of Curriculum and Instruction, Extension Division, University of Texas, Austin 12
Boren, Duralde, Primary Supervisor, Commerce
Boutte, Fay I., 3806 Sealy, Galveston
Brashear, J. T., Elementary Supervisor, 3213 Cochran St., Dallas
Buckley, J. L., Superintendent, Lockhart
Burke, Margaret E., Elementary School Principal, 720 W. Poplar St., San Antonio
Carruth, I. B., Superintendent, Waco Public Schools, Waco
Cassell, Mable V., Director of Curriculum, 1315 Eagle Ave., Houston
Childers, Zelma W., Supervisor, Jasper County, Jasper
Clough, G. O., Professor of Education and Director of Evening College, Southern Methodist University, 3532 Asbury Ave., Dallas
Cook, Harris M., Canyon
Cullin, Florence, Supervisor of Student Teaching, Box 5134 T C Station, Denton
Dent, Charles H., Assistant Superintendent of Elementary Schools, Dallas
Devin, Mattie, Teacher, 1302 W. 7th St., Plainview
Evans, Idris, Elementary Supervisor, Bonham
Fincher, M. E., Fort Stockton Public Schools, Fort Stockton
Fortescue, Z. T., Superintendent, Webster Bldg., Port Arthur
Fothergill, Mrs. Charles S., Primary Supervisor, McLeman County, Courthouse, Waco
Greene, P. H., Superintendent, Webster Independent School District, Webster
Haines, Hazel S, Box 181, West Columbia
Hale, Pauline, Rt. 1, Overton
Hall, Pearl, Principal, Box 63, South Houston
Hammock, Robert C., Assistant Professor, University of Texas, 2107—G San Antonio St., Austin
Harvin, Mrs., R. R., County Supervisor, County Department of Education, North St. Sta., Nacogdoches
Hatchett, Ethel L., Supervisor of Elementary Education, Hardin Simmons University, Abilene
Heflin, Bess, Department of Home Economics, University of Texas, Austin
Hendricks, Jake J., Educational Representative, Macmillan Company, 16 Enfield Road, Austin
Hill, J. Davis, Principal, Ball High School, Galveston
Holden, P. H., Burrus Junior High, 1820 Live Oak St., Houston
Hughes, J. Lyndal, Superintendent, Talco Public Schools, Talco
Humphrey, J. R., Municipal Bldg., Temple
Knowles, J. C., Principal, Box 551, Borger
Kuykendall, Ima, 4020 Clarke. Fort Worth
Lasater, I. L., Winters Public Schools, Winters
Lomax, Dorothy, Director of Secondary Curriculum, 3105 21st St., Lubbock
Mann, Sue B., Court House, Cleburne
Mason, C. C., Head of Department of Education, North Texas Agriculture College, Arlington
Matthews, J. Carl, Teachers College, Station Box 359, Denton
McDonald, Annie L., Supervisor of Elementary Grades, Senior High School, Amarillo
Miller, Perry Van, HQ. 16 BOTW, Biggs Field, El Paso, Texas
Nash, Corinne, Director of Elementary Education, 2500 Trice, Waco
Neal, Elma A., Assistant Superintendent, Elementary Division, 141 Lavaca St., San Antonio
Otto, Henry J., School Education, University of Texas, Austin 12
Peters, Hulda B., 701 Drexel Ave., San Antonio 3
Pledger, Maud Myrtice, Supervising Teacher, 1301 Monroe St., Commerce
Selby, Robert A., Director of Secondary Curriculum and Guidance, 837 Parker, Amarillo
Sister Adelaide Marie, Our Lady of the Lake College, San Antonio
Smith, Raymond A., Dean of the School of Education, Box 278, Texas Christian University, Fort Worth 9
Sparks, R. B., Principal, Robert E. Lee High School, Goose Creek
Stark, Helen V., 414 Florida St., San Antonio
Tallman, Pearle, Assistant Superintendent of a Junior High School, 1500 Louisiana St., Houston
Umstattd, J. G., Chairman of Curriculum and Instruction, School of Education, University of Texas, Austin 12
Von Roeder, H. S., 3150 S. 7th St., Abilene
Warden, Ocoee P., Elementary Supervisor, Friona Independent School District, Friona
Watson, Vesta I., Pasadena Independent School District, Pasadena
Williams, R. L., Superintendent, Sweetwater
Wilson, Edgar Ellen, State Director of Elementary Education, State Department of Education, Austin 11
Wood, Lt. Hugh B., Navy V-12 Unit, Southern Methodist University, Dallas
Youngblood, J. B., Principal Lake Jackson School, Lake Jackson

UTAH

Andrew, Cathryn M., Elementary Supervisor, Box 309, Provo
Arnesen, Arthur E., Supervisor of Curriculum and Research, 440 East 1st South St., Salt Lake City
Brockbank, Hazel, Assistant Professor of Education, University of Utah, Salt Lake City
Campbell, Jennie, State Director of Elementary Education, 223 State Capitol, Salt Lake City
Chipman, R. S., Superintendent, Emery County School District, Huntington
Glade, Melba V., 2610 Highland Drive, Salt Lake City
Green, Eva May, Supervisor of Kindergarten and Primary Grades, 440 East 1st S. St., Salt Lake City
Griffin, Nethella, Boulder

LIST OF MEMBERS

Hardman, Maud R., Supervisor of Art, 440 East 1st S. St., Salt Lake City
Jensen, Fredia, Primary Supervisor, 112 West 1st St. North, Sandy
Jensen, Norma, Primary Supervisor Board of Education, Brigham City
Kirkbride, J. W., Superintendent Board of Education, Cache County, 179 N. Main, Logan
Merrill, Ray S., Principal, Box 152, Pleasant Grove
Moffitt, J. C., Superintendent of Schools, Provo
Nuttall, Drayton B., Magna
Oscarson, J. E., Superintendent, Piute School District, Marysvale
Phillips, Virginia, Teacher Education, Utah State Agriculture College, Logan
Schwan, Myrtle A., Supervisor of Language Arts, 440 East 1st S. St., Salt Lake City 2
Simmons, E. Lee, Supervisor of Health, 440 E. 1st S. St., Salt Lake City 2
Valentine, Ruth, Elementary Supervisor, Carbon County School District, Price
Wheelwright, Lorin F., Supervisor of Music, 440 East 1st S. St., Salt Lake City
Williams, Margaret, Director of Elementary Education, Granite School District, 3234 S. State St., Salt Lake City
Winsor, Tillie, Elementary Supervisor, St. George
Worlton, James T., Assistant Superintendent of Schools, 777 10th St., Salt Lake City

VERMONT

Allen, Frederick Chase, Principal, Whitingham High School, Jacksonville
*Hall, Elizabeth, South Ryegate
Holden, A. John, Professor Education, 39 N. Pleasant St., Middlebury

VIRGINIA

Alexander, Marie, Supervisor of Elementary Instruction, 8 River Road, E. Hampton, Va.
Ayres, Sue, Supervisor, County Board, Prince William County, Manassas
Barksdale, Mary, Supervisor, Elementary Schools, Halifax
Bauserman, James E., Supervisor of Elementary Education, Fairfax
Beery, D. C., Counsellor, 201 Thornrose Ave., Staunton
Bennett, Ercelle, Supervisor, Box 92A, State Teachers College, Radford
Bibb, Elizabeth K., Principal, Jefferson School, Bristol
Bierbower, Ada R., Elementary Supervisor, Brunswick Ave., Blackstone
Bishop, Ruby, Elementary Supervisor, Floyd County Schools, Floyd
Blakey, Letitia, Elementary Supervisor, Buckingham County, Buckingham
Brimmer, Rose L., Elementary Supervisor, 119 College Ave., Danville
Brougher, John F., Acting Principal, Calvin Coolidge High School, Washington, D. C., 5804-11th St., North Arlington
Bryant, Alice G., Elementary Supervisor, Newport News, Va., 8 River Rd., Hampton
Bush, Bernice M., Bassett
Carter, Alice E., Supervisor, Campus Training School, 702 High St., Farmville
Charlton, Gladys G., Director of Elementary Education, School Administration Bldg., Band and Charlotte Sts., Norfolk
Coleman, Mery E., Amelia
Cushwa, Virginia, Supervisor, Louisa
Daniel, Blanche W., Director of Training, State Teachers College, 1405 Grove Ave., Radford
Dinwiddie, Mary, Rural Elementary Supervisor, Wellington Apts., Main St., Harrisonburg
Ellmore, Elizabeth, Supervisor of Instruction, Dinwiddie

*Honorary member for life.

Fellows, Jeanette Luther, Supervisor of Instruction, Fairfax
Freeman, Mrs. Philip, Supervisor, Sussex County Schools, Stony Creek
Gorham, Pauline C., Principal, Jefferson School, Alexandria
Gravatte, Florence, Elementary Supervisor, 4400 18th North, Arlington
Graves, E. Boyd, Associate Professor of Education, Mary Washington College, Fredericksburg
Graybeal, H. C., High School Counselor, Radford
Griffith, Barton R., Supervising Principal, Quantico Post School, Marine Barracks, Quantico
Hamilton, India, King William
Harrison, Anne, Apt. 1, 3 Lawrence Circle, Portsmouth
Hatcher, Ashton, Supervisor, Mathews and Middlesex Company, Urbanna
Heard, Mrs. L. Wallace, Fork Union
Henson, Elizabeth, 7104-B River Drive, Huntington Court, Newport News
Hewitt, Eva, Elementary Supervisor, 312 N. 9th St., Richmond
Irwin, Agnes J., Supervisor of Elementary Schools, Orange
Jett-Cranz, Flora, Elementary Supervisor, Rt. 1, Hopewell
Johnson, Edgar M., Director of Bureau of Teaching Materials, State Teachers College, Farmville
Johnson, Emily W., Research Assistant, 2139 N. Quebec St., Arlington
Johnson, S. P. Jr., Director of Instruction, School Administration Bldg., Petersburg
Joynes, Blanche N., County Supervisor, Onancock
Kizer, Elizabeth, Principal, 226 Norfolk Ave., Lynchburg
Keyser, Mrs. Leslie Fox, Elementary Supervisor, Front Royal
Lewis, W. A., Rural Supervisor, Melfa
Lowe, Edwin S., Principal, Callands School, Callands
Lunsford, H. C., Principal, Churchville High School, Churchville
Luxford, Louise, Elementary Supervisor, Princess Anne
Martinsen, Supervisor of Elementary Education, School Board Office, Court House Hill, Petersburg
McIlwain, Orene, Associated Director of Executive Committee of Religious Education and Publications, Presbyterian Bldg., Richmond
Merville, Gladys, Primary Supervisor, Norfolk City School Board, Norfolk 10
Miles, Agnes, Supervisor, Gloucester County Schools, Gloucester
Miller, Dessie R., Elementary Supervisor, 251 W. Gay St., Harrisonburg
Miller, Mrs. W. W., Fredericksburg School, Fredericksburg
Mitchell, Eva C., Supervisor of Elementary Student Teaching, Hampton Institute, Hampton
Moncure, Anne E., Rural Supervisor, Stafford
Nicholas, Annie F., Supervisor, Culpeper
Overton, Edward F., 211 Fifth St., N. E., Charlottesville
Penny, Blanche, Supervisor of School, Monterey
Peters, Mildred Dudley, 1406 Calvert St., Norfolk
Phelps, Mary O., Elementary Supervisor, Troutville
Pierce, Lottie Mildred, Educational and Vocational Counselor, Ferrum Junior College, Ferrum
Pratt, Dorothy I., Associate Professor of Education and Supervision, Randolph-Macon Woman's College, Lynchburg
Richmond, John A., Director of Institute, Lee County Board of Education, Jonesville
Rollins, Dorothy, Elementary Supervisor, Madison County, Criglersville
Root, Blake S., 412 N. Thomas St., Arlington

Savedge, Mary A., County Supervisor, Appomattox
Shull, Lucibel, 473 S. Mason St., Harrisonburg
Simpson, Blanche, Supervisor of Elementary Education, Administration Bldg., Roanoke
Sinclair, Katherine, Elementary Supervisor, City Point Court, Apt. 2, Hopewell
Smith, Gertrude, Supervisor of Schools, Roslyn Post Office, Arlington
Smither, Ethel L., General Editor, Johnson Publishing Company, Richmond
Stanley, B. L., Principal, 56 Cantrell Ave., Harrisonburg
Staples, Mrs. J. Kemper, County Supervisor, 550 S. Mason St., Harrisonburg
Starling, Preston, Rural Supervisor, Frederick County Board of Education, Winchester
Stoddard, Jane, Supervisor of Special Education, State Dept. of Education, Richmond 16
Sutton, Virginia, Supervisor, Tazewell
Tate, Virginia, Supervisor, Smyth County Schools, Marion
Taylor, Lola A., Supervisor, Shenandoah County, Woodstock
Thompson, Vergie, Supervisor, Patrick County Public Schools, Stuart
Townes, Margaret O., 214 E. Clay St., Richmond
Truitt, W. J. B., Principal, Brambleton School, 2930 Henrico St., Norfolk
Vaughn, Eva, Elementary Principal and Supervisor, Jefferson School, Pulaski
Ware, Juliet R., Supervisor of Elementary Education, State Department of Education, Richmond 16
Washington, Mrs. M. B., Elementary Supervisor, Crozet
Weeks, Helen Foss, Professor of Education, 616 Blair Ave., Williamsburg
Whaley, Frances T., Elementary Supervisor, Kilmarnock
White, Edna G., Holmes, Walkerton
Wilhelms, Fred T., Assistant Director of Consumer Education Study, 3111 20th St. N., Arlington
Wingold, Elsie, Elementary Supervisor, Box 196, Kenbridge
Wright, Nelle, Director of Instruction, 200 Maple Ave., Waynesboro

WASHINGTON

Actor, Charles M., Superintendent, Ritzville
Anderson, Mabel T., Central Washington College of Education, Ellensburg
Bloomer, Lillian M., Assistant Professor of Education, Central Washington College of Education, Ellensburg
Bush, Helen T., Principal, Helen Bush School, 405 36th Ave. N., Seattle
Crum, J. Wesley, Superintendent, Chehalis
DeYoung, Henry, Principal, Vancouver High School, Vancouver
Draper, Edgar M., Professor of Education, University of Washington, 4007 48th St., N. E., Seattle
Fitzgerald, Marie, Principal, Logan School, 915 E., Montgomery, Spokane
Furgeson, Paul, Superintendent, High School Bldg., Centralia
Goff, Mary Downer, Supervisor of Special Education, South Kitsap High School, Port Orchard
Goodwin, Dorothy, 4210 Brooklyn, Seattle
Hall, Robert C., Superintendent, Rt. 2, Box 99, Tacoma
Hammer, Irwin A., Chairman of Department of Education, Western Washington College of Education, Bellingham
Hanawalt, P. B., Superintendent, Box 327, Puyallup
Hankamp, Mrs. George, Lynden
Hassler, Arthur A., Assistant Superintendent, Battleground
Haugan, S. M., Principal, Rt. 3, Box 291, Port Orchard

Hayden, Alice H., Assistant Professor of Education, 113-G Education Hall, University of Washington, Seattle 5
Hebeler, Amanda, Director of Teacher Training, Central Washington College of Education, Ellensburg
Jackson, Dorothea, Director of Kindergarten and Primary Education, 810 Dexter, Seattle 9
Jespersen, C. G., Administrative Assistant, Public Schools, 3010 North Proctor, Tacoma 1
Johnson, Carl, Superintendent, Battleground
Johnson, Morton, Superintendent, Kirkland
Knowles, Joe C., Superintendent, South Kitsap School District 402, Port Orchard
Laurie, Helen, Supervisor of Elementary Education, 810 Dexter Ave., Seattle 9
Lavin, Leila, Director of Elementary Curriculum, 1117 Wall, Spokane
Lawler, Marcella R., High School Supervisor, State Department of Education, Olympia
Martin, Sarah, Director of Elementary Education, 606 W. 21st St., Vancouver
Meyers, Helene K., Primary Supervisor, Shoreline School District 412, Aurora Ave. at North 100, Seattle 33
Miller, Loretta M., Central Washington College of Education, Ellensburg
Minkler, Laura N., Primary Teacher, Columbian Bldg., 23rd and Kaufman, Vancouver
Neterer, Elizabeth, Elementary Principal, 10481 Maplewood Place, Seattle 66
Ohlsen, Merle M., Washington State College, Pullman
Olds, Dolph, Superintendent, Camas
Olsen, Edward G., Department of Education, Rt. 5, Box 577, Olympia
Olson, Helen F., Head of English Department, Broadway High School, Seattle
O'Neel, F. W., Health Coordinator, 2204 N. Cedar St., Tacoma
Patterson, Don S., Director of Instruction, Central School, 5th and Warren, Bremerton
Pool, William, King County Superintendent, 310 County-City Bldg., Seattle 4
Reese, Chester M., Principal, St. Helen's School, Longview
Robison, C. L., 3540 Ferdinand St., Seattle 8
Scheffskey, Dora B., Kessler School, Longview
Schmitkin, C. R., Curriculum Supervisor, Box 91, Ridgefield
Sherman, Ruth S., Box 997, Richland
Smith, W. Virgil, Assistant Superintendent, Seattle Public Schools, 810 Dexter Ave., Seattle 9
Thompson, Stanley I., Vice Principal, 512 2nd Ave. N., Renton
Tucker, Edith A., Department Assistant in Child Guidance, 4531 Latona, Seattle 5
Wagner, Jean, Supervisor, Western Washington College of Education, Bellingham
Wanamaker, Pearl A., State Superintendent of Public Instruction, Olympia
Wright, Paul W., Dean, College of Education, Seattle Pacific College, Seattle

WEST VIRGINIA

Conaway, Freda Y., Teacher Training Department, West Liberty State Teachers College, West Liberty
Hamrick, Lettie, Box 94, Webster Springs
Leckie, Margaret, 1716 Virginia St., Charleston
Leonard, Louise, Elementary Supervisor of Teacher Training, Fairmont State College, 726 Fairmont Ave., Fairmont
Musgrave, Paul N., Principal, Marshal High School, Huntington 1
Scott, Grace, Director of Reading, Jefferson County Schools, Charles Town

WISCONSIN

Bassett, Gladys B., Associate Professor of Physical Education, 26 Breese Terrace, Madison
Berg, Mabel L., Supervisory Teacher, Court House Annex, LaCrosse

LIST OF MEMBERS

Billings, Neal, Director, State Teachers College, Milwaukee
Brener, Olga, Supervising Principal, 417 S. Lafayette, Shawano
Bush, Maybell G., Supervisor of Elementary Schools, State Department of Public Instruction, State Capitol, Room 147 N., Madison 2
Caldwell, Jessie E., Supervisor in Elementary Education, 113 N. 22nd St., LaCrosse
Chenoweth, Margaret, Grade Supervisor, High School Office, Janesville
Christensen, Essie, Mt. Horeb
Cleary, Margaret E., Principal, Washington School, West Allis 14
Cronin, Katherine L., Associate Professor of Physical Education, University of Wisconsin, Lathrop Hall, Madison
Dawald, Victor F., Superintendent, Beloit
Eye, Glen G., Principal, Wisconsin High School, Madison
Georgiady, Alexander, Curriculum Consultant, Manitowoc Public Schools, Municipal Bldg., Manitowoc
Gleiter, Paul F., Superintendent, Darlington
Goodell, M. R., Principal, Columbia County Normal School, 725 S. Lewis St., Columbus
Hampel, Margaret, Director of the Division of Elementary Education, State Teachers College, Milwaukee
Henderson, Margaret G., Director of Elementary Instruction, Green Bay Public Schools, 523 Howe St., Green Bay
Hintgen, Josephine, Director of Educational Guidance, Teachers College, 1241 West Ave. S., LaCrosse
Horkheimer, A. P., Publisher, *Educators Progress Service*, Randolph
Howard, Virgie M., Supervisor of Elementary Grades, 8509 Stickney Ave., Wauwatosa
Hull, Marion, Supervising Teacher, Court House, Fond du Lac
Jenson, T. J., Superintendent, Fond du Lac
Johnson, Harold B., Principal of Elementary Schools, Lake Geneva
Johnson, Leslie W., Director of Curriculum, Public Schools, Superior
Jones, Alex M., Lancaster
Jones, George E., Superintendent, 214 Dayton St., Mayville
Kellogg, Lulu O., Waushara County Normal, Wautoma
Kelly, Florence, Supervisor, Primary Grades, 1111 N. 10th St., Milwaukee
Kibbee, Delia E., Supervisor of Elementary Schools, Department of Public Instruction, State Capitol, Madison
Kromrey, Edward G., Principal of Elementary School, Middleton
Krug, Edward, Associate Professor of Department of Education, 2222 Commonwealth Ave., Madison
Larke, R. R., Elementary School Principal, Clintonville
Larson, C. P., Superintendent, New London
Lee, Donald, Superintendent, Jefferson
Low, Camilla M., Assistant Professor of Education, Department of Education, University of Wisconsin, Madison
Mattson, Martha M., Elementary Curriculum Coordinator, Central School, Wausau
Mother M. Josina, F. S. P. A., Acting President, Viterbo Teacher Training College, 815 South 9th St., LaCrosse
Mulvaney, Ralph A., Principal, 5000 N. 53rd St., New Hampton School, Milwaukee
Nash, H. B., Superintendent, 7510 W. National Ave., West Allis
Nemec, Lois G., University of Wisconsin, Madison
Ooley, Ida A., Department of Public Instruction, Madison
Paukner, Lillian C., Supervisor of Elementary School Curriculum, 1111 N. 10th St., Milwaukee
Powell, Harley J., Superintendent, Watertown
Rawson, K. O., Principal, John Edwards High School, Box 172, Port Edwards
Reichert, C. Lorene, Principal, Longfellow Elementary School, 2134 Keyes Ave., Madison
Schmeeckle, F. J., Department of Chemistry, Central State Teachers College, Stevens Point
Sister M. Augustine, O. S. F., Alverno Teachers College, 1413 S. Layton Blvd., Milwaukee
Sister M. Justinia, S. S. N. D., 1324 N. Milwaukee St., Milwaukee 1
Sorensen, Martha, Grade Supervisor, 120 E. Harris St., Appleton
Stanford, Beth, 177 Everett St., Fond du Lac
Stuessy, Susan E., Assistant in Rural Education, 35 N. Washington, Platteville
Thayer, H. C., Teacher Training Supervisor, 2259 Fox Ave., Madison
Tibbits, Blanche, Supervising Teacher, County Superintendent of Schools, Jackson County, Black River Falls
Vander Beke, George E., Head of Department of Education, Marquette University, 615 N. 11th St., Milwaukee
Waehler, L. A., Principal, Central High School, Madison
Whelan, Lilian B., 1009 N. 18th St., Superior
Willing, M. H., Professor of Education, University of Wisconsin, Madison
Willits, Mary E., Elementary Supervisor, Washington School, Neenah
Wilson, Ada Louis, Superior State Teachers College, Superior

WYOMING

Anderson, Doris, Elementary Supervisor, 221 K. St., Rock Springs
Goodman, John O., Director of Instruction, Cheyenne Public Schools, Cheyenne
Hackett, Rosalie E., Sublette County Superintendent of Schools, Pinedale
Hunsaker, Myrtle L., County Superintendent, Basin
Keck, Cleta, Supervisor of Elementary Education, 247 Coffeen Ave., Sheridan
King, Luella M., Principal, Harding School, Casper
Schlaht, R. J., Superintendent, Gillette
Schunk, Bernadene, W. R. A., Heart Mountain
Sholty, Director of Placement and Elementary Education, 534 Boyd Bldg., Cheyenne
Stolt, Edna B., Director of the Division of Special Education, State Department of Education, Capitol Bldg., Cheyenne
Thompson, Mable Fisher, Primary Supervisor, 630 E. 5th, Apt. D, Casper
Whittenburg, Clarice, Primary Supervisor, University of Wyoming, Laramie

UNITED STATES POSSESSIONS

Canaday, Lotty V., Lihiliho School, 3430 Maunaloa Ave., Honolulu, Hawaii
Caro, Ida J., Assistant Professor of Education, 2345 Liloa Rise, Honolulu, Hawaii
Cary, Miles E., Principal, McKinley High School, Honolulu, Hawaii
Faulkner, R. M., Supervising Principal, 1227 Pensacola St., Honolulu 34, Hawaii
Gantt, Beth King, 2614 Terrace Drive, Honolulu, Hawaii
Gordon, Walton M., Principal, W. R. Farrington High School, 1564 N. King St., Honolulu 35, Hawaii
Hendry, Eva, Principal, Lincoln School, Victoria Street, Honolulu, Hawaii
Madden, Ward, Supervisor of Student Teaching, Teachers College, Intermediate School, University of Hawaii, Honolulu 10, Hawaii
Peterson, Francis, Principal, 1951 Vancouver Highway, Honolulu, Hawaii
Pickerill, Cicely P., Supervisor of Interne Teachers, Kawananakoa School, Honolulu, Hawaii
Sayers, E. V., Professor of Education, University of Hawaii, Honolulu 34, Hawaii

Sueoka, George, 2249 Seaview Ave., Honolulu, T. H.
Suzuki, Harriet, Lihiliho School, 3430 Maunaloa Ave., Honolulu, Hawaii
Traut, Gladys, Acting Principal, Teachers College, Elementary School, University of Hawaii, Honolulu, Hawaii
Vance, Agnes B., School Principal, Thomas Jefferson School, 324 Kapahulu Ave., Honolulu 30, Hawaii
Weatherbee, Gladys B., Principal, Lulalilo School, 810 Pumehana St., Honolulu 27, Hawaii
Conafay, Katherine, Insular Board for Vocational Education, San Juan, Puerto Rico
Rodriquez, Marina F., 3 Palacios St., Santurce, Puerto Rico
Salgado, S. Morales, Superintendent, San German, Puerto Rico
Segarra, Mrs. Rafael A., Elementary School Principal, 22 S. Aguastin Colemane St., Guayama, Puerto Rico
Velez, Ernestina Torres, Riera Palmer School, Mayaguez, Puerto Rico
Zuazaga, Carlos F., Superintendent, Arroyo, Puerto Rico

FOREIGN

Brown, J. E., Inspector of Schools, Department of Education, Victoria, B. C., Canada
Brown, Ruth, Quennel Bldg., High School Centre, Nanaimo, B. C., Canada
Campbell, H. L., Municipal Inspector of Schools, School Board Office, City Hall, Victoria, B. C., Canada
Crookes, S., Supervising Principal, Fernie Public Schools, Fernie, B. C., Canada
Frederickson, C. J., Inspector of Schools, Cranbrook, B. C., Canada
King, Major H. B., Chief Inspector of Schools, 701 Yates St., Victoria, B. C., Canada
Marriott, E., Supervising Principal, Creston Valley Elementary Schools, Box 21, Creston, B. C., Canada
McHugh, Michael F., College Teacher, 4 Lakeside Ave., Ottawa, Ontario, Canada
Norris, K. E., Principal, 1441 Drummond St., Montreal 25, Canada
O'Brien, A. A., Superintendent, Edmonton Separate School Board, 103rd St. School, Edmonton, Alberta, Canada
Sister Francis DeSales, Mt. Saint Vincent College, Halifax, Nova Scotia, Canada
Watts, Morrison L., Director of Curriculum, Department of Education, Edmonton, Alberta, Canada
Hills, W., Esquire, Teachers College, Hobart, Tasmania, Australia
Echegoyan, Ana Dra., Professor, University of Havana, Concordio 669, altos, Habana, Cuba
Vivanco, Martin Rodriguez, Professor of Education, Havana University, Goss 166, Santos Suarez, Habana, Cuba
Ramirez, Rafael, Head of the Department of Rural Schools, Ave. Ayuntamiento 78, Coyoacan D. F. Mexico
Manuel, Edith, Kindergarten Teacher, Bishop Spencer College, St. John's, Newfoundland
Coetzee, J. Chr., 20 Reitz St., Potchefstroom, South Africa
Driscal, Ione, Missionary Teacher, Kamabai, Via Mokeni, Siera Leone, West Africa

SCHOOLS AND LIBRARIES

Houghton Memorial Library, Huntingdon College, Montgomery 6, Alabama
Library, State Department of Education, Montgomery, 4
Library, Negro Department, Stillman Institute, Tuscaloosa, Alabama
College of Education Library, University of Alabama, University, Alabama
Wilson Public School, Wilson, Arkansas
Kern County Union High School Library, 1341 F. St., Bakersfield, California
Library, University of California, Berkeley 4, California
Chico College Library, Chico, California
Claremont Colleges Library, Claremont, California
Compton City Schools, 604 S. Tamarind St., Compton, California
Library, Fresno State Teachers College, Fresno, California
Hemet Union High School, Hemet, California
Teachers Library, Board of Education, 715 Locust Ave., Long Beach, California
Los Angeles Public Library, Serials Division, 530 S. Hope St., Los Angeles, California
Library, University of California at Los Angeles, 405 Hilgard Ave., Los Angeles, California
Teachers Library, Los Angeles County Public Library, 322 S. Broadway, Los Angeles 13, California
Manhattan Beach City School District, 1313 John St., Box 457, Manhattan Beach, California
Contra Costa County Library, Martinez, California
Monterey City Schools, Drawer 1031, Monterey, California
Oakland Public Schools, Administration Bldg., 1025 Second Ave., Oakland, California
Teachers Library, Room 201, Administration Bldg., Oakland, California
Pasadena Board of Education, Superintendents Office, 320 E. Walnut St., Pasadena, California
University of Redlands Library, E. Colton Ave., Redlands
Curriculum Department, Mr. Cress, Riverside City School District, 3450 9th St., Riverside, California
Professional Library, School Storeroom, 21st and L Sts., Sacramento, California
Sacramento City Schools, 1200 21st St., Sacramento City, California
Professional Reference Library, 825 Union St., San Diego, California
Superintendent of Schools, San Diego County, 209 Civic Center, San Diego, California
Library, State College, San Jose, California
Hillsborough School District, 303 El Cerrito Ave., San Mateo, California
Stanford University Library, Stanford University, California
Washington School Building, Gertrude Miller, Librarian, San Joaquin and Lindsay Sts., Stockton, California
College of the Pacific Library, Stockton, California
Ventura County Free Library, Box 771, Ventura, California
Whittier College Library, Whittier, California
Colorado Military School, 1984 S. Columbine St., Denver 10, Colorado
Department of Education, 127 State Capitol Bldg., Denver, Colorado
Library, Western State College, Gunnison, Colorado
Franklin School, Sterling, Colorado
Board of Education, Supervisor's Office, 249 High St., Hartford 5, Connecticut
Case Memorial Library, Hartford Seminary Foundation, Hartford 5, Connecticut
State Department of Education, C. D. Hine Library, Room 307, State Office Bldg., Hartford, Connecticut
Yale University, Department of Education, New Haven, Connecticut
Board of Education, Stratford, Connecticut
Howard University Library, Serials Department, Washington, D. C.
Lafayette School Faculty, Broad Branch Rd. and Northampton St., N. W., Washington, D. C.
Public Library, Periodical Division, 455 Pennsylvania Ave., N. W., Washington 1, D. C.

LIST OF MEMBERS

Lewes Special School District, R. A. Shields, Superintendent, Lewes, Delaware
General Library, University of Georgia, Athens
Teachers Reference Library, 13th Floor, City Hall, Atlanta, Georgia
Textbook and Library Division, State Department of Education, 217 State Office Bldg., Atlanta 3, Georgia
Glynn Academy Library, Brunswick, Georgia
War Relocation Authority, Hunt High School, Minimoka Project, Hunt, Idaho
Library, Eastern Illinois State Teachers College, Charleston, Illinois
Chicago Public Library, Teachers' Room, 78 E. Washington St., Chicago 2, Illinois
John Crerar Library, 86 East Randolph St., Chicago, Illinois
Joseph Schaffner Library, 339 East Chicago Ave., Chicago, Illinois
Library, Scott Foresman and Company, 623 S. Wabash Ave., Chicago, Illinois
Pestalozzi Froebel Teachers College, 410 S. Michigan Blvd., Chicago, Illinois
St. Xavier College Library, 4928 Cottage Grove Ave., Chicago, Illinois
Library, Northern Illinois State Teachers College, Dekalb, Illinois
Dupo Community High School Library, District 195, Dupo, Illinois
Deering Library, Northwestern University, Evanston, Illinois
Library, National College of Education, Sheridan Road N. of Isabella St., Evanston, Illinois
Row, Peterson and Company, 1911 Ridge Ave., Evanston, Illinois
St. John's Lutheran School, Circle and Warren Avenue, Forest Park, Illinois
Library, Illinois State Normal University, Normal, Illinois
Mooseheart Governors, Mooseheart, Illinois
Board of Education, 122 Forest Ave., Oak Park, Illinois
Peoria Public Library, 111 N. Monroe St., Peoria 3
Rockford College Library, Rockford, Illinois
Rockford Public Library, N. Wyman St., Rockford, Illinois
Illinois State Library, Springfield, Illinois
Periodical Division, University of Illinois, Library, Urbana, Illinois
New Trier Township High School, Physical Education Department, Winnetka, Illinois
School of Education, Bureau of Cooperative Research, Indiana University, Bloomington, Indiana
St. Francis College, Library, 2200 Spring St., Fort Wayne, Indiana
Gary Public Library, Fifth Avenue at Adams St., Gary, Indiana
Butler College Library, Butler University, Indianapolis, Indiana
Indianapolis Public Library, St. Clair Square, Indianapolis, Indiana
Indiana State Library, 140 Senate Ave., Indianapolis, Indiana
Library, Ball State Teachers College, Muncie, Indiana
Indiana State Teachers College Library, Terre Haute, Indiana
College Library, Iowa State College, Ames, Iowa
Administration Library, Garfield Bldg., 629 Third St., Des Moines, Iowa
State University of Iowa Library, Library Annex, Iowa City, Iowa
Library, Morningside College, Sioux City, Iowa
Teachers Library, 6th and Minnesota, Kansas City, Kansas
University of Kansas Library, Periodical Department, Lawrence, Kansas
University of Kansas, School of Education, Curriculum Laboratory, 119 Fraser, Lawrence, Kansas
Porter Library, Kansas State Teachers College, Pittsburg, Kansas

Educational Library, Board of Education, 506 W. Hill St., Louisville, Kentucky
Library, Eastern Kentucky State Teachers College, Richmond, Kentucky
Library, Orleans Parish School Board, 1835 Erato St., New Orleans, Louisiana
Caddo Parish, Materials Library No. 529, 1142 Texas Ave., Shreveport 6, Louisiana
Library, Johns Hopkins University, Homewood, Baltimore, Maryland
U. S. Public Health Service, Division of Public Health Methods, Wilson House, Room 101, Bethesda, Maryland
Library, Maryland State Teachers College, Towson, Maryland
Elementary Department, D. C. Heath and Company, 285 Columbus Ave., Boston, Massachusetts
Publicity Department, D. C. Heath and Company, 285 Columbus Ave., Boston, Massachusetts
Wheelock College Library, 47 Pilgrim Road, Boston, Massachusetts
Hills Library, Andover Theological School, 169 Institution Ave., Newton Centre, Massachusetts
Newton School Department, 40 Elm Rd., Newtonville, Massachusetts
State Teachers College, Library, Salem, Massachusetts
Wellesley College Library, Wellesley, Massachusetts
University of Michigan, General Library, Ann Arbor, Michigan
Detroit Public Schools Health Education Club, 467 W. Hancock, Detroit, Michigan
Reference Library, 1354 Broadway, Detroit, Michigan
Wayne University Library, 4841 Cass Ave., Detroit, Michigan
Educational Service Library, Western Michigan College of Education, Kalamazoo, Michigan
Mandelle Memorial Library, Kalamazoo College, Kalamazoo, Michigan
Library, Central State Teachers College, Mt. Pleasant, Michigan
Nazareth College Library, Nazareth, Michigan
Library, Central State Teachers College, Mt. Pleasant, Michigan
Hoyt Public Library, Saginaw, Michigan
Michigan State Normal, College Library, Ypsilanti, Michigan
Board of Education Library, Room 102 & 103, Jackson Bldg., 15th Ave. S. and 4th St., Minneapolis, Minnesota
Barton School, Colfax Ave. S. and 43rd St., Minneapolis 9, Minnesota
Fuller School, 48th St. and Harriet Ave. S., Minneapolis 9, Minnesota
Minneapolis Public Library, 10th and Hennepin Sts., Minneapolis, Minnesota
Librarian, State Teachers College, St. Cloud, Minnesota
St. Paul Diocesan Teachers College, 240 Summit Ave., St. Paul, Minnesota
Library, State Teachers College, Winona, Minnesota
Southeast Missouri State Teachers College, Library, Cape Girardeau, Missouri
General Library, University of Missouri, Columbia, Missouri
Kansas City Public Library, 9th and Locust St., Kansas City, Missouri
Social Science Department, Northwest Missouri State Teachers College, Maryville, Missouri
Christian Board of Publication, Editorial Dept., 2700 Pine Blvd., St. Louis 3
Division of Audio-Visual Education, 4466 Olive St., St. Louis, Missouri
Harris Teachers College Library, 1517 S. Theresa Ave., St. Louis, Missouri
Librarian, St. Louis University, Grand and Pine Blvd., St. Louis, Missouri
Normandy Consolidated School District, Board of Education, 6701 Easton Ave., St. Louis County, Missouri

St. Louis Public Library, 13th and 14th Sts., St. Louis, Missouri
Curriculum Library, Weaver School, Douglas and Division, Springfield, Missouri
Library, Montana State Normal College, Dillon, Montana
Eureka Elementary School, Eureka, Montana
Library, Montana State University, Missoula, Montana
Library, Nebraska State Teachers College, Kearney, Nebraska
Professional Library, Board of Education, 303 West 22nd St., Kearney, Nebraska
State Board of Education, State House Annex, Concord, New Hampshire
Cape May City Board of Education, Superintendent of Schools, Cape May, New Jersey
State Teachers College, Montclair, New Jersey
Library, New Jersey College for Women, New Brunswick, New Jersey
Public Library, 5 Washington St., Newark, New Jersey
Sylvan School, Sylvan St., Rutherford, New Jersey
State Teachers College, Library, Trenton, New Jersey
Catholic Teachers College of New Mexico, Indian School Road, Albuquerque, New Mexico
Library, University of the State of New York, Albany, New York
Brooklyn College Library, Bedford Ave. and Ave. H., Brooklyn, New York
Bureau of Libraries, Board of Education, 110 Livingston St., Brooklyn, New York
Bureau of Reference, Research and Statistics, Mr. Eugene A. Nifenecker, Director, Board of Education, 110 Livingston St., Brooklyn, New York
Union Free School District No. 5, Town of Dewitt, East Syracuse, N. Y.
The Jewish Center School, 1295 Far Rockaway Blvd., Far Rockaway, New York
State Normal School, Fredonia, New York
Library, City College, Serials Division, Convent Ave. & 139th St., New York, New York
Foley and Edmunds, Incorporated, 480 Lexington Ave., New York, New York
Jewish Education Committee, Library, 1776 Broadway, New York, New York
Riverdale County School for Girls, Evelyn Friend, Librarian, Riverdale-on-Hudson, New York, New York
Women's College Library, University of Rochester, Rochester, New York
Library, Syracuse University, Syracuse, New York
Wellsville Public Schools, Wellsville, New York
World Book Company, Yonkers 5, New York
Library, University of North Carolina, Chapel Hill, North Carolina
Western Carolina Teachers College, Library, Cullowhee, North Carolina
Bennett College of Women, Library, Greensboro, North Carolina
Library, East Carolina Teachers College, Greenville, North Carolina
Salem College Library, Winston-Salem, North Carolina
Library, State University of North Dakota, University Station, Grand Forks, North Dakota
State Teachers College Library, Mayville, North Dakota
Library, State Teachers College, Minot, North Dakota
Bierce Library, University of Akron, Akron, Ohio
Chubb Library, Ohio University, Athens, Ohio
Public Library of Cincinnati, Periodical and Serial Department, Cincinnati 1, Ohio
University of Cincinnati, Library, Cincinnati, Ohio
Public Library, Order Department, 325 Superior Ave. N. E., Cleveland, Ohio
Shaker Heights High School Library, Onaway and Aldersyde Rds., Shaker Heights, Cleveland, Ohio
University Library, Western Reserve University, Cleveland, Ohio
Capital University Library, Columbus, Ohio
University Library, Ohio State University, Columbus, Ohio
Albert Emanuel Library, University of Dayton, Dayton, Ohio
Superior School, 13560 Superior Road, East Cleveland, Ohio
Boys Industrial School, Lancaster, Ohio
Storeroom, Curriculum Workshop, 400 N. Walnut Ave., Oklahoma City, Oklahoma
Library, Oklahoma A. & M. College, Stillwater, Oklahoma
Oregon College of Education, Library, Dessa Hofstetter, Librarian, Monmouth, Oregon
Oregon State College Library, Corvallis, Oregon
Curriculum Library, 31 S. Penn Street, Allentown, Pennsylvania
McCartney Library, Miss Miriam Grosh, Librarian, Geneva College, Beaver Falls, Pennsylvania
Lehigh University Library, Bethlehem, Pennsylvania
Superintendent's Office, Junior High School, Bradford, Pennyslvania
Manumit School, RFD 2, Bristol, Pennsylvania
Library, State Teachers College, Clarion, Pennsylvania
Erie Public Library, William Bacon, Librarian, Erie, Pennsylvania
Messiah Bible College Library, Grantham, Pennsylvania
Library, State Teachers College, Lock Haven, Pennsylvania
Drexel Institute Library, Philadelphia, Pennsylvania
Finletter School, Front and Spencer Sts., Philadelphia 20, Pennsylvania
Free Library of Philadelphia, Periodical Department, Middle City West District, Philadelphia 3, Pennsylvania
Library, University of Pennsylvania, Philadelphia, Pennsylvania
Madison School, Newmarket and Green Sts., Philadelphia, Pennsylvania
Pedagogical Library, Room 301, Parkway at 21st St., Philadelphia, Pennsylvania
Temple University Library, Broad and Berks Sts., Philadelphia, Pennsylvania
Carnegie Free Library of Alleghany, Federal and Ohio Sts., Pittsburgh, N. S. Pennsylvania
Library, 160 Administration Bldg., Bellefield Ave., and Forbes St., Pittsburgh, Pennsylvania
Division of Industrial Education, Pennsylvania State College, State College, Pennsylvania
Library, Pennsylvania State College, State College, Pennsylvania
Library, State Teachers College, West Chester, Pennsylvania
Warwick School Department, Miss Irene E. Conway, Apponaug, Rhode Island
School Department, New Port, Rhode Island
The Library, Augustana College, Sioux Falls, South Dakota
Library, Eastern State Normal School, Madison, South Dakota
Library, East Tennessee State College, Johnson City, Tennessee
Library, University of Tennessee, Knoxville, Tennessee
Library, George Peabody College, Nashville, Tennessee
A-2018 Oak Ridge Schools, Anderson County Schools, Oak Ridge Division, Oak Ridge, Tennessee
Library, Abilene Christian College, Abilene, Texas
University of Texas, Health Education Bureau, Room 301, Extension Bldg., Austin, Texas
A. & M. College of Texas, Education Department, College Station, Texas
Library, A. & M. College of Texas, College Station, Texas

LIST OF MEMBERS

Southern Methodist University, Library, Dallas, Texas
Fort Worth Public Library, Fort Worth, Texas
Fort Worth Public Schools, Professional Library, 409 E. Weatherford St., Fort Worth, Texas
Horace Mann Junior High School, Goose Creek, Texas
Library, University of Houston, Houston, Texas
Library, Sam Houston State Teachers College, Huntsville, Texas
Texarkana College, 16th and Pine Sts., Texarkana, Texas
Board of Education, Box 506, Cache County, Logan, Utah
Weber County School District, 2324 Adams Ave., Ogden, Utah
Superintendent's Office, Provo City Schools, Provo, Utah
University of Utah Library, Salt Lake City, Utah
Huntington Memorial Library, Hampton Institute, Hampton, Virginia
Library, Willis-Syms-Eaton School, Ida Sinclair, 240 Victoria Ave., Hampton, Virginia
Library, Medical College of Virginia, Richmond 19, Virginia
Library, College of William and Mary, Williamsburg, Virginia
School District No. 5, K. Box 100, Aberdeen, Washington
Board of Education, Professional Library, Roeder School Bldg., Bellingham, Washington
Eastern Washington College of Education, Library, Cheney, Washington
Library, Central Washington College of Education, Ellensburg, Washington
Union High School District No. 1, 9th & Fulton, Mt. Vernon, Washington
State College of Washington Library, Pullman, Washington
Library, University of Washington, Seattle, Washington
Periodical Department, Public Library, 4th Ave. and Madison St., Seattle, Washington
Professional Library, 810 Dexter Ave., Seattle 9, Washington
School of Education, University of Washington, Seattle 5, Washington
Superintendent of Schools, Morgan School, 120 E. Harris St., Appleton, Wisconsin
Bureau of Visual Instruction, W. A. Wittich, 1204 W. Johnson St., Madison 6, Wisconsin
Curriculum Department, 351 W. Wilson St., Madison 3, Wisconsin

County Rural Normal School, 18th and Michigan Ave., Manitowoc, Wisconsin
Library, Stout Institute, Menomonie, Wisconsin
Dominican Sisters, 2214 E. Capitol Dr., Milwaukee 11, Wisconsin
Library, St. Clare College, 3221 S. Lake Dr., Milwaukee 7, Wisconsin
State Teachers College, Library, Milwaukee, Wisconsin
Racine Public Library, Racine, Wisconsin
State Teachers College, Stevens Point, Wisconsin
Education Department, University of Wyoming, Laramie, Wyoming
Seward Public Schools, Harold F. Roth, Superintendent, Box 240, Seward, Alaska
Kaiulani School, 873 N. King St., Honolulu 51, Hawaii
Kamehameha Schools, Preparatory Department, Bishop Hall, Honolulu 35, Hawaii
Kapalama School Library, N. School St., Honolulu 51, Hawaii
University of Hawaii, Mary P. Pringle, Librarian, Honolulu 10, Hawaii
Division Office Library, c/o Division Superintendent of Schools, Baguio City, Philippines
Puerto Rico Teachers Association, Box 1166, San Juan, Puerto Rico
Librarian, Teachers College, University Grounds, Newtown, Sydney, N. S. W., Australia
American Embassy, IAEF, La Paz, Bolivia
Biblioteca do Servico de Radiofusao Educativa, Praca da Republica 141 A, Rio de Janeiro, Brazil
Ministerio da Educao e Saude, Biblioteca do Departemento de Administrao, Palacio da Educao, 42 andar, Rio de Janeiro, Brazil
Edmonton Education Society, 11406 66th St., Edmonton, Alberta, Canada
Library, Macdonald College, Quebec, Canada
Superintendent of Schools, C. C. Goldring, Board of Education, 155 College St., Toronto, Canada
Library, University of British Columbia, Vancouver, British Columbia, Canada
American Embassy, Santiago, Chile
American Embassy, IAEF, San Jose, Costa Rica
American Embassy, IAEF, San Salvador, El Salvador
American Embassy, IAEF, Guatemala City, Guatemala
American Embassy, IAEF, Tegucigalpa, Honduras
American Embassy, IAEF, Lima, Peru
Librarian, University College of Orange Free State, Bloemfontein, South Africa